Distributed Leadership According to the Evidence

Although not new, the concept of distributed (shared) leadership has re-emerged in recent years as one highly promising response to the complex challenges currently faced by schools. Responding productively to these challenges far exceeds the capacities of any individual leader. If schools are to flourish in the future, they will need to enlist the collective expertise of many more of their members and stakeholders than they have in the past. The purpose of this volume is to both present and synthesize the best available evidence about the nature, causes and effects of distributed school leadership. The book also clarifies common misunderstandings about distributed leadership and identifies promising implications for practice and for future research. Key features include:

- Expertise–written by the most active and widely respected scholars engaged in research on distributed leadership, the book encompasses the very latest knowledge about the nature, causes and consequences of such leadership in schools.
- Comparative models–the book compares various approaches to distributed leadership and examines the conditions under which some approaches may be better than others in improving schools.
- Evidence-based–much of the popularity of distributed leadership is rooted in expectations unsupported by systematic empirical evidence. Virtually all of the available evidence about a distributed approach to leadership can be found in this book.

This book is appropriate for researchers studying school leadership, instructors and students in graduate-level school leadership courses and practicing administrators at the district and building level.

Dr Kenneth Leithwood is Professor of Educational Leadership and Policy at the Ontario Institute for Studies in Education at the University of Toronto, Canada.

Dr Blair Mascall is Professor of Leadership and Educational Change at the Ontario Institute for Studies in Education at the University of Toronto, Canada.

Dr Tiiu Strauss is currently a project director working with Kenneth Leithwood in the Department of Theory and Policy Studies at the Ontario Institute for Studies in Education at the University of Toronto, Canada.

Distributed Leadership According to the Evidence

Edited by Kenneth Leithwood,
Blair Mascall, and Tiiu Strauss

Routledge
Taylor & Francis Group

NEW YORK AND LONDON

First published 2009
by Routledge
270 Madison Ave, New York, NY 10016

Simultaneously published in the UK
by Routledge
2 Park Square, Milton Park, Abingdon, Oxon OX14 4RN

Routledge is an imprint of the Taylor & Francis Group, an informa business   ·

© 2009 Taylor & Francis

Typeset in Minion by Wearset Ltd, Boldon, Tyne and Wear
Printed and bound in the United States of America on acid-free paper by Edwards Brothers, Inc

Library of Congress Cataloging in Publication Data
Distributed leadership according to the evidence / edited by Kenneth Leithwood,
Blair Mascall, and Tiiu Strauss.
p. cm.
Includes bibliographical references and index.
1. Educational leadership. 2. School management and organization. I. Leithwood,
Kenneth A. II. Mascall, Blair. III. Strauss, Tiiu.
LB2805.D528 2008
371.2—dc22   2008001573

ISBN10: 0-8058-6422-9 (hbk)
ISBN10: 0-415-99217-6 (pbk)
ISBN10: 1-4106-1857-9 (ebk)

ISBN13: 978-0-8058-6422-9 (hbk)
ISBN13: 978-0-415-99217-6 (pbk)
ISBN13: 978-1-4106-1857-3 (ebk)

Contents

Figures

Tables

Contributors

Stephen E. Anderson is Associate Professor in the Educational Administration Program, Department of Theory and Policy Studies, Ontario Institute for Studies in Education, University of Toronto, Canada. His research interests include education policy and program implementation, school improvement and teacher development, and his work includes research and consulting activities in Canada, the United States, Africa, and Pakistan.

Eric M. Camburn is Assistant Professor in Educational Leadership and Policy Analysis at the University of Wisconsin-Madison. His research focuses on the improvement of leadership and teaching practice. His current research is primarily conducted in urban settings and focuses on programmatic efforts to improve school leadership and instruction; the organizational factors that support such improvement efforts; and the impact such change efforts have on leadership practice, instruction, and student achievement. Camburn's research has appeared in the *American Educational Research Journal*, the *American Journal of Education*, *Educational Administration Quarterly*, *Educational Evaluation and Policy Analysis*, and the *Elementary School Journal*.

William A. Firestone is Professor of Educational Policy and Leadership in the Rutgers Graduate School of Education, New Brunswick, New Jersey. His interests include the effects of a variety of policies on teaching, leadership distribution, and qualitative research methods. His recent books include *A New Agenda for Research in Educational Leadership* and *The Ambiguity of Teaching to the Test*.

Joseph J. Flessa is Assistant Professor in Educational Policy and Politics in the department of Theory and Policy Studies at the Ontario Institute for Studies in Education at the University of Toronto, Canada, where he teaches graduate courses in educational administration and teacher education courses in social foundations. His research interests include urban school leadership, schooling and inequality, and the professional preparation of school administrators. As a PhD student at the University of California, Berkeley he helped to found an innovative preparation program for urban school principals. Before graduate school he taught sixth grade in Houston, Texas, and taught fifth grade and later served as principal of a bilingual, bicultural school in Mexico.

Peter Gronn is a professor and the foundation chair in Public Service, Educational Leadership and Management, University of Glasgow, Scotland.

Previously, he held a personal chair appointment as Professor in the Faculty of Education, Monash University. He is the author of well over 100 publications. His most recent book is *The New Work of Educational Leaders* (London: Sage/Paul Chapman, 2003). In 2005–6 Peter was a consultant to the Australian Council for Educational Research on the project "Standards for School Leadership" and in 2006–7 he co-authored the Country Background Report for Australia which formed part of the OECD international project on school leadership.

W. Norton Grubb is a professor and the David Gardner Chair in Higher Education at the School of Education, the University of California, Berkeley. He is also the Faculty Coordinator for the Principal Leadership Institute, an innovative program to prepare urban school leaders. He has published extensively on various topics in the economics of education, public finance, education policy, community colleges and "second chance" programs including job training, and social policy for children and youth. His most recent book is about the vocational transformations of American schooling: *The Education Gospel: The Economic Power of Schooling*, published in 2004 by Harvard University Press. He received his doctorate in economics from Harvard University in 1975.

Alma Harris is a professor and holds the Chair in Educational Leadership at London Centre for Leadership in Learning, at the Institute of Education, University of London. She has previously held posts at the University of Warwick, University of Nottingham, and University of Bath. She is currently Associate Director of the "Specialist Schools and Academies Trust" and she is the editor of *School Leadership and Management*. Her research work has focused upon organizational change, particularly on ways in which leadership can contribute to school development and change. Her work has explored middle-level leadership, teacher leadership, and leadership in challenging circumstances. Her most recent work has focused on distributed leadership and her book *Distributed School Leadership: Developing Tomorrow's Leaders* is published by Routledge/Falmer Press in July 2008.

Kenneth Leithwood is Professor of Educational Leadership and Policy at the Ontario Institute for Studies in Education at the University of Toronto, Canada. His research and writing concerns school leadership, educational policy, and organizational change. Dr Leithwood has published more than 70 refereed journal articles and authored or edited more than 30 books. For example, he is the senior editor of both the first and second *International Handbook on Educational Leadership and Administration* (Kluwer Publishers, 1996, 2003). His most recent books (all with Corwin Press) include *Making Schools Smarter* (third edition, 2006) and *Teaching for Deep Understanding*

(2006). Among his current research projects is a large, five-year Wallace Foundation study, with colleagues, aimed at determining how state, district, and school-level leadership influences student learning. Dr Leithwood is the recent recipient of the University of Toronto's Impact on Public Policy award.

Karen Seashore Louis is Rodney S. Wallace Professor of Educational Policy and Administration at the University of Minnesota. Her work over the past several decades has focused on the intersection of teachers' work and school reform. Her most recent books include *Professional Learning Communities* (2007, with Louise Stoll), *Organizing for School Change* (2007), and *Strong Cultures: A Principal's Guide to School Improvement* (with Sharon D. Kruse, in press).

John MacBeath OBE is Professor Emeritus at the University of Cambridge and Director of Leadership for Learning: The Cambridge Network. He was a member of Tony Blair's Task Force on Standards between 1997 and 2001 and continues to advise a number of government bodies including the Hong Kong Education Department since 1997. Other consultancies have included OECD, UNESCO, and ILO (International Labour Organisation), the Bertelsmann Foundation and the European Commission. He is currently President of the International Congress on School Effectiveness and Improvement. His books on school self-evaluation and school improvement have been translated into 13 languages.

M. Cecilia Martinez is a post-doctoral fellow at the National University of Buenos Aires, in Argentina. As a research assistant at Rutgers University, she has worked on several qualitative studies analyzing how urban schools could improve math and science teaching. She has collaborated at the New Jersey Department of Education analyzing qualitative data from urban schools. She has also worked at Educational Testing Services at the Teaching and Learning Research Center. Currently, she is conducting an action research study that explores the role of professional communities in changing teachers' beliefs about their students and about their practices.

Blair Mascall is Professor of Leadership and Educational Change at the Ontario Institute for Studies in Education at the University of Toronto, Canada. He is currently working on a large five-year study funded by the Wallace Foundation, examining the link between leadership at the state, district, and school levels, and its impact on student learning across the United States. His current work on distributed leadership with Kenneth Leithwood and Tiiu Strauss builds on eight years of research on the role of leadership in implementing systemic reform.

David Mayrowetz is Assistant Professor of Educational Policy Studies in the College of Education at the University of Illinois in Chicago. His research interests include the formation and implementation of educational policy and how individual, organizational, and institutional factors shape those processes, especially in schools and classrooms. Mayrowetz earned an EdD in educational administration and an MS in public policy from Rutgers University. He has a BA from the University of Pennsylvania and he is a former US Education Department employee.

Nadeem Memon is a doctoral student in the Department of Theory and Policy Studies at the Ontario Institute for Studies in Education at the University of Toronto, Canada, and part-time faculty member at Centennial College. Among his research interests is the interconnection between distributed leadership and student leadership.

Shawn Moore worked as a Senior Research Officer at the Ontario Institute for Studies in Education of the University of Toronto from 1980 to 2005. His research and writing includes the following areas: developmental theory and children's understanding; the social organization, teaching, and learning implications of computers in the classroom; parents' involvement in schooling and their child's learning; teachers' intellectual and emotional experiences of educational change; structures and forms of educational leadership and the policy and process of principal succession. Mr Moore is currently a Research Consultant on the Wallace Foundation Study, "Learning from District Efforts to Strengthen Education Leadership."

Joseph Murphy is Associate Dean and Professor at Peabody College at Vanderbilt University. His area of research is school improvement, with an interest in leadership and policy. He is past vice president of AERA. His most recent book is *Turning Around Failing Schools: Leadership Lessons from the Organizational Sciences*.

Amber Stitziel Pareja, PhD is a post-doctoral fellow at the Institute for Policy Research (IPR) at Northwestern University and works on the National Institute for School Leadership (NISL) study. She is currently working to develop a multi-method research agenda aimed at examining the ways in which the composition of a school's student body affects principal practice. Dr Pareja's research interests include: inequality among children in educational achievement in particular and life chances in general; race/ethnicity and social class; educational policy, social policy, and the interaction between the two; and mixed-methods research (quantitative and qualitative).

Robin Sacks is currently working on her PhD in Child Development and Education at the University of Toronto with a focus on youth leadership and positive youth development. Robin's dissertation research involves the first ever Canadian national survey of youth leaders. She is developing curricula for schools to couple students' leadership and service experiences with positive self-identity development. She is the founder of Peace by PEACE Canada which trains university students to teach a 12-week conflict resolution and community-building curriculum in elementary schools. Since its inception, Peace by PEACE has trained 1500 university students and reached over 10,000 school children.

Mark A. Smylie is Professor and Chair of the Educational Policy Studies Department in the College of Education at the University of Illinois in Chicago. His research interests include urban school improvement, teacher and administrative leadership, and the relationship of school organization to classroom teaching and student learning. Smylie received his PhD in educational leadership from Peabody College at Vanderbilt University and his MEd and BA from Duke University. He is a former high school social studies teacher.

James P. Spillane is the Spencer T. and Ann W. Olin Chair in Learning and Organizational Change at Northwestern University, where he is a Professor of Human Development and Social Policy, Learning Sciences, and Management and Organizations. Spillane is a Faculty Fellow at Northwestern University's Institute for Policy Research and is a senior research fellow with the Consortium for Policy Research in Education (CPRE). With funding from the National Science Foundation, the Spencer Foundation, and the Institute for Education Sciences, Spillane's work explores the policy implementation process at the state, school district, school, and classroom levels, and school leadership and management. He is author of *Standards Deviation: How Local Schools Miss-Understand Policy* (Harvard University Press, 2004), *Distributed Leadership* (Jossey-Bass, 2006), *Distributed Leadership in Practice* (Teachers College Record, 2007), and numerous journal articles and book chapters.

Tiiu Strauss is currently a project director working with Kenneth Leithwood in the Department of Theory and Policy Studies at the Ontario Institute for Studies in Education at the University of Toronto, Canada. She has published in the areas of leader problem solving and distributed leadership. She is also involved in research projects related to leadership in turnaround schools.

Jingping Sun is a PhD student in Educational Administration at the Ontario Institute for Studies in Education, University of Toronto, Canada. She has published in the areas of school leadership and Chinese higher education reforms. Her research interests are school and district leadership and student learning, values theory, and comparative studies of leadership. Her dissertation is on meta-analysis of transformational leadership research.

Helen S. Timperley is a professor and holds an academic position at the University of Auckland, New Zealand. She has been involved in researching and evaluating the New Zealand Ministry of Education's initiatives to improve schooling for traditionally underachieving groups for a number of years. Her disciplinary background is organizational psychology, with a particular interest in promoting the learning of professionals, both teachers and leaders within schools.

Anna Yashkina is a PhD student in the Educational Administration program at the Ontario Institute for Studies of Education, University of Toronto, Canada. Her interests are educational leadership and learning communities. Before coming to Canada, Anna completed her bachelor's degree in Education and Foreign Philology at the Kharkov State Pedagogical University and worked as an English teacher and a curriculum manager in the public educational sector in the Ukraine.

Preface

Few concepts in the educational leadership field have garnered more popular attention over the past half dozen years than "distributed leadership." This popularity reflects the extent to which heroic images of leadership have become out of step with the more grounded – and decidedly unheroic – leadership experienced by many of those in schools. The current preoccupation with distributed leadership is also in response to the more complex mission facing schools, a mission which, if it is to be approximated, will require generous infusions of professional expertise wherever it can be found. The idea of distributed leadership is also aligned with a growing appreciation of just how much influence people not occupying formal administrative roles actually do have in schools, not to mention a widespread disaffection with formal office holders who often wield their power largely for their own benefit, at least in other sectors of society.

But being popular is not the same as being useful, effective, right, or valuable. Nor is being popular the same as being clear about the conditions under which distributed leadership has its most beneficial effects, how it is developed, what forms it might take, and whether there are different outcomes of enactment of different patterns of leadership distribution. Some systematic scientific evidence about these matters would seem to be very helpful at this point. And so we have assembled ten chapters describing the latest and best of the available science addressing a reasonably comprehensive array of important questions about leadership distribution. We have tried to synthesize this evidence, offer some additional clarity about some concepts, and extend the implications for research and practice in the first and last chapters for which we were responsible as editors.

Research on distributed leadership helps to advance a larger agenda about optimal forms of organizing. This is an agenda also reflected in research about collaborative cultures, teamwork, professional learning communities, communities of practice, and the flattening of bureaucratic structure. Indeed, these lines of research often overlap and intersect, suggesting that we are still behaving like the proverbial "blind man" trying to imagine what the elephant looks like by feeling its individual parts. This text reveals most of the parts of distributed leadership as we now understand it; "touching" each of them should significantly improve the readers' overall understanding about the nature, causes and consequences of distributed leadership in schools and districts.

We do not pretend to know what prompted each of our contributing authors' explorations of distributed leadership. For us editors, it grew "naturally" out of a long line of research concerned with many issues concerning leadership. We suspect this is the case for many of our contributing authors, most of whom are either senior scholars or were working with senior scholars on the research that appears in this volume. Some of us came together in order to produce a special issue on distributed leadership for the journal *Leadership and Policy in Schools*. Our mutual satisfaction with the outcome prompted a symposium at the American Educational Research Association's annual conference in April of 2006. One thing led to another – the idea of a book with others contributing, as well, was not much of a stretch from there.

The Editors

1

New Perspectives on an Old Idea

A Short History of the Old Idea

KENNETH LEITHWOOD, BLAIR MASCALL, AND TIIU STRAUSS

Current conversations about educational leadership have increasingly included questions about its sources. *Distributed leadership* is much in vogue with researchers, policy makers, educational reformers, and leadership practitioners alike (Hammersley-Fletcher & Brundrett, 2005; Storey, 2004). Not surprisingly, however, there are competing and sometimes conflicting interpretations of what distributed leadership actually means. As Harris (2004) has noted, the definition and understanding of distributed leadership varies from the normative to the descriptive. Some, for example, are attracted to increasing, or otherwise manipulating, the distribution of leadership as a possible strategy for school improvement. This perspective, reflected in most of the chapters in this text, encompasses "shared" (Pearce & Conger, 2003), "democratic" and "dispersed" (e.g. Ray et al., 2004) conceptions of leadership, as well. Others (e.g. Spillane et al., Chapter 5 in this volume) employ the concept as a means of "simply" better understanding the meaning and nature of leadership in schools. Not surprisingly, then, the literature about distributed leadership remains diverse and broad based (Bennett et al., 2003).

Although current interests in leadership distribution represent a shift in both educational leadership research and policy from a preoccupation with those in formal roles, the study of distributed sources of leadership can be traced back at least to the work of Gibbs in 1954 (Gronn, Chapter 2) and possibly as far back as the mid-1920s. As MacBeath's example of the counsel to Moses reminds us (Chapter 3), however, the actual practice of distributed leadership is as old as human efforts to organize. Pearce and Conger (2003) provide a very useful synopsis of the roots of research on leadership distribution and trace their evolution to the present. The significant shift in interest toward sources of leadership reflects, they suggest, disillusionment with "great man" conceptions of leadership and bureaucratic organizational structures. This shift also reflects growing appreciation for the contributions to productivity of the informal dimensions of organizations (Tschannen-Moran, 2004), the untapped and often unrecognized leadership capacities found among those not in positions of formal authority (Gronn, 2003), and the extent to which the capacities of those at the organizational apex alone have been overtaken by the complexities of the challenges they now face (Wheatley, 2005). Through a normative lens, leadership increasingly is conceptualized as an organization-wide phenomenon (Ogawa & Bossert, 1995) in which flatter organizational structures and leadership distributed over multiple people and roles are being advocated as solutions to these dilemmas (Manz & Sims, 1993).

Indeed, the overwhelming disposition of the contemporary, normatively-oriented literature on distributed leadership is enthusiastic optimism about its anticipated benefits. As compared with exclusively hierarchical or "focused" forms of leadership, distributed leadership is thought to more accurately reflect the division of labor which is experienced in organizations from day to day and to reduce the chances of error arising from decisions based on the limited information available to a single leader. Distributed leadership, it is argued, also enhances opportunities for the organization to benefit from the capacities of more of its members, permits members to capitalize on the range of their individual strengths, and develops among organizational members a fuller appreciation of interdependence and how one's behavior affects the organization as a whole. Through increased participation in decision making, greater commitment to organizational goals and strategies may develop. Distributed leadership, some claim, has the potential to increase on-the-job leadership development experiences and reduce the workload for those in formal administrative roles (presumably by increasing the workload of others). The increased self-determination believed to arise from distributed leadership may improve members' experience of work. Such leadership might allow members to better anticipate and respond to the demands of the organization's environment. Solutions to organizational challenges may develop through distributed leadership which would be unlikely to emerge from individual sources. Overlapping actions that occur in some distributed leadership contexts provide further reinforcement of leadership influence (e.g. Burke et al., 2003; Cox et al., 2003; Gronn, 2002; Grubb & Flessa, Chapter 7). England's *National College of School Leadership* is advocating more distributed leadership as a strategy for increasing both administrator and teacher retention, as well as minimizing the significant negative consequences typically associated with leadership succession (NCSL, 2004).

Empirical Evidence About the Consequences of Distributed Leadership

Positive Consequences

The above list of potential positive consequences of distributed leadership is impressive. One might reasonably expect that if even a few such outcomes materialized, the effects on the organization's bottom line would be signific-

ant. In point of fact, however, the evidence to justify a belief in these consequences is mixed and indirect. On the supportive side of the ledger, for
example, the effectiveness of democratic, supportive and shared forms of
organizational leadership (defined as control and influence) have received
support from research on teacher participation with peers in planning and
decision making (Talbert & McLaughlin, 1993) and from tests of shared
transformational leadership effects (Leithwood & Jantzi, 2005). A reasonably
strong case for the value of distributed leadership can also be found in studies
of organizational turnaround processes, as well. While focused leadership
seems most useful at the "crisis stabilization" stage, the subsequent "recovery"
stage demands widespread sharing of responsibility to be successful (Murphy,
in press; Nicolaidou & Ainscow, 2002).

Leadership succession studies also provide evidence in support of the value
of widely distributed sources of leadership, as NCSL's advocacy illustrates.
This line of research suggests that the often devastating effects of principals'
succession on school improvement processes can be significantly mitigated
when both the ownership and leadership of such processes is widely dispersed
(e.g. Fink & Brayman, 2006). In a recent study of teacher retention, as another
positive consequence of shared forms of leadership, Ingersoll (2007) found
that teacher leadership or control over some key decisions, in this case school
and classroom disciplinary policies, had striking effects on the willingness of
teachers to continue in their existing schools. More specifically, "Almost one
in five teachers in schools with a low level of teacher control over student
discipline issues were expected to depart, whereas only one in 20 were
expected to depart from schools with high levels of teacher control over such
issues" (p. 24).

Negative Consequences

Empirical evidence about the consequences of distributed leadership is not all
positive, however. For example, a recent, very comprehensive, review of
teacher leadership – one approach to the distribution of influence and control
in school organizations – found only a very small handful of studies which
had actually inquired about effects on students and these data were generally
not supportive (York-Barr & Duke, 2004). One of the few large-scale empirical studies directly testing the effects of *collective* school leadership on students (i.e. their engagement in school) also reported non-significant, negative
effects. The authors speculated that this might signify a non-linear relationship between the number of sources of leadership and organizational outcomes. Beyond some optimal amount, perhaps "more leadership actually
detracts from clarity of purpose, sense of mission, sufficient certainty about
what needs to be done to allow for productive action in the school and the
like" (Leithwood & Jantzi, 2000, p. 61). Others have offered similar specula-
tions (e.g. Bryk, 1998; Timperley, 2005). Ritchie and Woods (2007) allude to

the potential of distributed leadership to increase the burdens and responsibilities of teachers without actually increasing their power. Such leadership may simply be used as a subtle strategy for inculcating among staff the values and goals of more powerful members of the organization.

Additional evidence about the negative consequences of more widely distributing leadership can be found in research carried out in non-school contexts, especially research in which effectiveness is defined as some version of organizational productivity and assessed using objective indicators. For example, Tannenbaum (1961) was able to provide only limited support for his hypotheses about the contributions of "democratic" organizational control structures. And after about 15 years of programmatic research about "organic management," Miller and Rowan (2006) reported that "the main effects are weak and positive effects appear to be contingent on many other conditions" (p. 220). It is reasonable to conclude at this point, then, that the positive consequences of more widely distributing leadership in schools cannot simply be assumed; their precise nature remains unpredictable and likely depends on circumstances and conditions that we do not yet understand very well.

Theoretical Explanations for Distributed Leadership Effects

In addition to the empirical evidence exemplified above, a handful of different theoretical perspectives give rise to expectations about mostly positive associations between organizational effectiveness and the distribution of influence and control to more people, especially those not occupying formal leadership roles. We briefly describe four such perspectives, pointing out how each might be used to better understand the nature and consequences of leadership distribution. These perspectives include organizational learning, distributed cognition, complexity science, and high involvement leadership or management.

Organizational Learning Theory

According to this perspective, learning can take place outside individual brains (Weick & Roberts, 1996). An organization can be more intelligent than any one of its individual members, reflecting Gronn's (2002) concept of "concertive action" as a type of distributed leadership. This collective learning depends on the nature of a small set of key organizational conditions such as a culture of collaboration (Ritchie & Woods, 2007; Starbuck, 1996) in support of such learning. Hutchins' (1995) description of how the navigation team, on a disabled aircraft carrier, managed to bring the ship under control without being able to use their established routines and without any central direction, is often cited as the type of evidence capable of supporting these claims. Applied to the concept of distributed leadership, this line of theory raises the expectation that distributed leadership will lead to improved organizational capacity; it also suggests the need for implicit coordination, if not intentional planning, of leadership distribution if the superior capacity development assumed by collective learning is to materialize in practice.

Distributed Cognition

Theories of distributed cognition offer a set of ideas closely related to those found in theories of organizational learning as explanations for the potentially positive effects of distributed leadership (e.g. Salomon, 1993). This line of theory points to the different sets of capacities that exist not only within individual members of an organization but also in the technical and physical artefacts that constitute the setting in which people find themselves. From this perspective, capacities are distributed throughout both the social and material conditions which constitute the organization. When applied to the concept of distributed leadership, this line of thinking encompasses Jermier and Kerr's (1997) concept of "substitutes for leadership" – although it would be more accurate to describe what they have in mind as substitutes for leadership *by people*. These substitutes include the direction and influence on organizational members exercised by the technical and material artefacts found in organizations as, for example, its policies, procedures, culture, and shared mental models.

If our concept of leadership includes at least influence in pursuit of the organization's directions, such non-social features of the organization must count as forms of distributed leadership. In this text, the work of Spillane et al. (Chapter 5) makes explicit reference to distributed cognition theory, even borrowing and adapting Perkins (1993) "person plus" concept to label a pattern of distributed leadership as *leader plus*. This pattern captures instances in which members' individual contributions add up to more than the sum of their parts through the interdependent nature of relationships among them. Spillane and his colleagues, however, limit their purview, as do the writers of all other chapters, to the social sources of leadership and cognition within organizations.

Much like organizational learning theory, distributed cognition gives rise to the expectation that the existing capacities of individual members of the organization, along with the sources of influence to be found in the organization's technology and other artefacts, are radically underutilized in contexts of control firmly exercised by formal leaders at the organization's apex. Unlike organizational learning theory, however, distributed cognition is mostly about using existing capacities more fully, as distinct from learning new capacities; it leads to the assumption that considerable value could be added to the organization's effectiveness by simply making better use of the existing capacities without the additional investment required to learn new capacities. The most powerful forms of leadership distribution, from this perspective, would be founded on close knowledge of where in the organization was located the expertise needed to respond productively to a perceived challenge. Given such knowledge, the job of formal leaders is to bring those perhaps disparate sources of expertise together and insert a coordination function into their collective problem solving processes.

Complexity Science

Although its natural environment is the physical sciences, concepts from complexity science offer evocative metaphors for trying to better understand social organization. Complexity science appears to be a largely unused tool of some promise for unpacking the nature and consequences of distributed leadership. Indeed, this theoretical perspective has significant implications for focused leadership or those in formal leadership roles, as well. According to Uhl-Bien et al. (2007), for example, the rapidly changing context in which knowledge organizations (that would include schools) find themselves means that "organizations must increase their complexity to the level of the environment rather than trying to simplify and rationalize their structures" (p. 301). Citing the *Law of Requisite Complexity*, this means that:

> It takes complexity to defeat complexity.... Knowledge Era leadership requires a change in thinking away from individual, controlling views, and toward views of organizations as complex adaptive systems [CAS] that enable continuous creation and capture knowledge. In short, knowledge development, adaptability, and innovation are optimally enabled in organizations that are complexly adaptive (possessing requisite complexity).
>
> (p. 301)

Since bureaucracy and hierarchy are simplifying strategies, complexity science suggests that optimal adaptability is most likely when those closest to the action are empowered to shape the organization's responses. Such empowerment through, for example, the distribution of leadership to groups whose members work interdependently, is likely to generate rapid and innovative solutions when these groups are prompted to find solutions largely unconstrained by existing, widely-shared mental models and organizational structures (Osborn & Hunt, 2007). Thus empowered, such groups may self-organize themselves as they adjust their collective behavior to the environment in unpredictable ways. Moving between periods of stability and instability, these groups may be expected to produce emergent and creative actions or solutions as they approach disequilibrium, instability or the "edge of chaos" (Waldrop, 1992). As Osborn and Hunt (2007) explain: "In self organizing systems, order comes from the actions of interdependent agents who exchange information, take actions, and continuously adapt to feedback about others' actions rather than from the imposition of an overall plan by a central authority" (p. 343).

Formal leaders prompt emergent and creative actions among groups to whom leadership has been distributed by, for example, disrupting existing patterns within the organization, embracing uncertainty, creating and surfacing conflict and encouraging novelty (Plowman et al., 2007). From a complexity perspective, those in formal leadership roles "emphasize the management of interdependencies, rather than controls over process or outcomes" (Osborn & Hunt, 2007, p. 329).

So complexity science focuses our attention on the rich networks of relationships that are made more likely by distributing leadership more, and assumes that the complex adaptive systems likely to form and reform through their interdependencies will respond more rapidly and produce more innovative responses to organizations' challenges than would be the case without such distribution. But complexity science applied to social organizations also awards considerable importance to the facilitating actions of those in formal leadership roles. Useful solutions to organizational challenges do not emerge "for free" (Osborn & Hunt, 2007) from the naturally emerging interdependencies created by greater leadership distribution; such solutions require thoughtful nurturing and careful planning by those in formal leadership positions.

High Involvement Leadership

"Participative" leadership is among the lines of leadership research closely related to our meaning of distributed leadership. As Yukl (1994) has noted, "After supportive and task-oriented behavior, the largest amount of behavior research has been on participative leadership" (p. 159). This is research dating back to studies by social psychologists carried out in the late 1930s. Many of the same advantages claimed for participative leadership are to be found among the positive consequences anticipated for distributed leadership summarized earlier in this chapter. Yukl (1994) also points out, however, that participative leadership need not include the distribution of leadership; it may be limited to consulting with one's non-leader colleagues or to engaging them in joint decision making. Distributed leadership then, lies at the extreme end of what is typically thought of as a continuum of degrees of participatory leadership.

Not surprisingly, organizational theorists have, by now, generated a substantial array of alternative approaches to productively increasing involvement in the leadership of organizations. One well-known model for doing so, a model that has guided considerable research in schools (e.g. Wohlstetter & Mohrman, 1993), was developed and tested by Lawler and his colleagues (e.g. Lawler et al., 1992). This model stipulates greater organizational productivity emerging through the provision to employees of greater information about the organization and its work, greater knowledge among employees through better access to capacity building experiences, as well as significant access to both the power and rewards associated with the work of the organization.

Access to power in its many forms, in particular, is almost synonymous with many conceptions of leadership and is at least implicit in all of them. Research related to Lawler's model has, among other things, examined the consequences of different approaches to increasing employee power including "enriching" peoples' jobs by, for example, adding more variety to their jobs, and making the tasks people are required to carry out more meaningful. Giving people more autonomy over decisions of direct importance to how they perform their jobs is also a job enrichment strategy, one which Ritchie and Woods (2007) found to encourage greater leadership distribution in schools. In Chapter 8, Mayrowetz et al. explore the value of Hackman and Oldham's (1980) Job Characteristics Model for explaining consequences of the job enrichment anticipated by greater distribution of leadership in schools.

Distributed Leadership's "Problem Space"

Undeniably, a central problem for those adopting either a normative or descriptive lens on distributed leadership is some version of figuring out "Who does what?" For those aspiring to use leadership distribution as a strategy for school improvement, this encompasses questions about whether some practices are better carried out by some people or roles rather than others (Grubb & Flessa, Chapter 7) and whether some patterns of distribution are more productive than others (Leithwood et al., Chapter 10; Timperley, Chapter 9). Those with primarily descriptive or theoretical interests want to know, among other things: How does leadership distribution emerge in organizations?; and What accounts for the interactions that occur within and among those exercising leadership? (e.g. Gronn, Chapter 2). Examples of other important questions to be addressed, largely from a normative perspective, include how leadership capacities can be developed across members of the organization? (e.g. Anderson et al., Chapter 6), why people come to be attributed leadership qualities by their colleagues (e.g. Leithwood et al., Chapter 10), and what role formal leaders play in fostering greater leadership distribution in their organizations (e.g. Firestone & Martinez, Chapter 4).

An Overview of the Chapters

Part 1 provides a discussion of foundational information on what distributed leadership is. In Chapter 2, Gronn argues that since its emergence as a field of inquiry, leadership has displayed, and continues to display, extraordinary resilience and adaptiveness. Unlike other areas of the social sciences, for example, it basically managed to sidestep the paradigm wars of the 1970s–1980s and it has remained pretty much immune to the questions raised by post-modernists. The current state of the field is one in which the citadel of focused orthodoxy is under threat by a new kid on the block, distributed leadership. The question that is not clear here is: What happens next? A number of developments are possible. The one argued for in this chapter, is hybridization. This suggestion was first made by Day et al. (2006) in a recent co-edited special edition of *Leadership Quarterly* devoted to leadership in team-based organizations. Hybridization refers to empirically determined adaptational patterns of leadership; the various ways in which schools, for example, operating in policy environments of market devolution, configure their overall density of leadership resources to meet their site-based needs. This means that in some instances, for example, individuals may monopolize leadership while in others leadership will be shared; in others it will be emergent; in still others, organizational personnel may self-lead, while in some cases there may be complex patterns of role sharing and interdependence. Implicit in the idea of hybridization is an evolutionary view of change, implying some form of environmental selection, retention, mutation and discard of forms in response to changing circumstances. The chapter aims to identify some of the problems and possibilities opened up by a hybrid view of leadership, and the significance of this perspective for the future of the field.

MacBeath (Chapter 3) takes the view that distributed leadership remains a contested concept embracing a wide range of understandings and often bearing little apparent relationship to what happens in schools and classrooms. This chapter draws on a study in England carried out for the National College of School Leadership in which six forms of distribution were identified. These were co-constructed by researchers and school personnel working together to theorize practice, and in light of that, to revisit those practices with new levels of awareness. While these six forms of distribution may be regarded as a developmental sequence, evidence from shadowing, interviews, and workshops shows that in the complex and changing world of schools, things are rarely that simple, and leadership activity, whether individual or shared, has to be responsive to prevailing cultural conditions. This chapter argues that those who lead and those who follow can do so more intelligently, inviting of enhanced social capital, when they have a clearer theory-in-use of what leadership is and how it expresses itself in school life. This theoretical stance, it is argued, understands leadership as existing in different forms of activity and within differing activity systems.

In Part 2, we look at recent explorations of how distributed leadership works in schools and districts. From the perspective of Firestone and Martinez (Chapter 4), the growing interest in distributed leadership reflects an effort to reconceptualize leadership in schools by exploring how leadership is spread across a variety of roles and to explore the process of leadership. Using case studies of four schools in three districts, this chapter explores how leadership is distributed in school districts and asks about the role of teacher leaders in particular. It proposes that teacher leaders and districts can share three leadership tasks: procuring and distributing materials, monitoring improvement, and developing people. The district and teacher leaders play complementary roles. Districts tend to be distant forces, and teacher leaders are more personal. How effective teacher leaders are at people development will depend on the time they have, the knowledge they have, and their monitoring responsibilities. These conditions depend partly on their administrative support. The authors suggest that districts may have more opportunity to influence teaching practice than past research had indicated.

Chapter 5 (Spillane et al.) is the only chapter in the book to adopt a descriptive orientation to distributed leadership. Focusing on the school principal's day to day work, these authors inquire about who leads curriculum and instruction- and administration-related activities when the school principal is not leading but is participating in the activity. The study reported in this chapter also explores the prevalence of co-performance of management and leadership activities in the school principal's workday. Looking across a range of administration- and curriculum and instruction-related activities school principals participate in, we show that who takes responsibility for leading and managing the schoolhouse varies considerably from activity to activity and from one school to the next.

Chapter 6 by Anderson et al., presents an analysis of how leadership for school improvement was distributed in five schools in varying state and district contexts, with an emphasis on understanding the principal's role in the distribution of leadership. The analysis integrates concepts from research on core leadership practices (*setting directions, developing people, redesigning the workplace, managing the instructional program*) and on alternative patterns of leadership distribution in organizational settings. The findings highlight the need to distinguish between school-wide and goal-specific patterns of leadership distribution in schools, and to recognize that how principals interact with other sources of leadership may vary for different focuses of improvement in the same school. The principals' orientation toward state and district influences on school goal setting and toward the use of professional expertise (their own, teachers', and external sources) in the pursuit of school improvement goals, were key factors shaping leadership distribution.

In Chapter 7, Grubb and Flessa report the results of one of the very few studies that have been undertaken about the nature and consequences of a formal sharing of the principalship on the part of two or more people. Current federal, state, and local school accountability measures, as well as policy initiatives that call for improved leadership have placed increasing demands on principals. Many districts face shortages of appropriate candidates for the job; popularly, this shortage is explained by the fact that simply too few hero-principals exist for all openings available, particularly in high-needs districts. An alternative to finding the perfect – and rare – candidate for an increasingly untenable position is to restructure the job itself.

The study on which this chapter is based examined ten schools that had adopted alternative structures: schools with two principals, three principals, rotating principals, and a school with the principal's duties distributed among teachers. These ten sites provided examples of alternative ways of organizing school leadership with varying benefits and challenges. Data collection at the ten schools included site visits conducted by a team of researchers, interviews with principals, teacher leaders, and district supervisors. Observational and interview protocols were adapted from the Northwestern University Distributed Leadership Study. These protocols focus on uncovering not only how school site leaders explain their decisions but also on providing evidence of what those decisions are. Interview and observational data were organized into thematic codes to permit cross-case comparison.

The authors observed the idiosyncratic ways in which schools and districts approached the policy dilemmas associated with attempts to change the default administrative structure of principal and assistant principal. Some schools with co-principals, for example, thrived; others struggled. Where local school sites participated actively with the policy-making process that produced these arrangements, the alternative seemed viable. Where alternatives were imposed without school input, implementation floundered. The findings analyze the origins of the reforms, school site roles, costs and benefits, the role of the district, and the long-term stability of the approach.

Part 3 brings together several discussions of the effects of distributed leadership in a wide range of contexts. Chapter 8 (Mayrowetz et al.) offers us a theory of both why and how leadership distribution might be expected to have positive consequences for students. In recent years, the authors note, educators have been trying to create "distributed leadership" in their schools, often with the support of influential groups in the educational leadership policy community. Generally these reforms involve groups of teachers becoming formal leaders by undertaking tasks they would not traditionally have done, including some that would be perceived as administrative. In this chapter, they revive work redesign theory, specifically Hackman and Oldham's (1980) Job Characteristics Model (JCM) as a tool to examine these distributed leadership initiatives and to predict the success or failures of these efforts. Based on their early observations of six schools engaged in distributed leadership reform and a broad review of literature, including empirical tests of work redesign theory inside and outside schools, they retrofitted the JCM by: (1) adding more transition mechanisms to explain how changes in work could lead to the widespread performance of leadership functions; (2) accounting for the fact that distributed leadership reform is a group work redesign; and most important, (3) enumerating relevant contextual variables that should impact the development, shape, and success of such reforms. The authors conclude with suggestions for future directions in the research of distributed leadership reforms.

Chapter 9 reports the results of a study carried out by Timperley in New Zealand. This chapter presents a case for distributing leadership in particular ways that can have positive outcomes for students in a school improvement context in which varying success was evident. Grounding the theory in this practice context led to the identification of some risks and benefits of distributing leadership and to the challenge of some key concepts presented in earlier theorizing about leadership and its distribution. Concepts related to distributed leadership discussed in the chapter include embedding vision in activities and the social distribution of task enactment. Issues addressed within the latter concept include boundary spanning, relationships between leaders and followers, and the use of artefacts.

The study reported in Chapter 10 (Leithwood et al.) inquired about: patterns of leadership distribution, who performed which leadership functions, the characteristics of non-administrative leaders, and the factors promoting and inhibiting the distribution of leadership functions. This qualitative study was carried out in both elementary (4) and secondary (4) schools located in a district the authors considered to be an example of "best practice" for distributing leadership in ways likely to be productive in relation to the goals of the district. Results of this study suggest a four-fold classification of leadership distribution patterns with different consequences for schools and students. The results also describe the characteristics associated with those in schools who provide informal leadership, and identify the factors that both foster and inhibit the emergence of distributed patterns of leadership in schools.

Chapter 11 focuses on the relationship between distributed forms of leadership in schools and the processes of knowledge creation. Harris argues that knowledge creation is best supported and nurtured by forming communities of practice based on social processes where individuals collaborate and work together. These "micro-communities of knowledge" provide the shared space that encourages and nurtures participation on many different levels. The chapter provides illustrations from "development and research" (D and R) school networks in England that are actively seeking ways of restructuring and redefining leadership practice. Within these D and R networks, schools are focused upon deep and distributed leadership. Harris suggests that distributed leadership provides the "organizational circuitry" which can support knowledge creation within and between schools.

Our objective for this book was to draw together a body of current knowledge on the new practices of this old idea in schools and districts. The lack of empirical evidence about the practice and effects of leadership distribution has caused us to question the enthusiasm for this approach to leadership in schools. The research and conceptual rigor presented by the authors in this volume provide a much-needed empirical base for examining distributed leadership in today's educational climate. These chapters provide insights for those who are attempting to practice distributed leadership, as well as, considerable guidance for those doing research on the subject in the future.

References

Bennett, N., Harvey, J.A., Wise, C., & Woods, P.A. (2003). *Desk study review of distributed leadership.* Nottingham, UK: NCSL/CEPAM. Available at: www.ncsl.org.uk/literaturereviews.

Bryk, A. (1998). *Charting Chicago school reform: Democratic localism as a lever for change.* Boulder, CO: Westview Press.

Burke, C.S., Fiore, S.M., & Salas, E. (2003). The role of shared cognition in enabling shared leadership and team adaptability. In C.J. Pearce & J.A. Conger (eds), *Shared leadership: Reframing the how and whys of leadership* (pp. 103–122). Thousand Oaks, CA: Sage.

Cox, J.F., Pearce, C.L., & Perry, M.L. (2003). Toward a model of shared leadership and distributed influence in the innovation process: How shared leadership can enhance new product development, teach dynamics and self effectiveness. In C.L. Pearce & J.A. Conger (eds), *Shared leadership: Reframing the hows and whys of leadership* (pp. 48–76). Thousand Oaks, CA: Sage.

Day, C., Gronn, P., & Salas, E. (2006). Leadership in team-based organizations: On the threshold of a new era. *Leadership Quarterly, 17*(3), 211–216.

Fink, D. & Brayman, C. (2006). School leadership succession and the challenges of change. *Educational Administration Quarterly, 42*(1), 62–89.

Gronn, P. (2002). Distributed leadership. In K. Leithwood & P. Hallinger (eds), *Second international handbook of educational leadership and administration* (pp. 653–696). Dordrecht, The Netherlands: Kluwer Academic Publishers.

Gronn, P. (2003). *The new work of educational leaders: Changing leadership practices in an era of school reform.* London, UK: Paul Chapman.

Hackman, J.R. & Oldham, G.R. (1980). *Work redesign.* Reading, MA: Addison-Wesley.

Hammersley-Fletcher, L. & Brundrett, M. (2005). Leaders on leadership: The impressions of primary school headteachers and subject leaders. *School Leadership and Management, 25*(1), 59–75.

Harris, A. (2004). Distributed leadership and school improvement: Leading or misleading? *Educational Management and Administration, 32*(1), 11–24.

Hutchins, E. (1995). *Cognition in the wild.* Cambridge, MA: MIT.

Ingersoll, R. (2007). Short on power, long on responsibility. *Educational Leadership, 65*(1), 20–25.

Jermier, J.M. & Kerr, S. (1997). Substitutes for leadership: Their meaning and measurement – contextual recollections and current observations. *Leadership Quarterly, 8*(2), 95–101.

Lawler III, E.E., Mohrman, S.A., & Ledford Jr, G.E. (1992). *Employee involvement and total quality management: Practices and results in fortune 1000 companies.* San Francisco, CA: Jossey-Bass.

Leithwood, K. & Jantzi, D. (2000). The effects of different sources of leadership on student engagement in school. In K. Riley & K. Louis (eds), *Leadership for change and school reform* (pp. 50–66). London, UK: Routledge.

Leithwood, K. & Jantzi, D. (2005). A review of transformational school leadership research: 1996–2005. *Leadership and Policy in Schools, 4*(3), 177–199.

Manz, C.C. & Sims Jr, H.P. (1993). *Business without bosses.* New York, NY: Wiley.

Miller, R.J. & Rowan, B. (2006). Effects of organic management on student achievement. *American Educational Research Journal, 43*(2), 219–253.

Murphy, J. (2007). *Turning around struggling schools: Lessons from the organizational sciences.* Thousand Oaks, CA: Corwin Press.

National College of School Leadership (NCSL). (2004). *The five pillars of distributed leadership in schools.* Nottingham, UK: NCSL.

Nicolaidou, M. & Ainscow, M. (2002). *Understanding 'failing' schools: The role of culture and leadership.* Paper presented at the British Education Research Association Conference, Exeter, UK.

Ogawa, R.T. & Bossert, S.T. (1995). Leadership as an organizational quality. *Educational Administration Quarterly, 31*, 224–243.

Osborn, R.N. & Hunt, J.G. (2007). Leadership and the choice of order: Complexity and hierarchical perspectives near the edge of chaos. *Leadership Quarterly, 18*(4), 319–334.

Pearce, C.J. & Conger, C. (2003). *Shared leadership: Reframing the hows and whys of leadership.* Thousand Oaks, CA: Sage.

Perkins, N. (1993). Person-plus: A distributed view of thinking and learning. In G. Salomon (ed.), *Distributed cognitions: Psychological and educational considerations* (pp. 88–110). Cambridge, UK: Cambridge University Press.

Plowman, D.A., Solansky, S., Beck, T.E., Baker, L., Kulkarni, M., & Travis, D.V. (2007). The role of leadership in emergent, self-organization. *Leadership Quarterly, 18*(4), 341–356.

Ray, T., Clegg, S., & Gordon, R. (2004). A new look at dispersed leadership: Power, knowledge and context. In L. Storey (ed.), *Leadership in organizations: Current issues and key trends* (pp. 319–336). London, UK: Routledge.

Ritchie, R. & Woods, P.A. (2007). Degrees of distribution: Towards an understanding of variations in the nature of distributed leadership in schools. *School Leadership and Management, 27*(4), 363–381.

Salomon, G. (ed.). (1993). *Distributed cognitions: Psychological and educational considerations.* Cambridge, UK: Cambridge University Press.

Starbuck, W. (1996). Learning by knowledge-intensive firms. In M. Cohen & L. Sproull (eds), *Organizational learning* (pp. 484–515). Thousand Oaks, CA: Sage.

Storey, J. (2004). Changing theories of leadership and leadership development. In J. Storey (ed.), *Leadership in organizations: Current issues and key trends* (pp. 11–38). London, UK: Routledge.

Talbert, J.E. & McLaughlin, M.W. (1993). Understanding teaching in context. In D.K. Cohen, M.W. McLaughlin, & J.E. Talbert (eds), *Teaching for understanding: Challenges for policy and practice.* San Francisco, CA: Jossey-Bass.

Tannenbaum, A.S. (1961). Control and effectiveness in a voluntary organization. *American Journal of Sociology, 67*(1), 33–46.

Timperley, H. (2005). Instructional leadership challenges: The case of using student achievement information for instructional improvement. *Leadership and Policy in Schools, 4*(1), 3–22.

Tschannen-Moran, M. (2004). *Trust matters: Leadership for successful schools.* San Francisco, CA: Jossey-Bass.

Uhl-Bien, M., Marion, R., & McKelvey, B. (2007). Complexity leadership theory: Shifting leadership from the industrial age to the knowledge era. *Leadership Quarterly, 18*(4), 298–318.

Waldrop, M. (1992). *Complexity: The emerging science at the edge of order and chaos.* New York, NY: Simon & Schuster.

Weick, K. & Roberts, K. (1996). Collective mind in organizations: Heedful interrelating on flight decks. In M. Cohen & L. Sproull (eds), *Organizational Learning* (pp. 330–358). Thousand Oaks, CA: Sage.

Wheatley, M.J. (2005). *Finding our way: Leadership for an uncertain time.* San Francisco, CA: Berrett-Koehler.

Wohlstetter, P. & Mohrman, S.A. (1993). *School-based management: Strategies for success.* New Brunswick, NJ: Rutgers University.

York-Barr, J. & Duke, K. (2004). What do we know about teacher leadership? Findings from two decades of scholarship. *Review of Educational Research, 74*(3), 255–316.

Yukl, G. (1994). *Leadership in organizations* (3rd edn). Englewood Cliffs, NJ: Prentice-Hall.

Part 1
Distributed Leadership
What It Is

2

Hybrid Leadership

PETER GRONN

With the recent emergence of distributed leadership, a key question is: What happens next? One possibility is that a distributed understanding may replace traditional individualistic leadership approaches. Another is the polarization of the field around re-assertions of individualism and pro- ponents of distribution. A third development may be an accommodation between distributed and individualistic approaches. Another possible outcome is hybridity, the focus of the chapter. Hybrid leadership means mixed leadership patterns. Employing data from a case study, this chapter explains why such patterns arise and how hybrid leadership operates. The chapter also identifies some of the problems and possibilities opened up by a hybrid view of leadership, and the significance of this perspective for the future of the field.

A distinctive and enduring feature of leadership writings has been that commentators frequently frame and discuss their subject matter from a variety of prescriptive standpoints. Without resorting to caricature, this kind of predilection may be labeled as *normativism*, the first of two common leadership *-isms*. A normativist is someone who is comfortable inhabiting a realm of desirability. Normativism boils down to commentators taking upon themselves the role of advocates for conceptually grounded leadership models, approaches or styles which they find attractive or optimal (March, 2005, p. 113). I have in mind not merely the countless glossy covered titles that leap out with monotonous regularity as one is idly browsing along the shelves of airport bookshops, but also the tips that populate the regular advice columns of all manner of professional publications, occasional reflective pieces in more prestigious outlets like the *Harvard Business Review* and even writings in scholarly research journals. With remarkably few exceptions, these sources adopt a focused or concentrated view of leadership as a personal capacity, for which a high profile individual exercises a monopoly or near monopoly. The particular mission entailed by this normativist advocacy tends to be one of exhorting various readerships and audiences to implement an author's preferred type of focused leadership as a template for change-oriented action.

Normativism is a form of advocacy from "on high." I say on high, because insofar as it retains a connection with reality, the normative mindset tends (God-like) to dismiss or residualize practice as something that is ripe for discursive reconstruction. In this sense, normativism expresses a transcendental impulse. This predilection accounts in turn for the closely related second -ism: *adjectivalism* – the extraordinary resilience of leadership in being able to replenish itself by generating new categories and classifications through the simple device of substituting an endless supply of successive candidate adjectives (e.g. *great man* leadership, followed by *charismatic* leadership, in turn followed by *authentic* leadership and so on), these being differentiated mainly on the basis of conceptual fine-graining. Once again, these types are mostly grounded in a focused, individualist view of leadership. What this regeneration process yields is a range of adjectivalisms that acquire the status of elixirs or solutions in search of problems awaiting practitioner preferment in an intensely competitive leadership marketplace. To what extent, then, does the recent popularity accorded distributed leadership provide additional confirmation of this trend toward adjectivalism? In short, is distributed leadership simply one more normatively defined candidate solution-in-waiting?

Given the huge popular currency accorded leadership, the normativist's willingness to succumb to the temptation to try to transform practice by resorting to the kind of hortatory enthusiasm to which I have just alluded is perhaps understandable. If, on the other hand, one sees one's mission in the leadership field as the advancement of knowledge, then this kind of proselytizing both stretches credulity and is of questionable truth value. Complete avoidance by researchers of some degree of normativism is exceeding difficult, particularly for those of us whose names have come to be associated with a particular adjectivalism – in my case with distributed leadership. In this chapter, however, I try to eschew the role of advocacy in favor of a more naturalistic, organic understanding of leadership, with a view to elucidating some of the realities of leadership practice. My purpose is to advance the claim that such practice is best understood not as distributed but as hybridized, based on the argumentative reasoning in the next section. Although the enthusiasm for distributed or dispersed leadership may be recent, the idea itself is far from novel (as it was first articulated in small group research in social and organizational psychology in the 1950s and again later in the 1970s). What is new this time around, however, is that in the wake of the rampant individualist exceptionalism of the 1980s–1990s (Gronn, 2004, p. 352), distributed leadership has begun to function as a rallying-point for those commentators searching for "post-heroic" leadership alternatives.

Rudiments of a Theory of Hybridity

There are a number of possible responses to distributed leadership as a new leadership kid-on-the-block. First, this discrediting of previously dominant

approaches to leadership as heroic and the replacement of them by distributed leadership has accorded it a kind of counter-hegemonic status. My own
initial enthusiasm for distributed leadership, for example, prompted me to
trumpet the virtues of this strategy of replacement (e.g. Gronn, 2003a, pp.
286–288). The difficulty with this response, I now realize, is that by doing so
all one does is to perpetuate even more adjectivalism. A second, closely
related mode of response to the arrival of distributed leadership might be for
commentators in the leadership field to begin polarizing themselves combat-
ively as in favor of either revitalized focused approaches or distribution. The
initial result of this tendency might be an either/or stand-off situation with
the possibility of subsequent solidification into a much more hard-edged par-
adigmatic bifurcation. A third possible response to distributed leadership's
rise and diffusion as a category might be a begrudging live-and-let-live situation in which commentators, perceiving merit in each broad perspective (i.e.
focused and distributed leadership forms), try to find ways of accommodating
both sets of understandings. There was a precedent for this in the (pre-Fou-
caultian) 1970s debates in the social sciences about power, when a broad
elitism–pluralism polarity established itself among scholars. A decade or so
long tit-for-tat argument between political scientists and sociologists over the
competing merits of elitist and pluralist approaches to describing and analyzing power relations, especially in urban and industrial communities, seemed
to resolve itself (somewhat uneasily) with empirical evidence that power in
some locations was concentrated in the hands of a monolithic (or near monolithic) elite, while in others it was shared by a plurality of rival and competing
sets of decision-makers. Likewise with leadership: there may indeed be empirically demonstrable occasions when, and locations in which, leadership is
more likely to be concentrated for substantial periods of time in the hands of
one individual, while in others it will tend to be shared.

A fourth and final development, the one endorsed in this chapter, is
hybridity – a possibility I recently canvassed as co-editor of a special issue of
Leadership Quarterly devoted to leadership in team-based organizations (Day
et al., 2006). A situation of hybridity does not designate a new type of leadership, for it is a way of characterizing an emerging state of affairs. For this
reason, it avoids the pitfalls of normative adjectivalism. Hybridity encompasses the third possibility just summarized and it also allows for the likelihood that, over time, in each organizational context where leadership may be
manifest, different kinds and degrees of *both* individualized-focused and distributed patterns of leadership will co-exist. Taken at face value, a recent
observation of the Scottish Inspectorate (HMIE, 2006) to the effect that
leadership "is therefore both individual and shared" (p. 93) suggests that it
may have had this possibility or something akin to it in mind. Moreover,
there are likely to be occasions during which each leadership form will be
present simultaneously while for other periods of time their presence may be

sequential. If I am on the right track here, then in any particular organizational setting it would make sense to speak of a constantly shifting leadership mix or configuration, the overall composition of which should be understood as an adaptive or emergent response to wider environmental and immediate situational challenges that are specific to that context. Thus, in policy environments of quasi-market devolution of schooling (with OECD countries, especially, in mind), schools are likely to arrange what, for want of a better term, might be referred to as their overall density of leadership resources in ways that they believe best accommodate their site-based needs.

These on-the-ground realities experienced by people in schools are considerably more complex than can be captured by such blanket leadership descriptors as *distributed, transformational, visionary,* and so on. They also require more imaginative explanations for their occurrence. Two (potentially rival) candidates worthy of consideration are evolution and emergence. Evolutionary or quasi-evolutionary explanations have been invoked for some time (although not developed theoretically in great detail) to account for sector- and site-based variations in leadership practice which deviate from expectations of individualism. One example is Senger's (1971, pp. 79–80) early discussion of the demands of dual leadership in the military and co-management in US corporations. Another is Whisler's (1960, passim) analysis of the administrative "assistant-to" phenomenon. The idea of emergence, on the other hand, is more recent and originates from research into the behavior of complex physical and biological systems. Changes in organizational practice may occur through deliberately planned actions, but they may also arise partly as a result of unintended and unforeseen consequences of numerous previously accumulated decisions and actions, or even inaction on the part of agents. Such possibilities include consideration of structural levels, and their emergence through processes and mechanisms of structuration. More detailed consideration of each approach is held over to the discussion section of the chapter.

Hybridity – Some Tantalizing Preliminary Examples

Consistent with the above line of reasoning, then, the aim of the present chapter is to identify some of the problems and possibilities opened up by a hybrid view of leadership, and the significance this perspective might have for the future development of the field. In the main part of the discussion, I draw on some data from research on leadership patterns in Australian schools. By way of introduction to my detailed consideration of that material, I want to illustrate more concretely what I mean by hybridity, by reviewing three short pieces of indicative evidence.

The first is taken from a history of nineteenth-century Scottish secondary education. While the author (Knox, 1953, pp. 39–40) makes no mention of "leadership" per se, he nonetheless depicts a highly disparate overall pattern of school administration in which, for much of the period, hierarchical and collegial authority imperatives were in contention:

> In general [in the widely diverging forms of Scottish schools], it had not been customary to grant the headmaster (or "rector," as he was traditionally called) any very extensive authority over his other colleagues on the staff. Though nominally in charge of the internal affairs of the school, he had only limited powers of discipline, hardly any control of appointments to the staff, and little to do with regulating the work done, since there was no compulsory course of studies and normally a separate fee was charged for each subject taken, at the option of the parent.

The extent of this situation of "inherent anarchy" was compounded following the fusion of grammar schools and academies, for:

> In some places two rectors were retained, as in Perth, and in others the office of rector was abolished, as in Dundee. In either case there was a tendency for the virtually independent heads of the separate departments to form a council of masters, sometimes presided over by each in turn, to manage the internal affairs of the school in republican fashion. Even to this day [1953], though notions have changed and a fully-fledged rector sits in authority over all, the head of each department of study at Dundee High School (so called since 1859) retains the title of headmaster (e.g. of mathematics, modern languages, etc.). Strangely enough, this competitive system seemed to commend itself to Scottish opinion as good for the school, and in some cases local sentiment was resolutely against consolidation of the work under one headmaster.

Despite strong community endorsement for it, this variegated "system" was beginning to experience strong countervailing pressures:

> As the century advanced, however, it became more usual to appoint a rector with a good deal of influence in all matters affecting the school, as in Inverness Royal Academy and in Glasgow in both High School and Academy. In a few cases, on the other hand, particularly where English influence made itself felt, as in the case of Edinburgh Academy, the headmaster was from the first granted supreme authority over the working of the whole school, with the power to appoint and dismiss his staff almost at pleasure. Thus the variations within the system were great.

Although the precise timing of the administrative transitions in each of these schools is unclear, what this lengthy extract (sub-divided into three for ease of reading) highlights is the quintessence of a hybrid developmental pattern. That is, rarely does there appear to have been one preponderant pure type or form of Scottish school administration. Instead, different patterns grew up over the course of time, the impetus for their emergence being distinctly bottom-up, as is indicated by mentions of "local sentiment" and "customary." There are also hints (especially in the third extract) that some schools were becoming aware of practices followed in other schools, and that while pressures toward standardization were beginning to mount (e.g. from south of the border), there was still no uniformity. In short, rather than convergence around an imposed standardized norm or model, there was an overall pattern of divergence which manifested differences (in kind and degree) of administrative practice, and plenty of mixed (or hybrid) arrangements. Pending the outcome of a more detailed enquiry, the overall pattern seems to have been a range of adaptations to locally generated demands and constraints, perhaps under the influence of explicit democratic values (as evidenced by the use of "republican" in the second extract).

The second, contemporary, example is taken from a recent column by Will Hutton in the *Guardian* (March 21, 2007). With the United Kingdom (and probably the rest of the Western world and beyond) then poised for an announcement by the Prime Minister, Tony Blair, of his likely retirement from office (and now confirmed), Hutton was commenting on the Prime Ministerial succession. His remarks were written shortly after the presentation of the final budget of the Treasurer, Gordon Brown, to the House of Commons, while speculation had been mounting for some time about whether or not Brown was "a shoo-in" to succeed Blair. Of the relationship between the two men during their party's decade in office, Hutton describes Brown as the "pre-eminent political and economic strategist of his generation." Then, in his next passage, Hutton switches focus away from the two men as rival titans contending for the highest political office (which, essentially, was the text of the British media's ongoing morality play about these politicians' handover plans) to the dynamics of the relationship between them:

> Blair had the sense to recognize it [i.e. Brown's pre-eminent strategizing] and stayed yoked to his difficult chancellor, whatever. Now the partnership is over, and Brown [as prospective Prime Minister] will reap the inheritance. It is not at all bad. But Brown needed Blair as much as Blair needed Brown – an interdependence that Blair recognized, if not his chancellor. Brown now urgently needs to find someone to complement his skills at the top of government.

One reason why this passage is interesting is that it demonstrates how, from time to time, dimensions of the power and influence relations that operate between leaders percolate through the surface layers of the "star" culture that consumes political leadership. Whereas stardom status reinforces a public figure's view of him or herself as "separate, disconnected, or independent from others," the real irony of what it means to be powerful in public and organizational life is pithily captured by Hutton's example, namely that: "powerholders are highly connected to, embedded in, and dependent on social relationships and the social context" (Lee & Tiedens, 2001, p. 45). In short, leaders in charge of governments and leaders in charge of the financial resources of governments are reciprocally influential and need one another.[1] In relation to hybridity, this phenomenon provides additional evidence of an improvised response to circumstances. In this instance, the structural patterning of relations in the guise of dyadic partnering arises out of the exigencies of public office holding. Clearly, Hutton's example is far from being a textbook illustration of the conventional paradigm of individualist leader–follower relations. And while in some senses it might approximate the holistic version of distributed leadership for which I have previously made allowance (Gronn, 2002, pp. 429–432), the fact that Blair and Brown each operate as individual leaders within their own separate spheres of ministerial responsibility while at the same time they also partner one another, demands a much more subtle explanation of the significance of their relationship dynamics.

The Blair-Brown case is far from an isolated one. A not dissimilar understanding between two leaders is evident in the third example of the Indian Prime Minister, Manmohan Singh, a Sikh, and the president of the Indian Congress Party, the Italian-born Roman Catholic, Sonia Gandhi. It was Ms Gandhi who headed a 20-party coalition that swept the former BJP government from office in 2004, but she renounced the Prime Ministership. Since then, according to political journalists (*Straits Times*, April 30, 2005): "The alliance chair [woman] and the prime minister have settled into a comfortable relationship that, despite drawing-room gossip, seems to show little sign of fraying." Their partnership works as follows: "They meet on Friday evenings at the prime minister's residence, either alone or accompanied by aides. At other times they are frequently talking on the telephone. Sometimes, he simply drops in to see her." The difficulties of trying to hold together a fragile and tenuous 20-party alliance means that these two politicians have little choice but to agree to a spread of leadership between them. And that is the point for, as with Blair and Brown, circumstances have once more dictated the genesis of the partnership. As a general rule, then, what counts in the working practices of executives and leaders is less their conformity to first principles of soundness than those leaders' "constant improvisation and adaptation" (Whisler, 1960, p. 182). The kinds of complexities brought to light by these examples are next considered in more detail in relation to some evidence from secondary schooling.

Identifying Hybrid Patterns of Leadership

For the project entitled "Patterns of distributed leadership in Australian schools" there were three participating government sector secondary colleges located in two Australian states. Two of the three were stand-alone or single campus schools, anonymized here as: "Single Secondary College 1" (SSC1), and "Single Secondary College 2" (SSC2), while the third was a multi-campus college, or "Multi Secondary College" (MSC). This section of the chapter draws on sociometric, documentary, interview and observational data obtained during intensive fieldwork at SSC1 particularly in relation to informants' perceptions of forms of leadership and the dynamics of leadership relations. (Data on SSC2 and MSC are to be reported elsewhere.)

Research Background

As is implied by the project title, the avowed aim of the research was to pinpoint some of the forms taken by distributed leadership. Because case study designs preclude, by definition, the procurement of large scale incidence-related data, it was hoped when drafting the bid proposal to compensate for the absence of this particular dimension of the distributional phenomenon by surfacing at least some of the structural properties and cultural dimensions of this form of leadership through relying on short bursts of intensive site-based fieldwork. The five-year delay in reporting the data (i.e. 2003–7), while partly accounted for by a range of competing pressures and projects, is mainly due to the dawning recognition on my part as the principal investigator that, notwithstanding the original intention of the research, what was being documented in the fieldwork was not merely evidence of distributed leadership but a qualitatively different phenomenon. Intellectual honesty dictated that I should re-think some of my initial (cherished) assumptions. How could the data be indicative only of distributed leadership when, as I show shortly, our informants were simultaneously describing both individual leaders and a conterminous range of "small number" (Alvarez & Svejenova, 2005, p. 2) structures? Thus, while I commenced the project committed to finding distributed leadership, while the original application protocol for the research grant had made a persuasive case for its existence, and while I had already empirically documented a case example (Gronn, 1999) – with another to follow shortly (Gronn & Hamilton, 2004) – the SSC1 data yielded a picture of practice not encompassed by existing categories, the explanation for which stemmed from the unique form taken by the division of labor.

Researching Leadership

There are a number of candidate terms with which scholars characterize human conduct and relations in organizations, including exchanges, transactions and interactions. Likewise, as part of each of these forms of conduct there is a variety of ways of designating the dynamics of the relations between the agents, such as influence, power, persuasion, manipulation, coercion and leadership. The present discussion is not an occasion for reviewing the appropriateness and merits of these rival candidate terms, except to say that having chosen "leadership" from among the available alternatives, I sought in my research design to provide opportunities for the informants to verbalize their assumptions about what the concept in practice meant to them (see below).

In order to answer two of the key questions for each of the cases at the outset of the fieldwork (namely, who were the leaders and what were the criteria for identifying them?) I had proposed a variation of Hunter's (1963) approach to locating community leaders in "Regional City." Because some Regional City leaders were likely to be publicly prominent individuals, and others not so prominent, Hunter (1963) believed that locating position-holders in community organizations (based on evidence accessible from media reports and other documentary sources) would be "a good start toward turning up leaders who might operate behind the scenes" (p. 256). To this end, he devised lists of "persons presumed to have power" in civic, business, governmental and social activities in Regional City (Hunter, 1963, p. 11). A panel of 14 judges was then asked to decide from the pool of 175 names "who were top leaders on each of the lists" (Hunter, 1963, p. 261). A broad consensus on these rankings yielded a sample of 40 persons, of whom 27 were interviewed. These 27 were then requested to rank the top ten of the 40, with various sociometric diagrams being used to represent the informants' scores, relationships between the nominated leaders, mutuality of selections and nomination weights.

The variation on Hunter's approach that I proposed for the first part of the research was to dispense with judges, and to combine the sociometric exercise with an initial interview in the following way. After an invitation to all staff in each school to participate in the project, in one-on-one interviewing, volunteer informants were asked two questions intended to elicit their implicit assumptions about leadership. Our presumption was that our teacher informants operated (at least partly) within a framework of expectations of leadership and its potency in influencing their work in relation to improving students' learning. While Leithwood (2003, p. 105) used a questionnaire to ascertain teachers' nominations of people who provided school leadership, I was extending this approach, in effect, by allowing for leadership to be sourced from work units as well as individuals. The two questions with which the interviews began were:

1. When you think of leadership in general terms, do you normally associate it with action on the part of an individual, a number of different individuals, a group or something else?
2. What does leadership in general terms mean to you?

Our informants were then handed school documents listing the names, titles and work contact details of their colleagues along with the titles of a series of bodies responsible for various areas of school policy and operations, and they were requested to indicate (by shading with a highlighter pen):

3. Which roles would you associate with leadership in this school?
4. Which groups or committees would you associate with leadership?

Following these questions, they were then asked:

5. Are there any other informal groupings of people or relationships which you would associate with leadership?
6. Have these groups and committees changed much in their style of operation since you have been working here?

Finally, as cross-checks on their responses to these questions, respondents were also asked:

7. If you were to initiate a policy or curricular change in your area, who would you approach? How would you go about it?
8. Here are some words (i.e. management, direction, guidance, head-ship, authority, control) commonly associated with leadership. How would you rank them in importance?
9. Is there anything else which you wish to add?

For the purpose of analysis, the responses to questions 1, 3, 4 and 5 were scored numerically, while for the remaining questions the responses were transcribed verbatim.

Hybrid Leadership Practice at SSC1

SSC1 is a co-educational government secondary school located in a leafy middle class residential suburb in the capital city of a mainland Australian state. It had been established in the mid 1950s. At the time of the research, there were about 850 students enrolled in Years 7–12. The majority of these were boys (in a boy-to-girl ratio of approximately 5:3). The main feature of the school's enrolment pattern since the late 1990s was that student numbers had been trending upwards such that, in the words of one informant, SSC1 was "getting to the stage where we can pick and choose a little bit in terms of who comes to the place" (Interviewee #4). Moreover, the overall demographic profile of the clientele was reasonably homogenous: apart from a small number of international students, only a quarter of the students were from homes where languages other than English were spoken and more than 80 percent of students had been born in Australia. SSC1 offered a comprehensive range of curriculum subjects at all year levels, supplemented by programs for student support, extension and accelerated learning, including some select entry provision. Its enriched curriculum for students included drama, debating, choral music, vocational training, study tours to the Asia and Pacific regions, and specialist youth development initiatives. There were about 60 teaching staff members at SSC1 and a dozen or so non-teaching staff (SSC1 Planning and Review documentation).

Division of Responsibilities

The first point of significance for my argument concerning hybridity concerns the formal status accorded leadership and management at SSC1. Despite whatever the wider scholarly community might insist about the nature of, and relationship between, these two domains of activity, overwhelmingly at SSC1 the highest priority was accorded to management, with leadership embedded within it. While the aforementioned term division of labor refers to the working practices used to accomplish the totality of the work of an organization, division of responsibilities encompasses the overall arrangement of authority and accountability, lines of reporting and duty statements. The formal division of responsibilities at SSC1 was strongly biased towards management. Leaving aside a small handful of non-teaching front office staff and the business manager, the titles of the dozen or so senior level teachers next in seniority to the principal and assistant principals, for example, were *manager* or *assistant manager*. Likewise, the duty statements for the two assistant principals (the one responsible for student management [APSM] and the other curriculum [APC]) and the description of their relations with the principal (to whom they were accountable as members of the *overall Principal Team*) were quintessentially managerial. Thus, only once does leadership appear in the preface forming the general introduction to the role statement and not at all in the 13 dot points specifying the job particulars ("Assistant Principal Job Descriptions, 2002"). In three statements outlining assistant principal roles, "to lead" appears only twice in 15 dot points in the first, "lead" and "take a leading role" are to be found once each in the nine dot points for the second assistant and there is no mention at all of leadership in eight dot points in the third ("Specific Areas of Responsibility" – assistant principals, educational services, student management and human resources).

Attributing Leadership

The next point to be made in relation to the hybridity thesis is that when they were asked about leadership specifically, the thinking of our SSC1 informants displayed a mixture of wildly disparate assumptions about both individual and shared leadership. This generalization derives from the teachers' aggregated sociometric interview responses to Qs 1–4. Thus, for Q 1, while the teachers in Spillane's (2006, pp. 47–48) study of distributed leadership attributed the status of leader to a range of colleagues, SSC1 teachers' attributions included formal and informal groupings as well as individuals. Of 15 sociogram respondents, for example, only two associated leadership with individuals (with one nominating the *individual* option and one *a number of different individuals*), 12 selected *a group*, one nominated both an individual and a group, and no one chose *something else*. As if to confuse matters, those with a preference for the group option mostly used the word "team" and of these, three cited the principal and the two assistants as an example. For Q 2, leadership was either anchored in a range of nominated entities or it was entity-free. Those entities were singular ("Someone who has the ability to lead a group towards achieving goals"), plural ("People who can motivate the teachers, being good organizers – making sure the school runs properly") or collective ("Working as a team"). Entity-free assumptions were mostly expressed in participle form, as in "Planning…," "Taking responsibility…," or "…identifying and fulfilling needs, looking toward the future."

These responses are evidence of an attributional tangle. The answers to Qs 3 and 4 further tangle the skein. Thus, for Q 3, when provided with a list of 18 roles occupied by individuals – 12 of these referring to a designated person (e.g. the *principal*) and six expressed more generally (e.g. *school manager, teacher, year level coordinator, librarian*) – respondents made 118 nominations. The pattern evident here was distinctly hierarchical, for 60 of these nominations (or about 50 percent) were received by just five incumbents: *principal* (13), *assistant principal* (i.e. two persons), (13) *school manager* (12), *a manager with operational responsibilities* (11), followed by *teacher* (11). For Q 4, by contrast, a list of 11 groups and committees (with nine being structures that were specifically titled, representative or quasi-representative) received 89 nominations, for which the most frequently cited groupings were three with responsibilities for student welfare, advice to the principal, and teaching and learning, along with the council of the college (and one of its sub-committees). "Team" was the preferred way of referring to groupings. Because structural informality tends to be a feature associated with teams and teaming, it was hoped that the question about informal sources of leadership (Q 5) might have brought to light some actual examples of SSC1 teams. Respondents, however, could only come up with a mere five examples, each of which received just one nomination.

For Q8, the rankings of words commonly associated with leadership provided an interesting footnote to this broad pattern. Based on a calculation of each person's first ranking scored as 6, the second 5, and so on, the rankings and totals were:

1. Management   58
2. Direction   52
3. Guidance   49

4. Headship   34
5. Authority   24
6. Control   24

There is a clear split in this list between the three highest ranked terms taken as a group and the lower ranked set of three. While re-inforcing the close link between leadership and management just summarized, the choice of the first three terms also indicates that respondents associate leadership with guidance and direction setting. It is not clear why headship, authority, and control were grouped together, although their connection with leadership in respondents' minds is clearly weaker. Finally, if one was to highlight an emblem of the overall pattern of interwoven leadership and management in the minds of respondents at SSC1, there was no better example than the title of one of the teacher-manager portfolios, which was "Manager, Educational Leadership."

Managing and Leading "On the Hoof"

In addition to these differing assumptions expressed by the informants, observation of a number of individuals and groups in action provided further confirmation of hybrid leadership activity at SSC1. This was especially evident in the cases of the most prominent of the attributed leaders, the principal and assistant principals. Nineteen (discontinuous) days of shadowing members of the principal team yielded a picture that was broadly consistent with the outcomes of about three decades of field research on leader-managers (synthesized by Gronn, 2003b, pp. 72–81) – intensified, fractured, variable and interrupted work routines and rhythms.

First, in relation to the principal, much of her energy was devoted to activities normally associated with being a manager. To begin with, she worked punishingly long hours. Consistent with her usual pattern, on the night before the first day of the fieldwork, for example, she had left the school at 10 pm and was back as early as 7.30 am on the following morning (Field Notes [hereafter FN], p. 1). She also often came in to work on weekends. For much of her working day she fulfilled a stewardship role as the person who was in charge, by having to: constantly sign documents, receive reports of students, tour the site (while invariably gulping down her lunch and occasionally bawling out students for indiscipline), attend off-site meetings, be accessible to teachers and parents, be on show at public gatherings, put out occasional personnel-related spot fires and work through the mountains of paperwork associated with items like insurance claims which, as she lamented, was "so utterly boring" (FN, p. 31). For this regime of activity, she may have been her own worst enemy because, although she delegated many duties to the assistant principals and managers (e.g. FN, pp. 1, 2, 4, and 7), she micro-managed such matters as the removal of graffiti and procurement of some school supplies (FN, pp. 13, 29), and also permitted the parents to have direct e-mail access to her (FN, p. 6). Even though she succumbed to occasional depressed moods – triggered by a particularly high profile and intractable issue within the school community (at one point the subject of parliamentary questions in the state legislature) – regular jocularity with fellow team members helped relieve the tension (FN, pp. 19, 10).

Such a listing of tasks necessarily emphasizes individual actions, yet these were part of the principal team's shared labor. The principal described the team as a "very equal triumvirate" (Interviewee #6), except that during the fieldwork period the membership of this role constellation or role set was in transition. With the departure of one assistant and the arrival of another, therefore, there was a "need to rearrange the deck chairs" (FN, p. 9). Because role interlocking in a constellation is not necessarily automatic (Hodgson et al., 1965, p. 391), the senior person's expectations are crucial in framing its operations. Such expectations define what a manager "should do or avoid doing" (Fondas & Stewart, 1994, p. 85). Two weeks into the job, the new assistant confirmed that the principal wanted each of them to "share the responsibilities and regard each other as equals," insisting that "we do consult regularly," and treat one another "as equals and support each other" (Interviewee #12). These expectations were cemented by the adoption of one overall performance plan for the team (instead of three separate plans) which, following joint consultation, had been drafted by the principal (FN, p. 33). Within the overall plan and framework of expectations, her two assistants operated autonomously within their particular spheres of expertise, the principal explained, and needed only to consult her if and when there was a problem. Thus APSM would announce the adoption of a wet day timetable (due to inclement weather) after confirming this decision with the principal (FN, p. 7). Cheque signing was a task that all three of them shared and, in order to keep a tight rein on school funds, each colleague monitored what the others had signed (FN, p. 11). Regular weekly team meetings were conducted informally, without a set agenda and with no meeting chair. A similar air of informality was observed in meetings of a formally representative body, the principal's advisory committee, both when the principal herself was present and in her absence (FN, pp. 18, 20–21). Outsiders' perceptions of this grouping as working "pretty collaboratively together" (Interviewee #4), "really well as a team" and maintaining "a degree of interdependence among the team itself" (Interviewee #8) confirmed the triumvirate's view of itself.

Within the threesome, there were two main sub-sets of relations. While the recently departed assistant may not have been especially "good at listening to others [outside the role set] and tended to just make decisions based on what he thought was the best thing" (Interviewee #8), both APC and APSM worked interdependently. As in the Blair–Brown and Singh–Gandhi examples, then, this pattern of cheek by jowl working relations, in which two individuals familiar with each other's thinking "simply divide the work more or less at random, handling incoming work and information independently for long periods of time and checking with one another at intervals" (Whisler, 1960, p. 199), turns out to be far from unusual. The implicit understanding of APC and APSM was likened by the latter to a natural world example of hybridity:

> My area is student management, overseas students, emergency manage-ment. But the issue that APC just called me out [of the interview room] on is a student management issue. Now the teacher had called him down and therefore, there is a good example of where we cross-pollinate. In the same way that if APC had an issue, a PD [professional development] or curriculum issue, he would sit down and go through it with me first before he worked through it. So we very much work in that leadership level where we would nut out an issue first and then work through it.... The student management policy issues would come through me, but the day to day running of the discipline would be a shared responsibility. I have the final say, role in that area, that portfolio, in the same way that if it's a curriculum issue APC would have the final say. If it is an overall school issue the principal would have the final say.... So there are very discrete areas but we would make very much shared decisions.
>
> (Interviewee #13)

On other occasions, the two assistants might exit the school together to confer at length on common concerns over a coffee (FN, p. 24). APSM believed that staff saw her as "a fairly approachable person, but a person who will make a decision," and they "expect me to follow through" (Interviewee #13). She and the principal also formed a strongly bonded dyad, and each could contact the other "almost anytime day and night" to discuss issues. Such was the extent of their friendship that, when telephoning her boss from overseas during a trip to recruit students, the principal addressed her off-sider rather familiarly as "darling" (FN, pp. 9, 19).

Attributed Leaders and Perceptions of Leadership

While evidence of the kind of sustained change normally associated with leadership requires more than four working weeks of fieldwork to document, there were glimmers of it in some of the responses to Qs 6–9 and in inter-views. Although not necessarily sourced to the influence of a particular indi-vidual or group – after all, as Sociogram Interviewee #13 noted, leadership "doesn't have to be overt" – overall assessments of the school's recent progress were positive. Interviewee #9, for example, whose arrival at SSC1 had preceded that of the principal by about 18 months, believed that an unfortu-nate "them and us" relationship that existed between teaching and non-teaching staff when he arrived was "much better now" and was a "really good" outcome. And, as a resident living near the school who later became a school council member, Interviewee #5 had observed the school progress from circumstances "of apparent decline" to a situation "which is moving forward with great rapidity."

The same mixed pattern of individualism and partnering that was evident within the principal team was manifest elsewhere in the school. First, it typi-fied relations among the school managers. On the one hand, said Interviewee #7, managers took initiatives singly, because in the student management area, for example:

> You've got to deal with things straight away. Sometimes if you wait until the other person has made a decision it loses its effect. So in that respect we are independent. And that comes from, I guess, the trust that the hierarchy has put into us when they employed us for the position.

On the other hand, when working together within a common framework of goals:

> I think as teachers and as individuals we have a lot of respect for each other's opinion.... We kind of feed off and bounce off each other. In terms of decision-making ... it's the three of us [in the student manage-ment domain] who make the decision.

Second, because of various situational pressures, a similar dyadic pattern per-sisted between principal team members and other colleagues. These dyads were both enduring and temporary. As an illustration of the former type, the school council president and principal maintained regular e-mail contact with one another (FN, p. 19). Examples of the latter were the regular meetings between the council vice-president and the principal in her office to draft media briefings during the long-running issue in the school community (FN, p. 16), with the vice-president attesting to the principal's willingness to consult and "take and seek advice when necessary."

The question of whether informants had experienced changes in the oper-ation of collective sources of leadership, such as various committees and groups (Q 6), yielded a mixed set of responses. In general, while elements in the existing structure were seen as being granted more autonomy, some of them (e.g. the Education Committee) were also thought to have slightly lost their way. On the other hand, the overall apparatus was perceived as having been extended and become more fluid. With the regular utilization of focus groups, for example, colleagues described by the peers as working on the fringes of the staff now had a voice. One interviewee (#7) noted how:

> Now and then you have little teams forming off the main ones. And I think that's increased. Which I think is a good thing because you are

better off having the people that are directly related to, coming up with the ideas rather than coming just from … a select group of people.

All of this lends weight to the idea of emergent practices, for which there was further evidence in the responses to Q 7 (about strategies for initiating curriculum changes). These were equally diverse as for Q 6 and no doubt reflected the respondents' differing levels of experience and organizational know-how. Essentially, most informants nominated a key go-to-person in authority as a first step while a mere handful suggested they would assemble a group of colleagues to take soundings of peers' opinions. On the other hand, the preferred approach of most respondents tended (perhaps unremarkably) to depend on the nature of the particular issue.

Hybridity – Unfinished Business

At least two main considerations arise from the preceding analysis. First, given that there may be no way of confirming whether the case of SSC1 is in some sense representative, although there is also no obvious reason for dismissing it as an outlier, what might be the wider significance of this pattern of hybridity? Second, assuming that hybridity does have a more general application as a way of characterising the reality of leadership practice, how is such hybridity to be accounted for?

Significance of Hybridity

Two key features of the division of labor stand out in the fieldwork data. First, both in their assumptions about, and descriptions of, their practice, in the minds of SSC1 informants, leadership was mostly subsidiary to management. Second, within that overall subsidiary relationship, the leadership of individuals co-existed comfortably alongside various pairings, threesomes, and similar formations, with the leadership of individuals concentrated mostly among a few senior level position-holders, while in the simultaneous case of committees and groups it was spread more evenly across a range of instances. Important consequences follow from these features.

First, as was foreshadowed at the outset of this chapter, there are shortcomings with adjectival categories that are restricted to the inclusion of either the individual or distributed aspects of the overall mix. For this reason, then, when the overall configuration of practice defies convergence on a discrete leadership category or type, the characterisation of such practice as hybrid makes a good deal of sense. To the extent that patterns of hybridity may constitute the norm across an entire system of schools, then a developmental trajectory of divergence can be said to predominate over a trajectory of convergence and opens up the likelihood of a potentially infinite variation of versions of practice. This possibility highlights the need for a more illuminating way of coming to terms with leadership practice than can be accommodated by existing categories and formulae. Second, the reality of hybrid practice also casts doubt on the validity of existing leadership categories in relation to their presumed normative potential. What point is served, for example, by the espousal of a desirable type when that type is at best only a part, and possibly even a small part, of the overall mix? Take transformational leadership. Suppose that a researcher, committed to this type as an instrument of change, wanted evidence of the impact of a transformative individual at SSC1, then who, given the numerous individuals and groups nominated as sources of leadership, would be the designated agent of transformation? It makes little sense to think in sole agency terms. Likewise with a normative espousal of distributed leadership: what would be the justification for privileging dispersed practices ahead of (and perhaps instead of) individual agents when the demonstrable influence of individuals counts for at least some of the time?

Third, the presumed correspondence between aspects of practice and categories associated with leadership may be fraught when the framework of practitioner assumptions and sensemaking about leadership is so highly indiscriminate and muddled. As illustrated by this next extract, for example, respondents seemed to be entirely at ease with ignoring possible differences between management and leadership, and moved seamlessly back and forwards between each category:

> Obviously the people we've selected in managerial positions such as Level 4 [of the career structure] are leaders in certain ways. But some of them don't necessarily lead in the way that you could perceive as natural leaders. And there are some of the younger members of staff who are turning out to be natural leaders, like [names]. They're our first year teachers in the school. They're going to be natural leaders and they will pick up. But I think the principal and I, the principal is the leader of the school, and me in support, is doing a terrific job in targeting certain people, for certain jobs. We have got a good leadership team.
>
> (Interviewee #13)

Not only were management and leadership blurred here, but in relation specifically to leadership this short passage jumbles up natural leaders, the principal as "the" leader and "good" leadership – an implied reference to its overall spread across the school. Interviewee #13 continued:

> [The principal's advisory committee is] really the only leadership committee in the school. The student management team certainly has total leadership in respect of student management. It runs the student management so that's the discipline and welfare side of the school. And that's made up of the real movers and shakers of the school.

Here in this second extract, an advisory grouping has been nominated as the sole source of leadership, except that the real hub of initiative turns out to be a management team. These examples indicate that practitioners' categories simply do not map neatly onto the conceptual niceties preferred by scholars. This difference suggests the need for a re-think of the relationship between conceptual thinking and the division of labor that operates in schools.

Accounting for Hybridity

The occurrence of hybrid leadership practice, its potential diffusion across school systems and the divergent trajectories it may or may not be taking require a much more complete account than can be provided here. Extrapolating from the example of SSC1, however, my working hypothesis is that hybridity represents an attempt by schools to accommodate contingency.

While the recent neo-liberal inspired movement for the reform of schooling in many countries may not have followed a strict blueprint or timetable, under the broad rubric of devolution, it has increased significantly every school's responsibility for the deployment of resources (especially finances and staffing), management of risks, and a range of accountabilities associated with teaching and learning through a vast apparatus of performativity targeting and auditing regimes, as has been fairly well documented. Such reform has also required schools to tap into or establish their own specialist student markets. An unintended consequence of these kinds of imperatives has been the inescapable improvising of patterns of localized arrangements that are intended to meet increasingly uniquely experienced site-based needs. In the absence of reliable roadmaps for handling contingency, schools have had little option but to continually experiment to find what works best for them. And what works best may have a reduced shelf life in the face of relentless central pressures to implement new initiatives and to be simultaneously responsive to local markets to try to ensure a school's future viability. One of the ways in which schools cope is to make do by adopting ad hoc structures and relationships, or by grafting these on existing longstanding arrangements. In short, the likelihood is increased of the occurrence of a pattern of variation in practice that is not dissimilar to that described earlier in nineteenth-century Scotland, prior to the uniformity of site-level control prescribed by a then bureaucratizing state.

In these circumstances, the clue to understanding hybridity may be the need for schools, and particularly the people in charge of them, to try to maximize their means of acquiring knowledge. It was Hayek (1945, p. 526) who claimed that the idea of an omniscient mind was a fallacy. In circumstances of fragmented, dispersed and incomplete knowledge, and in the absence of such a mind, Hayek saw a problem of knowledge co-ordination. Writing with competitive market relations in mind, his solution was the communication of knowledge through the price mechanism. In the realm of corporate organizational relations, the solution to the problem of dispersed knowledge favored by his like-minded contemporaries, such as Polanyi (1951), was the mechanism of mutual adjustment – a kind of self-derived and self-imposed mode of coordination by a range of units, minus any central control or oversight. In this vein, Interviewee #3 said at one point: "No one has a monopoly on wisdom." The principal was also alert to the significance of knowledge and its relationship to leadership:

> While I ultimately will be the person who bears responsibility if things go astray, I try very much to share the leadership with my colleagues because I think that is very much the right way to operate and is best for their development as well. I certainly share all the knowledge of the school with them on the basis that … if for some reason I was ill or an accident occurred and I disappeared that they could pick up the baton and continue without me, without any hesitation.
>
> (Interviewee #6)

While possession of knowledge is typically understood to be a source of power, the lack of it recasts a leader's relationship with colleagues as one of dependence on them, as much as their dependence on a leader, as the principal also realized (Interviewee #6):

> I very much try to let people run their own show. I've been in schools where the principal basically intervened over the top of everything the leaders did, and often changed decisions and often changed direction. I appoint people to positions and very much I regard them as the experts of those areas. I wouldn't have any way of gathering the level of knowledge that they have. An example of that would be [name] who's our manager of careers and VET [Vocational and Educational Training] and pathways. That is a huge body of knowledge she has and I expect her to advise me. I certainly wouldn't be going in and telling her how to run her operation, it's the other way round.

There is a clear resonance here between these sentiments and those of Hayek and Polanyi, except that any individual and group self-adjustment at SSC1 took place within a framework of trust and expectations of knowledge sharing.

The trigger for hybrid leadership practices, then, appears to be the need for intelligence. The various individual, paired and grouped leadership units at SSC1 that are part of its division of labor may be understood as the functional equivalents of networked nodes of an integrated cognitive system occupying an infinite information space. As small intelligence units, such nodes are activated in conjunction with the various activity systems that inter-lock within the school. One example was the overseas program for which APSM said that, although it operated through her, she relied on an administrative assistant for day to day operations and she was "very dependent on teachers under the program to administer the actual teaching part of it" even though it "operates through me" (Interviewee #13). Collective intelligence in the ongoing leadership units comprised shared tacit understandings built up over time (Interviewee #15):

> The leadership team here [unspecified], most of us would have been working together for about six years or so.... There have been new people coming in obviously, but that's been a, you know, one at a time kind of thing. So I think there is a certain, I suppose reliance we have on each other and you know that we sort of understand each other and how we operate.

As Leithwood (2000, p. 5) notes, in comparison with the advantages bestowed on work environments relying on outside-the-head technologies, the distributed cognitive capacity of schools is heavily reliant on people. As a consequence, personnel changes have a rapidly detrimental effect on the collective memory (Interviewee #15):

> We lost a couple of key people from [the senior school] who had real experience ... and there was nothing written down really to help anybody coming in to the job and it really was.... I mean we got through it, it was a team effort though in a way to help the people that were new here.... So, one of the things I am actually trying to do is get a whole lot of stuff to put on the intranet for those sorts of eventualities.

Temporary membership units such as focus groups, on the other hand, were more akin to intelligence gathering devices designed to facilitate "more grassroots type initiatives" (Sociogram Interviewee #14).

On the basis of this analysis, then, it is likely that the division of labor in schools comprises an overall set of arrangements which, within the constraints of school system policy, they have the discretion to establish, reconfigure or rationalize as they, and when they, deem appropriate. Moreover, it is certainly plausible to characterize such alterations in the overall configuration as adaptations, as Whisler (1960) and Senger (1971) have proposed, along with the claim that these kinds of short-term adaptations may be undertaken for survival needs (Alvarez & Svejonova, 2005, p. 40). What is less clear is whether this characterization implies a genuine evolutionary mode of reasoning. Unlike genetic evolution, which is concerned with the reproduction of species and selection mechanisms which produce new species (i.e. varied effects from similar phenomena), cultural evolution is about changes in states of mind (Kennedy & Eberhart, 2001, pp. 14–15). In the absence of knowledge of the history of a particular organization or of organizational forms and transitions between forms across epochs, evolutionary arguments of this kind have little explanatory value. In this sense, while the fieldwork data provide limited access to the collective state of mind prevailing at SSC1, this was restricted to a limited and specific slice of time.

Emergence, on the other hand, does offer some explanatory purchase for what was happening at SSC1. There are two senses of emergence. The first refers to the genesis of social and organizational structures. Here, the actions of micro-level phenomena build complexity at a higher level, with the emergent higher level phenomena manifesting holistic properties not evident from the isolated behavior of the lower level individual elements that comprise them. In this way, for example, "a bird flock has properties over and above the properties of the birds themselves" (Kennedy & Eberhardt, 2001, p. 25). The emergent structures with such holistic properties that comprise the outcome of this structuring act, in turn, with causal force on the individual member elements. It was in this sense that the principal team at SSC1, for example, shaped the behaviors of its individual members. The second sense refers to mobilization or the arrival from time to time of new entities, such as decision-making fora that made their first appearance. These emerged as the solution to a problem or a need. Provided these structures endure, temporary or incipient entities (such as the management teams and the focus groups at SSC1) take their place as part of the overall mix of relationships in the formal decision-making apparatus. Otherwise, they come and go. For these reasons, at any one time in the life of the leadership of a school, the existence of emergent arrangements, in both of these senses of initial mobilization followed by subsequent potential transition to permanence, guarantees that a hybrid division of labor has the status of an ongoing work-in-progress. As with SSC1, this division of labor is most usefully understood as comprising a mélange of leadership units that are both top-down, or hierarchically ordered and legitimated, and bottom-up, or heterarchically emergent and entangled (Kontopoulos, 1993, pp. 230–231).

Conclusion

Recently, Hartley (2007, p. 202) has cited a number of authors (myself included) as suggesting that distributed leadership is an idea whose time has come. It might be more accurate to say that if any idea's time may really be said to have come, then it is the generic one of distribution, because instances of distributed phenomena continue to multiply. In the not so distant mythical past, the notion of distribution was confined mainly to the realm of political economy, and used principally in relation to the socialist objective of left-wing political parties. In the Australian case, this meant something like "state ownership of the means of production, distribution and exchange." Also, there were (and still are) well-rehearsed references in political and social theory to "the distribution of power" or "the distribution of influence." Latterly, however, one keeps encountering distribution not merely in relation to leadership, but in numerous guises, such as distributed information systems, distributed cognition, parallel distributed processing, distributed decision making, distributed learning and even (as in the recently documented retaliatory move by Russia against Estonia for the offence to national pride caused by its removal of a wartime statue) distributed denial of service – meaning the impairment of computer network servers as a result of calculated internet traffic flooding.

In relation to this distribution notion, what I have tried to do in this chapter is to introduce a small note of caution regarding the recent growing attention accorded distributed leadership. As someone who is closely identified with the provenance of this idea, by doing so I am probably leaving myself vulnerable to the accusation that I am acting in denial of my own self-interests. Perhaps I am, in which case, so be it, for there are occasions when, to use an old-fashioned expression, needs must, and this just happens to be one of them. Setting aside this possible consequence of what I have written, there is some consolation to be had in that the position I have articulated is broadly consistent with the stance adopted by the originator of the distributed leadership notion, C.A. Gibb. That is, while Gibb (1954) did not articulate the kind of hybridity argument that I have been advancing here, he by no means jettisoned the idea of focused leadership in preference for distributed leadership and merely allowed for the presence of both forms in group and organizational contexts. As to the uptake of new ideas in scholarly circles, it is well known that some ideas take off, some are stillborn, and still others fizzle out or come to nothing for a variety of reasons. For me to try to predict the fate of the idea of a hybrid leadership mix in light of these eventualities would be speculative at best and pointless at worst. On the other hand, if the possibility of hybrid or mixed forms of leadership in schools and organizations succeeds in sparking debate about the continued legitimacy and value of adjectivalism and normativism in leadership, with which I commenced the chapter, along with the significance of mixed forms and explanations for their occurrence, then this contribution might just have served a useful purpose.

Acknowledgments

Funding for the project "Patterns of distributed leadership in Australian schools" was gratefully received from the Australian Research Council for 2002 (Discovery Project number DP0210752).

I wish to thank Dr Felicity Rawlings-Sanaei for collecting the data from Single Secondary College 1 (SSC1).

Note

1 Similar examples of Prime Ministerial-Treasurer tag-teaming have surfaced in Australian federal politics, on both the Labor and Coalition sides – Bob Hawke and Paul Keating (1983–1990) and John Howard and Peter Costello (1996–2007).

References

Alvarez, J.L. & Svejenova, S. (2005). *Sharing executive power: Roles and relationships at the top.* Cambridge, UK: Cambridge University Press.

Day, D.V., Gronn, P., & Salas, E. (2006). Leadership in team-based organizations: On the threshold of a new era. *Leadership Quarterly, 17*(3), 211–216.

Fondas, N. & Stewart, R. (1994). Enactment in managerial jobs: A role analysis. *Journal of Management Studies, 31*(1), 83–103.

Gibb, C.A. (1954). Leadership. In G. Lindzey (ed.), *Handbook of social psychology, Volume 2* (pp. 877–917). Reading, MA: Addison-Wesley.

Gronn, P. (1999). Substituting for leadership: The neglected role of the leadership couple. *Leadership Quarterly, 10*(1), 41–62.

Gronn, P. (2002). Distributed leadership as a unit of analysis. *Leadership Quarterly, 13*(4), 423–451.

Gronn, P. (2003a). Leadership: Who needs it? *School Leadership and Management, 23*(3), 267–290.

Gronn, P. (2003b). *The new work of educational leaders: Changing leadership practice in an era of school reform.* London, UK: Sage/Paul Chapman.

Gronn, P. (2004). Distribution of leadership. In G.R. Goethals, G.J. Sorenson, & J. MacGregor Burns (eds), *Encyclopedia of leadership, Volume 1* (pp. 351–355). Thousand Oaks, CA: Sage.

Gronn, P. & Hamilton, A. (2004). "A bit more life in the leadership": Co-principalship as distributed leadership practice. *Leadership and Policy in Schools, 3*(1), 3–35.

Hartley, D. (2007). The emergence of distributed leadership: Why now? *British Journal of Educational Studies, 55*(2), 202–214.

Hayek, F.A. (1945). The use of knowledge in society. *American Economic Review, 35*, 519–530.

Her Majesty's Inspectorate of Education (HMIE) (2006). *Improving Scottish education: A report by HMIE on inspection and review, 2002–2005.* Livingston, Scotland: HMIE.

Hodgson, R.C., Levinson, D.J., & Zaleznik, A. (1965). *The executive role constellation: An analysis of personality and role relations in management.* Boston, MA: Graduate School of Business Administration, Harvard University.

Hunter, F. (1963). *Community power structure: A study of decision makers.* New York, NY: Anchor Books.

Kennedy, J. & Eberhart, R.C. (2001). *Swarm intelligence.* San Diego, CA: Academic Press.

Knox, H.M. (1953). *Two hundred and fifty years of Scottish education.* Edinburgh, Scotland: Oliver & Boyd.

Kontopoulos, K.M. (1993). *The logics of social structure.* Cambridge, MA: Cambridge University Press.

Lee, F. & Tiedens, L.Z. (2001). Is it lonely at the top?: The independence and interdependence of powerholders. In B.M. Staw & R.I. Sutton (eds), *Research in organizational behavior, 23* (pp. 43–91). Amsterdam, NL: JAI Press.

Leithwood, K. (2003). Teacher leadership: Its nature, development, and impact on schools and students. In M. Brundrett, N. Burton, & R. Smith (eds), *Leadership in education* (pp. 103–117). London, UK: Sage.

Leithwood, K. (2000). Introduction: Understanding schools as intelligent systems. In K. Leithwood (ed.), *Understanding schools as intelligent systems* (pp. 1–15). Stamford, CT: JAI Press.

March, J.G. (2005). Mundane organizations and heroic leaders. In J.G. March & T. Weil, *On leadership* (pp. 113–121). Malden, MA: Blackwell.

Polanyi, M. (1951). *The logic of liberty: Reflections and rejoinders* (pp. 111–137). London, UK: Routledge & Kegan Paul.

Senger, J. (1971). The co-manager concept. *Sloan Management Review, 13*(3), 77–83.

Spillane, J. (2006). *Distributed leadership.* San Francisco, CA: Jossey-Bass.

Whisler, T.L. (1960). The "assistant-to" in four administrative settings. *Administrative Science Quarterly, 5*, 181–216.

3

Distributed Leadership

Paradigms, Policy, and Paradox

JOHN MACBEATH

Distributed leadership remains a contested concept embracing a wide range of understandings and often bearing little apparent relationship to what happens in schools and classrooms. This chapter draws on a study in England carried out for the National College of School Leadership in which six forms of distribution were identified. These were co-constructed by researchers and school personnel working together to theorize practice and in light of that to revisit those practices with new levels of awareness. While these six forms of distribution may be regarded as a developmental sequence, evidence from shadowing, interviews, and workshops shows that in the complex and changing world of schools, things are rarely that simple and leadership activity, whether individual or shared, has to be responsive to prevailing cultural conditions. This chapter argues that those who lead and those who follow can do so more intelligently, inviting of enhanced social capital, when they have a clearer theory-in-use of what leadership is and how it expresses itself in school life. This theoretical stance, it is argued, understands leadership as existing in different forms of activity and within differing "activity systems."

Tracing the History

The earliest written record of distributed leadership is the counsel to Moses: "This is too heavy for thou cannot bear it alone," (Exodus 18: 17–18). It is a counsel with a strong contemporary relevance whether in a business or in an educational context. The belief in the power of the charismatic leader to single-handedly turn around an ailing business or a failing school has been undermined by too many examples of heroic failure (Berliner, 2001; Bevan, 2002, MacBeath et al., 2007). Assumptions as to what may have served well in the past have been confronted by accelerating global change which challenges conventional wisdom about the very nature of institutional life. As Alvin Toffler famously wrote, it is not simply the rate of change that is different but that the nature of change itself is changing. Change is the constant and demands a rethinking not simply of what leaders are or do but of what we understand by the very notion of leadership itself.

What we might term "the Moses dilemma" was a pragmatic response to the multiplicity of tasks and the pressure on a single individual. In that context distribution implied a downward delegation, relieving Moses of some of the burden of leading his people. It was a carefully selective, hierarchical model of multi-level leadership with a considered judgment as to the nature of the task at hand:

> And it shall be that every great matter they shall bring unto thee but every small matter they shall judge so shall it be easier for thyself, and they shall bear the burden with thee. Thou shalt provide out of all the people able men, such as fear God, men of truth, hating covetousness; and place such over them to be rulers of thousands, and of hundreds, rulers of fifties and rulers of tens.
>
> (Exodus 18: 21 and 22)

When we focus on leadership itself as opposed to what the "big leader" is doing, we begin to see things differently and begin to understand distribution in a new way. We may see it as "spread out" (Hargreaves, 2005), as embedded in the flow of activities in which as school is engaged (Gronn, 2000), as the "glue" of engagement in a common task (Elmore, 2000), as measured by the "density" of penetration (Sergiovanni, 2001), or in Jim Spillane's terms (2005), something existing before our very view if we have eyes to see it.

While *distributed leadership* as a term has tended to be preferred to *dispersed* leadership, the latter term seems to capture more accurately the nature of an environment which is "fertile" (Leverett, 2002) and one in which people, irrespective of status or rank, are prepared to assume responsibility according to the nature of the task, are able to take the initiative and respond creatively to meaningful change.

Towards a Practical Theory: The National College Study

This small-scale study, undertaken with funding from the National College of School Leadership (NCSL) in England, set out to explore the following questions:

- What is understood by the term "distributed leadership"? What meanings are attributed to the term "distributed leadership" by headteachers (principals) and by other staff?
- Who does that definition encompass and where does the initiative for distributed leadership lie?
- What are the processes by which leadership is distributed?
- What issues do headteachers meet with in trying to distribute leadership or trying to create environments in which it may be realized?
- What different forms may such distribution take? (For example, is it

conferred, delegated, invited, assumed, by election or by subversion?)

- How do people in formal leadership positions deal with the multiplicity of leadership roles within a school?

In addressing these questions the project took the form of case studies involving eleven schools (four secondary, two middle, three primary, and two junior/infant) within three English local authorities. The schools, which were located in urban and rural settings, were purposively chosen, based on recommendations from their local authorities as schools which either exemplified distributed leadership and/or were interested in becoming more distributive in their practice. All headteachers of the 11 selected schools were closely involved in the study, in most cases with three or four other staff who participated in attending meetings and interactive workshops. Prior to the commencement of the study, three separate meetings were held with representatives from each of the schools, forums which gave the Cambridge research team (i.e. J. MacBeath, G, Oduro, and J. Waterhouse) opportunities to establish rapport with school personnel and negotiate the rules of engagement.

Subsequently, drawing on three primary sources of data – questionnaires, interviews, and shadowing of headteachers – we held a series of workshops in which five staff from each school (including the headteacher) came together to work with us in making meaning from the data and helping to shape a typology of distribution.

Shadowing can be a powerful research instrument, not only allowing the researcher to observe the activities at first hand but, with a degree of trust between shadower and shadowee, it can create an atmosphere for a communal reflection on the activities of the person being shadowed and the context in which that activity is carried out. We followed each of the headteachers for a working day in their schools, focusing on actions and transactions and noting the frequency of their interactions with different individuals and groups, as well as the focus, or object, of that interaction. We quantified the time they spent with individuals and groups of people, for example, members of the management/leadership team, teachers, students, or visitors, and the contexts in which those meetings occurred. In Engestrom et al.'s terminology (2002) the focus was on the *activity system*, exploration of which enabled us to establish patterns of activity which were then discussed with the respective headteachers, at first on an individual basis and then at a later stage as a group dialogue. These workshop conversations helped them, and us, to amplify, to problematize and to theorize the nature of leadership activity that we had observed.

Interviews were semi-structured, in the case of headteachers primarily focused on issues emerging from the shadowing; while interviews with teachers focused mainly on issues emerging from the questionnaires that had been analyzed and returned to them. In both cases interviews explored similar themes although from different starting points:

- how people perceived and understood leadership;
- the people they saw as leaders in their schools;
- the nature of leadership practised by the headteachers;
- the meaning that they attached to the notion of distributed leadership;
- the processes through which leadership was distributed in their schools;
- factors that promoted distributed leadership and those that hindered it;
- the people/groups they considered to be the initiators of distributed leadership;
- the perceived relationship between leadership and learning.

Workshops

Workshops were a significant aspect of the research in each of the three local authorities, providing forums for feedback, dialogue, and inter-school networking. Time was scheduled to allow each school to tell its own story of how it understood distributed leadership prior to the project beginning and then at different stages over the course of the project's relatively short life (just over one year). Participants were encouraged to consider their stories in terms of factors that had aided the distribution of leadership and factors which they had perceived as barriers. The final workshop included an activity in which the teachers and headteachers interrogated samples of the data in order to test the developing theory.

This collaborative effort, in itself a genuine sharing of leadership, arrived at six categories which represented different ways of thinking about leadership and which reflected differing processes of distribution in practice. These were seen not as pure or discrete types but as capturing a tendency, or prevalent form of thinking and practice in a given school. While in some instances, the nature of leadership fell fairly neatly into one of the six categories, more typically leadership was distributed (or "distributive") in response to the task at hand, or in response to external events and policy imperatives.

We described these six forms of distribution as occurring *formally*, *pragmatically*, *strategically*, *incrementally*, *opportunistically*, and *culturally*. In Figure 3.1 we have portrayed these as a taxonomy, or continuum, to suggest a flow among them, but also in order to signal their situational character. While each of these different manifestations of leadership may be appropriate at a given time and in a given context, the most successful leadership would, we believe, convey an understanding of all of these different expressions of distri-

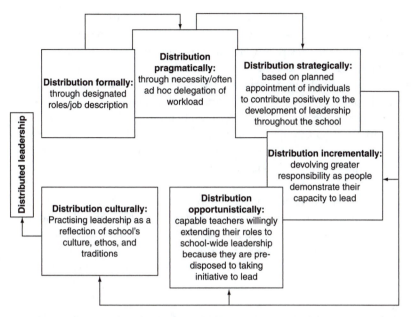

Figure 3.1 Six Forms of Leadership Distribution

bution and would be able to operate in each mode as appropriate to the situation and to the stage of development of the school.

Distribution Formally

Schools in England, as in many other countries of the world, are by history and nature hierarchical. They have a single principal, in recent years called a headteacher. When appointed to a school he or she comes, increasingly, with formal qualifications for headship, with a mandate from the school board of governors and with a set of expectations from staff and parents as well as from local authorities and from the Inspectorate. A new headteacher inherits a structure in which there are formally designated leadership and management roles and it is through these that the head then delegates responsibility. In primary schools there are few, if any, teachers without some management or leadership role. In this formal model distributed leadership is seen as allocating responsibility and encouraging a sense of ownership while at the same an agency constrained within the remit and boundaries of one's designated role.

> Well I think it's still important to have structure in leadership but distributed enough so that everybody feels that they've got ownership of something and that they feel empowered to be able to do something that's their own. I keep coming back to subject leadership. I can't talk about it in any other context really.
>
> (Special Needs Coordinator, Primary School)

The sense of "ownership" and "empowerment" – two key words in the lexicon of distribution – derive, in this model, from occupying a designated role within the formal structure and in most cases in relation to a subject area. A newly appointed headteacher may make little change in formal responsibilities and most heads tread warily in their first months, assessing the quality of people in positions of leadership, normally feeling obliged to accept the status quo, at least in the short term, as well as attempting to make explicit his/her expectations of staff in their given roles. This also holds true for others external to the school, for example, parents, visitors, or school inspectors who expect to find leadership explicitly demarcated in terms of formal structures.

> When people come into the school, they want to see the headteacher. If it's the press, they'll want to see the headteacher. That's fine, I'm glad to be the head figure. But internally, within the school, I've got a hierarchy of staff – deputy heads, assistant heads, year four leaders and a significant number of subject coordinators and I expect those people to lead.
>
> (Headteacher, Middle School)

New headteachers may, on the other hand, wish to restructure roles and responsibilities, re-designating job descriptions, particularly within the senior leadership team in which each member has a very specific area of responsibility. Responsibility as structurally delegated carries with it an attendant expectation of delivery and lines of accountability are clear. It may be accompanied by recognition that others have expertise that you do not have and that when responsibility is distributed in this way the headteacher's role is to "support and provide."

> If I give somebody responsibility, I expect them to get on with the job …. There're some generic things I can do but in terms of how to teach English better, it's the English specialist's job so I distribute responsibility. If they tell me what they need then my job is to provide.
>
> (Headteacher, Middle School)

This formal process of distribution has the advantage of lending a high degree of security not only to staff who occupy those formal roles but also to other staff who know where they stand, while parents know who it is they should speak to on any given issue. One headteacher who had recently taken over a "failing school" spoke of the need for a hero leader, bringing tight and clearly demarcated structures into a chaotic situation in which students and staff were unclear of the boundaries. It was, he believed, an essential precondition for a more radical developmental process on which the school might embark in the future.

Distribution Pragmatically

Pragmatic distribution is characterized by its ad hoc quality. It is often a reaction to external events. In these circumstances a headteacher may ask people to take on responsibility to ease the long jam and to spread the workload. Decisions as to who is given leadership responsibility, when and where, are made in response to demands from government, local authority or district, neighborhood events, or parental pressures. Distribution in this ad hoc sense plays an increasingly large part as pressures on schools mount and initiatives multiply. Jethro's advice to Moses about small and great matters determines largely what aspects of the burden may be shared and who the right people are to share that burden. The essence of pragmatic distribution was captured by a member of staff in a primary school: "I think only one person can take so much. Only one person can do so much. So therefore, distributing it to the right people helps everybody – helps the children, helps the teachers, helps everyone. It helps everybody" (Nursery Nurse, Primary School).

In an environment of increasing demands, decisions about the right people is often a pragmatic one, informed by a knowledge of staff capable of sharing the burden and judging how far individual capacity can be further squeezed. In a pressured high stakes environment such decisions tend to be marked by playing it safe, avoiding risk, and not courting failure by testing untried staff. Judgments are made in relation to those who can be entrusted with a leadership role, those who can be talked into some form of cooperation as against those who simply "divert your energy":

> You've got to be clear about those you can trust to do a good job. If all of them, that's great, but that's not possible. Bring the positive ones up with you and tap their talents, talk to the negative ones if possible. If they don't change, ignore them because they can divert your energy.
>
> (Headteacher, Primary School)

This view is reminiscent of two leadership aphorisms – "Know your people" and "Don't water the rocks." Both imply a capacity to discern latent energy in a high stakes pressured environment in which talent is at a premium. So it requires a form of cost–benefit analysis as to where growth is most fruitfully nurtured as against where it seems least likely to bear fruit. Characteristic of pragmatic distribution is its immediacy and short-term nature, not necessarily with a longer-term view to succession or building capacity.

This pragmatism was often justified by the contention that many staff did not wish to be given leadership roles or to take on responsibility beyond their own class teaching. This stemmed, in part, from perceptions of what a teacher is and does, but it may also be seen as a response to an impatient policy environment. "When there's so much pressure on teachers in the school they'll definitely avoid taking leadership responsibilities," as one junior school headteacher remarked. This is the "The Responsibility Virus" as described by Roger Martin (2002), a comfortable and collusive process in which leaders and followers assume fixed and complementary roles. In a sense it may be seen from teachers' perspectives as holding on to the right to be told but also the right to complain. In fact, with a wider distribution of leadership tasks it may in fact serve to alleviate pressure and lessen the differential between leadership as a given within a formal hierarchical structure and leadership as arising from need and opportunity.

Distribution Strategically

If formal leadership adheres to structure and protocol, and pragmatic leadership is ad hoc, the distinguishing feature of strategic distribution is its goal orientation. It is not about pragmatic problem solving but focused on a longer-term goal of school improvement. It is expressed most saliently in a carefully considered approach to new appointments. With longer-term strategy in mind these may be couched not so much in terms of individual competencies but more in terms of people as team players, perhaps with potential to fulfill certain roles that are still only a gleam in the eye of the headteacher or senior leadership team. Thinking in the longer term, one head challenged the notion that roles within a school can be neatly packaged and farmed out to particular people because, he argued, this would be inimical to sustainability.

> But one of my biggest worries, and I don't think it will ever go away, is the thought that if you give a particular specialism to any one individual, that the institution is weakened – not necessarily because of the way that individual is fulfilling that role but the consequences of that individual, for whatever reason, not being there next year or the year after to do that.
>
> (Headteacher, Secondary School)

By this argument, distribution assumes strategic importance because when expertise becomes concentrated rather than distributed it weakens school culture and sustainability.

> The role of examinations officer, for example, network manager – you can see that you need those positions to be filled but you don't want the expertise to be concentrated on just one person because we would be weaker as an institution once those people leave.
>
> (Headteacher, Secondary School)

This strategic thinking about leadership recognizes its quality as distributed between people, as joint or team leadership. As Katzenbach and Smith

(2003) argue, team leadership works across the grain to hierarchical delegation to individuals. Team leadership, it was argued by one of the school heads, celebrated individual differences because this is what fostered collective strengths. Gronn's (2000) distinction between additive and holistic distribution is relevant here. Additive distribution is nothing more than the sum of leadership roles, lacking the synergy, or "added value" that comes from a holistic view in which leadership is a "concertive action," activities which "stretch leadership function across the social and situational contexts of the school" (Gronn, 2000, p. 656).

Distribution Incrementally

Incremental distribution is distinguished from *formal, pragmatic,* and *strategic* leadership by a quality of letting go of top-down control, by widening the compass of leadership potential through a primary focus on professional development, building talent from within. It may be contrasted with strategic distribution by comparing two distinctively different stances: "Talented individuals create great organizations," (Michaels, 2001, p. 1) as opposed to "Great organizations create talented individuals" (Gladwell, 2002, p. 28). In other words, its focus is less on recruitment than on professional development, spotting and nurturing talent within. As heads become more comfortable with their own authority and feel more able to acknowledge the authority of others they are able to extend the compass of leadership and to gradually let go.

> I think initially from top-down through delegation and as it progresses it becomes both bottom-up and top-down. People who show willingness to take some levels of initiative from any direction are really encouraged. And I love to see it really happen and that's when I become happy. I believe everyone has a role to play in the school.
>
> (Headteacher, Junior School)

Its orientation is essentially a professional development one in which, to the degree that people demonstrate their ability to exercise leadership, they are able to assume more.

> Staff who have only been in the school for a short time could also be leaders in that they show by their personality, by their vision, by their jobs, commitment, expectations, and values that they have got the capacity to lead.... In a sense, anyone can be a leader. Leadership isn't hierarchical. It's a process that a lot of staff can demonstrate.
>
> (Headteacher, Secondary School)

This, it is claimed, is a less hierarchical view of leadership capacity than implied in the search for talent. It holds that capacity is inherent in everyone, but cannot be released without the crucial ingredient of confidence and self-belief. A middle school headteacher develops this theme:

> When people come out with new ideas, I ask them if they're prepared to carry out the idea.... I try to make people feel confident about what they can do because most people have the ability to lead. What they need is confidence.

People become confident when they are made to feel confident. Interpersonal relations, therefore, assume a particular significance because, as one secondary head put it, "Distribution can be seen in terms of how we relate to one another.... It's about our attitudes which are more important." The headteacher's emphasis here is on attitudes and relationships rather than roles. It implies a people, rather than a job, orientation, "a bringing on of experience" which extends limits and is professionally renewing:

> I don't really think there are too many limits because at worst, what you're doing ... is you're bringing on experience. You're encouraging contributions and I think you're benefiting. If people feel empowered if they are contributing, if opportunities for progression, for promotion don't exist here that means they will look for it elsewhere.
>
> (Assistant Headteacher, Secondary School)

Distribution Opportunistically

As we move from top-down to bottom-up the emphasis in leadership shifts from what the big leader is doing to what others in the school are doing, not by mandate but opportunistically. In this category leadership does not appear to be distributed at all. It is dispersed. It is taken rather than given. It is assumed rather than conferred. It is of the moment, opportunistic, rather than planned. It points to a situation in which there is such strength of initiative within the school that capable, caring teachers willingly extend their roles to new realms of leadership, sometimes on a school-wide basis. It stems from a natural predisposition to take a lead, to organize, to see what needs doing and make sure it gets done. Headteachers spoke of becoming aware of something dynamic happening, often surprising and unexpected, but prompting them to support that initiative. "It might not be necessarily my initiative. It might be somebody – anyone with a suggestion about something to be tried out. My job will be to support" (Headteacher, Junior School). It involves a symbiotic relation in which ambitious and energetic members of staff are keen to take on leadership roles and receive encouragement from senior leaders. Heads commented that they had learned to see something that was always there but which had previously escaped their notice:

Until this research project, I wouldn't have given it any attention but I think that's what we need in our schools. It's distributed at every level and it's not delegated leadership. Equally, there'll have to be opportunities for anybody who has ideas that fit in with the purpose of where we're going. We've got leaders at every level whether in subject areas, whether members of our teaching assistant teams or the pupils.

(Headteacher, Junior School)

A clarity of purpose or pulling in the same direction was seen as a precondition for leadership as dispersed and opportunistic. Without this common direction members of staff might exert strong leadership roles at cross-purposes to the school's mission or core values. This raises complex questions as to: Whose values? and Whose mission or vision? In an opportunistic climate there is always scope for subversion and that is both a risk and a strength. When values, priorities and direction are open to challenge and change they test a critical aspect of a school's formal leadership – how it responds to divergent views, its ability to manage conflict.

Opportunity may also be seen as extending to anyone who grasps the opportunity to take a lead, including pupils.

It's important that pupils can have a say and that, that they do actually feel involved as well, that it's not all just teacher-directed, it's not all coming from the teacher or the person who is at the top but that they do feel that they can have a say in it and sometimes they come up with a really good idea so it makes us think then, as adults. You know, perhaps we ought to be considering this; we ought to be taking this on board.

(Headteacher, Primary School)

The extension of leadership to pupils is described by one headteacher as integral to the school's purposes, the school in a sense as a laboratory for the development of their skills.

Sometimes the business stops with me but it can stop with someone else as well. Anyone in this school who has the opportunity to be the leader at some stage might be because that is what their job says; being a teacher involves leadership. I think everyone in this school should have the opportunity to do so; from the youngest child throughout and not just a selected few. The children will need these leadership skills in their development, future working, etc. It helps them to listen, value what other people say and be willing to come out with their ideas and try them out and be able and willing to persuade others.

(Headteacher, Junior School)

The metaphor for opportunistic leadership was described by one head-teacher, as the football (soccer) team. When the ball goes out of play the nearest player runs to retrieve the ball and get it back into play. Taking a free kick or penalty is typically decided on the pitch by players opportunistically. The flow is within an overall strategy but, in the event, it is intuitive, inter-dependent and implicit.

Distribution Culturally

There may seem little room left for a sixth conceptual category. When leader-ship is intuitive, assumed rather than given, shared organically and oppor-tunistically it is embedded in the culture. The sixth category, however, is distinctive by virtue of its emphasis on the *what* rather than the *who*. In other words, leadership is expressed in activities rather than roles or through indi-vidual initiative. Distribution as a conscious process is no longer applicable because people exercise initiative spontaneously and collaboratively and there is no clear demarcation between leaders and followers. The lines are blurred by what Rogers (1969) refers to as symbiosis, founded on mutual respect and reciprocity of value. Symbiosis is a term used to describe a form of reciprocal relationship in which there exists an implicit give and take and a level of mutual respect. This is by definition different from the concept of "delega-tion," which underpins much of thinking about distributed leadership. While delegation is expressed in "giving" responsibility to others or allowing responsibility by structural default, symbiosis has a more organic quality. It deserves a sixth discrete category because it switches the emphasis from indi-vidual leaders to a community of people working together to a common end with all the tensions and challenges that real vibrant communities display. This is what Gronn (2000) is referring to when he describes leadership as flowing in and around people, "the potential for leadership is present in the flow of activities in which a set of organisation members find themselves enmeshed" (p. 331).

This is premised on a culture in which it is safe to venture, one which breeds confidence and high self-esteem: "People must have high self-esteem because people need the confidence to engage in distributed leadership. I feel there must be a safe environment where people feel secure enough to venture, where they know they'll be encouraged" (Headteacher, Junior School). Culture is a word to which we are so inured that we tend to lose sight of its metaphoric origins. The metaphor is one of growth, which takes place in a nurturing set of conditions, seeding, grafting, and cultivating ideas and prac-tices. Team working, leading and following, and looking after others are reflections of culture, ethos, and traditions in which shared leadership is simply an aspect of "the way we do things round here." Distribution cultur-ally sees the strength of the school as located in its collective intelligence and collective energy.

Trust, confidence, a supportive atmosphere, and support for risk taking – a culture that says you can take a risk – you can go and do it. If it doesn't work, we learn from it. I think there's a range of cultural issues that support distributed leadership and create a climate; high levels of communication, willingness to change and to challenge; a climate that recognizes and values everybody's opinion.

(Headteacher, Secondary School)

Within another frame of reference this may be described as social capital. It is a form of capital described as "bridging" (Szreter, 2004). Whereas "bonding" social capital tends to emphasize strong internal and mutual links, which can often be exclusive and become inward looking, bridging social capital is characterized by many and weak links, a fluidity of relationships which is always alive to something new and challenging. In open, boundary-less relationships leadership moves fluidly and un-self-consciously among people.

Clearly in such a perfect anarchy distribution does not just happen. There are structures and expectations that create and infuse a certain kind of climate. In our conversations with teachers leadership activity was often simply invisible. "It just is," teachers said when asked, "It is simply the way we do things round here." From a headteacher's point of view, however, the creation and maintenance of such an environment was not accidental or serendipitous but likely to have been carefully wrought, underpinned by a value system and a sophisticated conception of leadership as a cultural artefact.

Paradoxes and Dilemmas

What emerged most clearly from the qualitative data, discussions, and follow-up workshops, was that no schools and no leaders could be fitted neatly into one of our six categories. Although in theory we would like to think that as schools and leadership mature they move through the six stages from formal to cultural distribution, life in schools is never that elegantly simple. In practice leaders at all levels of an organization draw on a repertoire of response modes, dependent on the situation in which the need for leadership is called upon.

Sometimes we delegate leadership roles. Sometimes people find themselves in situations where they assume leadership themselves. Sometimes it is frankly an executive decision but then again it also comes from the school's culture where people can simply assume leadership roles.

(Headteacher, Secondary School)

Embedded within this statement are different modes of distribution, as delegation and as opportunistic or cultural, underlining leadership as a situational process, highly sensitive to a range of contextual factors in a continuing state of flux. A number of factors will always appear in the mix:

- Factors to do with the headteacher himself/herself, for example, personality, experience, confidence, length of experience in the school and experience of other schools, influence of other leaders and models emulated.
- Factors to do with the school's history and culture, its stage of development, previous incumbents of headship, legacies of previous administrations and expectations, organizational memories, recruitment and retention.
- Factors to do with external pressures, the range and strength of these locally, regionally, and nationally. National policies, national agencies and how one is placed to respond to them.

As these factors bear upon a school at any given time the process of distribution finds differing expression. While it may be assumed that the most expert of heads have a capacity for reading situations and audiences and can choose their responses accordingly, in reality the breadth and flexibility of a headteacher's repertoire is necessarily constrained by a complexity of factors, unpredictable events within and outside the school and the management of paradox. As one headteacher commented, a progression toward the kind of leadership you aspire to cultivate never follows a simple trajectory. Progress is always shadowed by regress, a step back for every few steps forward.

This is why competency frameworks and individual assessment are so fallible. They only capture a moment, or an ideal state. As we found from the shadowing exercise, and as reported by headteachers themselves, they were different people in different places: "I am a different person on the second floor from who I am on the first floor" (Headteacher, Secondary School). While the outer body may remain, no matter which part of the building one inhabits, the inner self and its outward expression respond to the nature of relationships, expectations and past emotional histories. Toughness and tenderness, command and consultation, holding on and letting go, may be carefully considered or may simply be reflex responses. "No matter how I try to achieve a consistent approach to distribution," said one deputy head, "events always conspire to throw me into another mode."

Each encounter, each event may be viewed, in Engestrom et al.'s (2002) terms, as an activity system with its own objects ("the horizon of problems"), with access to its own relevant tools and divisions of labor. That is, with a clear view of the issues, an embrace of tools for deepened thinking about the relationship of the actors within the system and how those relationships might be otherwise, each encounter feeds progressively into a more developed, coherent theory-of-practice with regard to distributed leadership. As this happens, interactions previously boundaried within one activity system may then transfer from one space to another, helping those affected to respond in new ways and more creatively, in Sachs' words, leading to "norms of reciprocity, collective action and the development of broader identities" (2003, p. 10).

Whether this held true for the participants in this short-term project, whether they learned new skills or changed their practice is something that will only be measured over time. What they did profess to benefit from, however, was a higher state of self awareness and awareness of one's impact on others. Toward the end of the project staff who were involved were becoming more confident to talk about the leadership in action in their settings. They were more assured in recognizing and assigning behaviors and skills to varying forms of leadership. Some were expressing clear ideas about how they intended to further promote and develop a more agreeable climate for innovation and creativity. In promoting understanding and reflection it was serving to make action possible and potentially more effective.

One headteacher had been concerned that staff who had been given encouragement to lead were not fulfilling their potential or making the most of the opportunity. Through the shadowing, follow up feedback, and workshop discussion he became aware that he himself was part of the problem. As an instinctive, natural leader he admitted that he had never thought through either his own impact on other people or the skills and behaviors he expected from them. He reported a few months later that he was now better at facilitating and leading the learning of others and that the potential for a more thoughtful distribution of leadership was now being realized.

Trust and Accountability

The leadership discourse returned persistently to the issue of trust, counterpointed with the imperative of accountability. Together these defined the most acute of dilemmas. While there was an almost reflexive insistence on the importance of trust, senior leaders struggled with the resolution between a commitment to trust as growth promoting juxtaposed with the constraining nature of external accountability. The government mantra of "raising standards," portrayed by politicians as accountability to pupils, did not sit easily with school staff who saw the narrow standards agenda as disenfranchising young people and disenfranchising teachers too, distorting their work, undermining their professionalism, and eroding trust at every level from the micro-interaction in the classroom to the macro-decision making of school policy and priority.

Without mutual trust among teachers, the latitude for a more opportunistic or cultural form of distributed leadership was undermined. Getting people to participate in leadership activity, to share ideas and adventure into pedagogic territory is problematic. For senior leaders this presented a dilemma.

How could they create a culture of mutual trust within a distrustful policy environment? Some had too many experiences of trust betrayed or misplaced.

The dilemma was portrayed as a "force field" or a push-pull of factors, volatile and shifting, pushing leaders back to more coercive styles when trust was betrayed or when risk-taking proved too risky. These push and pull factors applied to members of the school leadership team, among staff generally, with pupils, between pupils and teachers, between teachers and support staff, with governors and with the parent body. Conversations in interviews and workshops depicted a continually shifting balance in relationships in which confidence and trust were in constant and precarious balance.

This was in large part a reflection of policy and accountability pressures, but this was not the whole story. How leaders struggled with these issues was relevant to the form or stage of distribution in a school. In what we have described as *distribution formally*, trust was balanced by systems of control and by what Bottery (2002) describes as "calculative trust" – a considered weighing up of the measure of trust that could be allowed to any individual in any given context. This may also be the form of trust characteristic of pragmatic and incremental distribution. Bottery's notion of "professional trust" – a confidence in the role someone is expected to fulfill – comes into play more perhaps in strategic distribution. Here trust is invested in role and status with a presumption of competence, until proved otherwise. As distributed leadership matures and evolves into distribution culturally, it would be reasonable to expect a high level of mutual trust in the school at least among staff, what Bottery described as "identificatory trust." This describes an ability and willingness to put oneself in other people's shoes, to realize the moral imperative (do unto others as you would have them do unto you) and to treat others with integrity. This latter level of trust may be more aspirational than real but it is a goal toward which many leaders strive.

So, while working to generate trust, at the same time senior leaders tried to convey the message that holding staff to account through monitoring, scrutiny of data and performance management could build, as opposed to eroding, trust. To accomplish this, however, implied creating opportunities for lateral learning and collegial exchange, peer mentoring and evaluation and a greater openness to critique and challenge, modelled by those in senior and middle leadership positions. It rested on a trustworthiness at the individual level, trust at the organizational level, and alignment at leadership level – alignment being measured by the congruence that exists between individual trustworthiness and organizational trust. This form of alignment is what Elmore (2003) has referred to as "internal accountability."

> Internal accountability is constructed as a deliberate contrast to external accountability. That is, internal accountability describes the conditions in a school that precede and shape the responses of schools to pressure

that originates in policies outside the organization. The level or degree of internal accountability is measured by the degree of convergence among what individuals say they are responsible for (responsibility), what people say the organization is responsible for (expectations), and the internal norms and processes by which people literally account for their work (accountability structures).

(Elmore, 2003, p. 17)

Without a strong sense of internal accountability, accountability to external agencies will always run at cross purposes to the generation of trust and distributed leadership. What is at stake is, in Elmore's words, how leaders account for their work, how they frame and tell their story, to one another, to their students, to parents and to the larger world outside.

References

Berliner, D. (2001, April). *The John Dewey lecture.* Paper delivered at the American Educational Research Association, Seattle, WA.

Bevan, J. (2002). *The rise and fall of Marks and Spencer.* London, UK: Profile Books.

Bottery, M. (2002, November). *The leadership of learning communities in a culture of unhappiness.* Paper presented at the Economic and Social Research Council (ESRC), University of Warwick, UK.

Elmore, R.F. (2000). *Building a new structure for school leadership.* Washington, DC: The Albert Shanker Institute.

Elmore, R.F. (2003). *Agency, reciprocity and accountability in democratic education.* Consortium for Policy Research in Education, Harvard University.

Engeström, Y., Engeström, R., & Suntio, A. (2002). Can a school community learn to master its own future? An activity-theoretical study of expansive learning among middle school teachers. In G. Wells & G. Claxton (eds), *Learning for life in the 21st century* (pp. 211–224). Oxford, UK: Blackwell.

Gladwell, M. (2002). The talent myth: Are smart people overrated? *New Yorker, 22,* July, 28–33.

Gronn, P. (2000). Distributed properties: A new architecture for leadership, *Educational Management and Administration, 28*(3), 371–338.

Hargreaves, A. (2005). *Dimensions of leadership* [video]. Retrieved May 10, 2007, from http://www.nationalpriorities.org.uk/-dimensions of leadership.

Katzenbach, J.R. & Smith, D. (2003). *The wisdom of teams: Creating the high-performance organization.* New York, NY: Harper Collins.

Leverett, L. (2002). Distributive leadership to foster equity. *National Clearinghouse for Comprehensive School Reform (NCCSR) Newsletter, 3*(7).

MacBeath, J., Gray, J., Cullen, J., Frost, D., Steward, S., & Swaffield, S. (2007). *Schools on the edge: Responding to challenging circumstances.* London, UK: Routledge.

Martin, R.L. (2002). *The responsibility virus.* London, UK: Prentice-Hall.

Michaels, E., Hartford-Jones, H., & Axelrod, B. (2001). *The war for talent: How to battle for great people.* Boston, MA: Harvard Business School Press.

Rogers, C. (1969). *Freedom to learn.* Columbus, OH: Charles Merrill.

Sachs, J. (2003, September). *Teacher activism: Mobilizing the profession.* Paper presented at the British Educational Research Association Conference, Herriot Watt University, Edinburgh, Scotland.

Sergiovanni, T. (2001). *Leadership: What's in it for schools?* London, UK: Routledge.

Spillane, J. (2005). *Distributed leadership.* San Francisco, CA: Jossey-Bass.

Szreter, S. (2004). The state of social capital: Bringing back in power, politics, and history. *Theory and Society, 31*(5), 573–621.

Part 2
How Distributed Leadership Works in Schools and Districts

4

Districts, Teacher Leaders, and Distributed Leadership

Changing Instructional Practice

WILLIAM A. FIRESTONE AND M. CECILIA MARTINEZ

The growing interest in distributed leadership reflects an effort to re-conceptualize leadership in schools by exploring how leadership is spread across a variety of roles and to explore the process of leadership. Using case studies of four schools in three districts, this chapter explores how leadership is distributed in school districts and asks about the role of teacher leaders in particular. It proposes that teacher leaders and districts can share three leadership tasks: procuring and distributing materials, monitoring improvement, and developing people. The district and teacher leaders play complementary roles. Districts tend to be distant forces, and teacher leaders are more personal. How effective teacher leaders are at people development will depend on the time they have, the knowledge they have, and their monitoring responsibility. These conditions depend partly on their administrative support. We suggest that districts may have more opportunity to influence teaching practice than past research had indicated.

The growing interest in distributed leadership reflects an effort to re-conceptualize leadership in schools by exploring how leadership is spread across a variety of roles and to explore the process of leadership (Spillane et al., 2004). However, most research on distributed leadership has examined its distribution within schools and not looked beyond them. This chapter seeks to expand the reach of distributed leadership research by exploring how leadership is distributed within school districts. It explores three questions:

- How do districts influence teaching practice?
- How do teacher leaders influence teaching practice?
- What is the relationship between teacher leaders and districts in educational change efforts?

These questions are explored through case studies of four schools in three school districts that collaborated with a university-based program to improve the teaching of mathematics and science.

Evidence from these cases suggests that districts may be able to have more influence on teaching practice than past research coming out of the loose coupling tradition (Bidwell, 1965; Meyer & Rowan, 1977) has indicated. Using these cases, we also propose that a distributed leadership framework can suggest how teacher leaders can be integrated into a district-wide change effort and complement district leadership. More specifically, we identify the leadership tasks that the district and teacher leaders conduct jointly – procuring and distributing resources, monitoring implementation, and developing people – and the conditions under which teacher leaders are most effective at contributing to the final task.

Research

Leadership is notoriously difficult to define but it usually involves the exercise of social influence, often in the service of some collective end such as organizational productivity (Leithwood et al., 1999; Smylie et al., 2002). Distributed leadership moves away from individual- and role-based views of leadership to those that focus on the organization and on leadership tasks (Smylie et al., 2002).

The term *distributed leadership* has been used in two ways. One is normatively, as a quasi-synonym for democratic leadership and as part of an effort to either expand the administrative apparatus of schools or to give more authority to teachers (Harris & Muijs, 2005). It is much like corporate research on shared leadership (Pearce & Conger, 2003). The other is as an analytic perspective to understand how leadership work is spread among leaders, followers, and the situation (Spillane et al., 2004). This second usage is intended to have no normative loading. There is to be no advocacy for (or against) teacher leadership or any particular pattern of leadership distribution. Rather the task is to describe different ways in which leadership is distributed and their causes and consequences.

Whichever orientation is taken, however, most examinations of distributed leadership have focused on the school and explored the spread of leadership among principals and teachers without exploring the role of the district (Gronn & Hamilton, 2004; Hatcher, 2005; Spillane et al., 2004). This chapter expands the focus of leadership distribution to the district. Our intention is not so much to ignore the role of the principal – which we hope to pursue in future analyses – as to bring out the role of the district office. We focus on three questions.

The first is: How do districts influence teaching practice? While there has been a range of views on this issue, expectations for district influence have been low. Some have viewed districts as structurally loose entities that gave teachers considerable autonomy (Bidwell, 1965). Others have pointed to a zoning of authority in which the district had more authority over curriculum than instruction but expected teachers to have substantial autonomy in the classroom (Lortie, 1975). Yet, even when the district has had authority over curriculum, observers doubted that it was used effectively (Floden et al., 1988).

More recently, observers have noted that districts have been willing and able to bring about changes in some kinds of practices, but not others. They have been more likely to and able to ensure the implementation of practices that can be brought about through the enforcement of a clear, unambiguous policy (Rowan & Miskel, 1999). Practices that require the re-education of teachers appear more difficult to implement (Fairman & Firestone, 2001). Districts' willingness to influence teaching practice appears attributable to growing accountability pressures from state and federal government (Firestone & Shipps, 2005; Stecher & Barron, 1999).

What tools or influence mechanisms do districts use to influence teaching? Reviews of the available research point to several possibilities (Leithwood et al., 2004; Marsh, 2002). One important thing they can do is adopt a curriculum that structures the way teachers use their time in class and order which topics are addressed by students (Togneri & Anderson, 2003). Centrally developed curriculum is most effective if it is supported by a capacity to analyze data and data are used to select the curriculum and monitor its implementation (Cawelti & Protheroe, 2001; Togneri & Anderson, 2003). However, there has been a long history of efforts to implement centrally mandated curricula, and these have often been unsuccessful. It appears that district guidance works more effectively when curricula are accompanied by the provision of time to learn new instructional approaches, including the use of new curricula, and if the district provides or supports professional development to teachers and administrators working in schools (Stein & D'Amico, 2002). If these operational changes are accompanied by a change in the district culture, in particular a focus on student learning and a concentrated effort to build professional communities among teachers, they are more likely to be successful (McLaughlin & Talbert, 2002; Togneri & Anderson, 2003). A few case studies of improving districts illustrate what happens when these factors all come together in one place (Elmore & Burney, 1999; Stein & D'Amico, 2002; Togneri & Anderson, 2003).

The second question concerns the influence of teacher leaders. While the idea of teacher leadership is not new, there is little consensus on what it should mean, although there is a common understanding that teacher leaders are peers with no authority over other teachers (Harris & Muijs, 2005). Some formalized teacher leader roles, like department chairs, are quite well established, but have traditionally been administrative and part of the regular structure of schools. Smylie and colleagues (2002) note a change in reformed uses of teacher leadership from the 1970s to the present. The formalized teacher leader roles of the earlier era established individual teacher leaders in order to decentralize school structures and empower and professionalize teachers. The emphasis in these reforms was on empowering individuals and professionalizing the teacher workforce (Lichtenstein et al., 1992). Through these changes, the goals were to increase the incentives to recruit high quality individuals into teaching and to change how decisions were made in schools rather than to work directly on improving instruction (Smylie et al., 2002).

Attention shifted in the 1990s to new strategies that included teacher research, leadership of teams and maintaining professional communities (Smylie et al., 2002), and coaching other teachers (Timperley, 2005). The intention was more on having teachers work with peers to improve their practice. In addition, informal teacher leadership has always existed, although teaching tends to be an isolated occupation in which individuals have relatively little opportunity to share what they do with other adults during the working day (Lortie, 1975).

Teacher leadership tasks are as diverse as teacher leadership roles (Harris & Muijs, 2005). Some teacher leaders are involved in administrative work like setting standards for student behavior, deciding on budgets, and addressing personnel issues. Some serve as go-betweens or liaisons between administrators and teachers. Of most interest, others focus on issues of curriculum and instruction and help their peers improve their own teaching.

The evidence on how teacher leaders help their peers improve their teaching is quite weak, perhaps because teacher leadership takes so many forms, but also because of the poor design of past research (York-Barr & Duke, 2004). Nevertheless, some conditions seem to facilitate teacher leader influence. For instance, teacher leaders who have the time and opportunity to interact with their peers appear more likely to influence them (Gigante, 2006; Harris & Muijs, 2005). Those who have an understanding of teaching practices and the content in the area where they are providing assistance may simply have more to offer to their peers and, therefore, be better able to build a relationship with them (Manno, 2005). Finally, because teaching is isolated, autonomous work, the assistance that accompanies coaching may require teachers to disclose potentially embarrassing information. Thus, trust may be a prerequisite for an effective helping relationship (Bryk & Schneider, 2002; Louis & Kruse, 1995).

The third question concerns the relationship between the district and teacher leaders. At the extreme, these relationships could be oppositional. Some recommend that school districts centralize more and hold principals and teachers accountable for their practice (Cawelti & Protheroe, 2001; Ouchi, 2003). Meanwhile, some writing on teacher leadership is explicitly anti-hierarchical, focusing on teacher empowerment (Silva et al., 2000). Others examine teacher leadership where administrative leadership has to some extent fallen short. Heller and Firestone (1995) describe teachers helping to maintain the vision for a program in part because administrators did not.

Yet, districts and teacher leaders may also be complementary. On the one hand, teacher leaders may depend on their district for some of the conditions that facilitate their work. These include the time, materials, and opportunities to interact with teachers. District leaders may also affect teacher leaders' relationships with teachers depending on what demands they place on the latter for monitoring teaching practices (Gigante, 2006; Harris & Muijs, 2005).

On the other hand, the district may depend on teacher leaders to improve teaching practice and support its initiatives. Many of the district's sources of influence are substitutes for leadership (Kerr & Jermier, 1978). As artefacts, schedules, or shared understandings, they operate at a distance to shape interaction. They lack the personal and informal touch that teacher leaders can offer and that may be extremely helpful in facilitating individual learning. Teacher leaders may be especially useful in contributing this missing piece.

Distributed leadership provides a way of thinking about how the work of school districts and teacher leaders may or may not complement each other. One growing point of consensus in theorizing about distributed leadership is that leadership work is carried out through a series of tasks or activities, although there remains considerable disagreement about what those activities might be (Leithwood et al., 2007; Spillane et al., 2004). These tasks may be a means of influence. A representative list of leadership tasks would include developing and maintaining a vision of an effective school or district; developing and managing a culture to support that vision; providing encouragement; procuring and distributing resources; supporting the growth and development of people in the organization; and monitoring instruction, innovation, and the overall climate (Heller & Firestone, 1995; Spillane et al., 2004). The challenge becomes distributing the work of accomplishing these tasks across roles and ensuring an appropriate alignment between people in diverse jobs. The theoretical and practical challenge for research on distributed leadership in school districts is to identify what constitutes an appropriate pattern of task distribution and to clarify what factors affect how those tasks are distributed. To cast further light on that issue, we turn to our cases.

Methods

This study draws on a larger study conducted at the Center for Educational Policy Analysis (CEPA) at Rutgers University of schools partnered with the New Jersey Math Science Partnership (NJ MSP). The NJ MSP engaged two local universities and eleven school districts in the improvement of math and science teaching. Funded by the National Science Foundation (NSF), NJ MSP sought to increase district and school capacity to adopt an inquiry-oriented approach to teach math and science. NJ MSP provided the unique opportunity to explore how teacher leadership roles, which were supported by the MSP, developed differently in each district and schools.

This study focuses on four schools in three districts and their district contexts. The four schools were all those in the larger study that had teacher leaders. All were in *Abbott Districts* (i.e. districts designated by the State Supreme Court to receive special state aid to equalize funding with the wealthiest districts in the state because of their poverty). The schools were poor, but they varied in their demographics, although most students were Latino or African American (see Table 4.1).

In each school an average of eight teachers were interviewed along with principals and teacher leaders. Teachers were selected to represent different levels of experiences and grade levels. Teachers' credentials varied among the schools from Madera where only 16 percent had master's degrees to Kahlo where half of them did. Six percent of the teachers in Marti School had emergency certificates.

The study used data from two consecutive years. Data collection for the MSP study started in the fall of 2003 and continued in the schools through the spring of 2005. Additional data were collected through spring 2006. Data were collected in each school through observation, interviews, and document analysis. Each teacher was interviewed six times, after math or science classroom observations. Data also included two interviews with a principal and teacher leaders.

In the spring of 2006, we interviewed district math and science supervisors. We also observed a two-day retreat with district and MSP leaders and teachers' meeting at each school. Semi-structured open-ended interviews (Patton, 1990), allowed gathering data about the roles and performance of district and school leaders. In addition, the study relies on data collected from previous studies of professional development and the effects of testing in the same districts. Moreover, in his role as principal investigator of the NJ MSP, the senior author informally obtained information as a participant observer during MSP meetings with district and school leaders. This information provided valuable insights about district history and context. Multiple sources of data allowed triangulation, which increased the validity of the study. The fact that the

Table 4.1 School Sample

Categories	Lopez	Kahlo	Marti	Madera
District	Riverside	Riverside	Victorian	Sandyfield
Grade Range	K-8	K-8	PreK-5	K-5
Enrollment	829	400	541	308
Free or Reduced Lunch	86%	93%	87%	82%
Hispanic	88%	84%	47%	15%
African American	11%	16%	52%	52%
White	n/a	0%	1%	32%
Students' Mobility Rate	13%	6.3%	1.7%	44%
Teachers with Emergency Certificate	0%	0%	6.4%	0%
Teachers with Masters Degree or Higher	37%	50%	27%	16%

interviews with different actors addressed the same issues allowed further triangulation.

Data identification includes sorting the data into analytically meaningful and easy to find segments (Reid, 1992). Through the process of coding, the researchers could assign analytical categories to segments of data. Coding allowed for retrieval of specific parts of the data later on during the analysis and enabled the researchers to combine and compare information from different sources. Transcribed interviews, observations and field-notes were coded using the software N6 for qualitative research.

The analysis consisted of rich descriptions and summaries of combined analytic categories. We wrote school based descriptions and cross-case comparisons. The analysis described the different ways teacher leaders and district influenced practice. To increase validity, the analysis looked for disconfirming evidence. Prolonged engagement with the schools and districts, as well as multiple visits to the teachers, teacher leaders, and administrators contributed to building trust with the participants (Cresswell, 1998).

Our findings suggest that teacher leaders complement the district efforts. Teacher leaders and districts contribute to the same leadership tasks: procuring and distributing materials, monitoring the improvement effort, and developing people. However, they do so in different ways. Districts operate at a distance and rely on formal authority and substitutes for leadership while teachers rely more on close relationships to lead. Moreover, teacher leaders are constrained by the time they have for this part of their work, their own experiences and knowledge, and the tension between monitoring and providing professional development where monitoring can diminish the trust needed for the latter. To provide the basis for these conclusions, we first introduce the districts studied. Then in turn, we describe district influence on teachers, teacher leadership influence on teachers, and how the districts affect teacher leaders.

Three Districts

Riverside

Riverside had had the same superintendent and deputy superintendent for 20 years at the start of fieldwork. Like all urban districts in New Jersey, leaders worried about raising test scores and reducing achievement gaps. They therefore, sought to exercise considerable control. Early in this superintendent's tenure, they had mandated quarterly topic plans to get teachers to follow the required curriculum for their grades.

The district also provided learning opportunities for teachers. These included a corps of teacher leaders who were content area specialists to assist elementary teachers. The math specialists taught one course and had free time for a variety of assignments, including working with other teachers in their classrooms, providing teachers with the calculators and manipulatives they needed, running after-school test preparation programs, and developing materials that teachers could use in the classroom. Other specialists supported the teaching of science.

While the district was very sensitive to test scores and maintained a strong central discipline, this discipline had a constructivist bent. The mathematics supervisor said that the deputy superintendent wanted district curricula "to be much more kid-centered, to be more focused on the child and ... engaging the child in the activity." The math and science education leaders of the district saw their constructivist approach as a way to prepare for the state tests but recognized that people in the schools did not. One teacher leader gave the following example:

> At one school, I remember they said, "We're doing Trailblazers but one day a week we're doing test prep." And I was like, "Look. Trailblazers is teaching the stuff on the test." And test prep was, a drilling, you know. They did not understand that Trailblazers was building thinking and the kids who could think mathematically could do that test. But they still had that because ... we hadn't reached a critical mass at that point where enough teachers believed it worked to sort of say to other ones, "You've got to stop doing that."

During the first year of fieldwork, the superintendent and deputy superintendent left the district, and the mathematics supervisor left the next year. The team that replaced them maintained the specialist positions but did not have the same understanding of curriculum or its relationship to testing. The district developed a narrower focus on raising test scores. According to a principal, "This year, unlike past years, every school, at the direction of the superintendent, will be concentrating on one goal and one goal alone, which is student achievement, which can be interpreted as 'pass the test.'" While the curriculum remained the same, special test preparation programs became more common.

Victorian

Ten years before the start of fieldwork, Victorian hired an outside new superintendent. This individual brought in a cosmopolitan team of change agents with an ambitious agenda for improvement. Initially, it sought to reform instruction in several subject areas, but it soon focused on improving literacy achievement. After about three years, the effort was expanded to include mathematics. Its approach was to combine long-term efforts to build teachers' knowledge and understanding and implement state standards with shorter-term efforts to raise test scores. Speaking to its interest in standards, the director of mathematics stated:

I think that the children of Victorian deserve the same math and science experiences that everybody ... else has. It should be standards-based. It should be high-level, it should be interactive, it should be hands-on. But I just think that that's best practice for everybody.

In these early years, district leaders cited teachers' low motivation to engage in new learning and limited knowledge of mathematics and science as a problem for achieving those standards (see also Bulkely et al., 2004).

Even before the district began focusing on improving mathematics education, it participated in a major NSF program to improve the mathematics teaching of selected teachers. This was the prelude to an effort to identify and groom informed teachers who would become math coaches, full-time teacher leaders who would be available to help their peers improve their teaching of mathematics. When the district did shift more attention to mathematics, it hired one full-time coach for each elementary school. These steps were part of the district's larger vision of where its mathematics program should go. Implementing that vision also entailed professional development, which was linked to the implementation of new curricula.

In the first year of fieldwork, the superintendent took a job in another district and the deputy superintendent resigned. A new superintendent with experience in mathematics education was hired from outside the district.

Sandyfield

Shortly before fieldwork began, Sandyfield promoted its assistant superintendent to superintendent. The superintendent promoted the science supervisor in the high school to district wide math and science supervisor. He saw three main challenges. One was to raise teachers' expectations for students. The second was helping teachers, even at the elementary level, better understand the math they would be teaching. The third was moving to more of "an inquiry or a discovery approach" in math as well as in science. He said, "I'm a great fan of the inquiry approach and discovery approach. I think students learn far more from their failures if they're allowed to fail and allowed to learn from it and move on, than simply by a teacher handing them answers." The district leaders saw these changes as compatible with the pressure to raise test scores and reduce achievement gaps. As a teacher explained, test scores are "important to the district as a whole ... statistics are out and you know, the facts are in the newspaper ... so it is very important."

These goals were supported by ten teacher leaders, but these individuals had no release time to work with their peers. One, who worked with thirty teachers, said her job was to "be communicator between the district level and our school level, as far as new initiatives, materials, supplies, information. Lately it's been to celebrate test scores, we got an increase in test scores."

District Influence on Teaching

Some of the activities the districts engaged in fell clearly into well defined leadership tasks such as monitoring instruction, procuring and distributing resources, and supporting the growth and development of people. We discuss curriculum development separately because it fell across tasks and included other elements. Finally we discuss administrative succession because of its implication for the tasks of developing and maintaining district vision and culture.

Monitoring

An important part of influencing teaching was monitoring, which happened directly through direct observation in supervision and indirectly through the use of testing. This was done with more or less reliance on formal authority. Victorian used a procedure called a *walk-through*, modeled on an approach used in District 2 in New York. Supervisors came into the classroom with a checklist that included the types of posters and graphics teachers needed to have and the types of teaching strategies they needed to be using. In the other two districts, supervisors would check to ensure that teachers were following the curriculum and to ensure its implementation. At Riverside, checking involved a joint visit with the teacher leader to make sure that:

> Children are actively engaged in the lessons, using the materials from the kits, that the teachers are doing the [brand] kits, that in the lesson plans, teachers are planning for instruction and planning to use the kits. And they'll be moving through the units you know in a timely way.

The math supervisor at Riverside would stop by the classrooms without any previous notice. Teachers said that she usually observed a lesson and sometimes would provide immediate oral feedback to the teacher. A teacher mentioned that she had to hide some of the materials she was not allowed to use because the supervisor showed up frequently. One of the teachers reported:

> [The math supervisor] is always coming in and whenever I was in the lab, I always saw her coming in to check up.... She's always talking to [teachers] and [the teacher] goes to trainings regarding the [computer program]. And he was taught how to use it.

At Sandyfield, the supervisor called, e-mailed, or showed up in person not only to make sure teachers were using the materials, but also to inquire about how the pacing of the curriculum was being implemented. In this district following the pacing of the curriculum was highly valued as a way to deal with the high student mobility within and across the district.

At the same time, the district supervisors would work to build teachers' trust and knowledge by showing what they knew. As the new supervisor in Sandyfield explained:

> The elementary teachers were a little concerned three years ago when I got the job because they said, "Oh, he doesn't understand elementary. He's a secondary guy." So I made it a point to get out in the classrooms in front of them as soon as I could, and every elementary teacher whose classroom I've been in has said the same thing to me. "We're really surprised how good you are with the kids."

They often did this during their supervision visits by teaching part of a lesson or offering useful suggestions. The math supervisor in Riverside said she told teacher leaders to tell teachers:

> [The district supervisor] will come and observe. And she will sit and do the check-off. However, at some point, she will probably ask if she can ask a question. And she may even teach for a few minutes. Do not think that that means she doesn't think you're doing a good job. It's just that she's someone who is very passionate about teaching and very passionate about math. And so, if she has another strategy, she's going to get up and model it for you. She's not going to write you up.

Direct supervision was supplemented by monitoring test scores. All three districts adopted a commercially developed test and implemented a district test to assess district benchmarks. Thus, most children took two tests, either the commercial test or the State test, and the district test. The district, teacher leaders and principals analyzed commercial test results and showed results to teachers. Leaders analyzed specific areas, such as open-ended questions, from the test. The district's tests allowed leaders to monitor the implementation of the curriculum. The district test was also a way to ensure that the teachers were following the required pace. This was particularly true at Sandyfield where curriculum pacing was a response not only to the need to reform mathematics and science, but to deal with high student mobility.

Procuring and Distributing Resources

Districts managed two kinds of resources that were important to teachers. The first was instructional materials. While materials were available in all three districts, communication around materials varied. Teachers at Madera, in Sandyfield district, could call the district supervisor as needed. At Riverside and Victorian teachers saw their supervisors during meetings, walk-throughs, and professional development events, but felt they had less influence than in Sandyfield.

All three districts also provided the teachers with practice test materials that influenced instructional strategies and content coverage. Talking about how these materials influenced her teaching, a teacher reported: "Practice testing material [is] very influential because the New Jersey [test] is the priority in fourth grade. The format in the practice book is a help for them."

The second was time allocated for instruction. Districts had the authority to allocate time to different subject areas. In Riverside and Sandyfield, the district increased the time to teach math. This affected how time was distributed in other areas. Madera School allocated 70 minutes for math every day. The two Riverside schools increased the time for math and decreased the time for science by ten minutes.

Moreover, the districts allocated more time for test preparation. At Madera, the district organized an After School Club that met twice a week for math, and twice a week for literacy. Students who scored below certain criteria on district-administered tests were encouraged to attend. In order to have this club, the district eliminated another after school program that was open to all the children who needed help with homework. In Riverside, the district replaced an after-school enrichment program with a test preparation program provided by a private company. In addition, a large part of the program targeted English language learners, and instruction consisted of English vocabulary that might be on math tests.

Growth and Development of People

Districts addressed the growth and development of people primarily through professional development.[1] The quantity and quality of district professional development varied. In Riverside, teachers had been learning about constructivist pedagogy for eight years through on-going, in-depth professional development events. Teachers reported discussing content, pedagogy, and the reason behind teaching strategies during these events. They had monthly district workshops, and some were part of Lesson Study Groups led by the MSP liaison that discussed, implemented, and reflected on lesson plans. Generally, Riverside teachers showed more knowledge of the pedagogy when they spoke about the intentions of the lesson and the reasons behind the strategies they used.

Sandyfield began continuous professional development with a strong focus on how to implement the textbook with the introduction of that textbook. Teachers reported learning the new pedagogy and being aware that they needed more time to change their practice. They had monthly district-wide grade level meetings and had four workshops provided by a consultant. In addition, teachers often talked among themselves. Because the program was new, teachers had difficulties integrating knowledge about the pedagogy with their expectations for their students. Teachers transformed inquiry-oriented tasks (such as allowing students to come up with different ways to solve a problem) into direct instruction (lecturing about the different ways to solve problems).

Victorian introduced two new textbooks during the fieldwork period (see below). Each year, the district provided three days of summer workshops on the use of each one. For most teachers, professional development began with the introduction of the first textbook, although some had participated in an earlier intensive program that provided a general introduction to constructivist approaches to teaching mathematics. In this new program, teachers met for three full days of hands-on workshops to perform tasks that their students would be required to do. Teachers mentioned that this kind of professional development increased both their knowledge of content and teaching strategies to implement the program. Some teachers reported not receiving as much professional development for the second math series. The emphasis in the second workshops was more on pacing, classroom management, and lesson planning than math content.

Curriculum

All three districts had centrally mandated mathematics curricula. They also expected teachers to use science kits to teach certain lessons in specific grades. These functioned as a material resource, much like manipulatives or other teaching materials. Their introduction became an occasion for the development of people. However, they were also key artefacts for controlling how teachers used their time. They also represented a vision of effective instruction so district leaders used them as a way to establish a new direction and build a culture of instruction.

The districts had several ways to control the implementation of the textbook. One was using formal authority to require teachers to follow the textbook. In all three districts, teachers reported that they were mandated to use math textbooks and to follow a specific order in how they used them. In Riverside, a teacher mentioned, "[They] encouraged us to follow it step by step," and said that they had to teach from the book because it was assigned to them. A teacher from Sandyfield said, "Everything I need is in the 'Everyday Math' manual.... You're not supposed to do anything extra. You're supposed to do exactly what the book asks you to do." And a Victorian teacher said that they were required to follow the book "to the letter" so that the company was to blame if test scores did not go up. Much of the monitoring described above was about the use of textbooks and materials.

The mandate to follow the book influenced both teaching strategies and the content teachers needed to cover. One teacher reported that the district leaders had pushed her to "move all the way through the book." And this feeling was shared among teachers from the three districts. Five Sandyfield teachers said that because of the new math series, they were teaching content that they had not taught before. For instance, a second grade teacher said she had never taught division before. But Sandyfield was the only district where that happened.

Most teachers from the four schools said that they used hands-on materials because the book suggested presenting the topics with manipulatives. When asked why a teacher had chosen to use straws and pins to make geometric figures, she said she was "following the 'Everyday Math' format." All three textbooks – "Everyday Math," "Investigations," and "Math Trailblazers" – provided many materials that allowed children to use multiple representations such as individual boards, manipulatives, and so forth.

While the district made the ultimate decision about which textbook to adopt, teachers' input varied. In Sandyfield, a few teachers brought back the idea of using "Everyday Math" – a moderately constructivist text – from professional development they received at a nearby university, and tried it out at Madera before the math supervisor led a curriculum selection process. Through that process, "Everyday Math" was ultimately selected in part because of those teachers' endorsement. Riverside held a similar committee process that led to the selection of "Math Trailblazers," another moderately constructivist text. At Lopez and Kahlo schools, some teachers felt they had had some input in the process, reviewing and comparing the textbooks, but most teachers felt that the textbook was imposed. At Victorian, teachers said they had no input at all in the selection of "Everyday Math." Nevertheless, through informal communication with parents, they influenced the district to end the use of a previous textbook which they deemed too constructivist and got the superintendent to bring together a committee of experts to recommend the change of text.

Regime Succession

Regime changes affected the districts' capacity to change teaching in several ways. They influenced people development activities, for instance, and stability of curriculum. They also upset district vision and culture. Riverside had been moving its math program in a constructivist direction before its superintendent retired. When the new administration came in, some individuals said there was clearly a shift to more short-term test preparation activities. Beyond that, the district seemed to lose its instructional vision. The Victorian administration had been in place for almost a decade, and had been working on mathematics reform for about five years with a link to the local university for most of that time. "Investigations" – the previous textbook – had been part of that change. In the middle of fieldwork, the superintendent took a job in another district amid rumors of declining board support. The new superintendent was more willing to listen to parent and teacher complaints. She introduced an expert review that allowed the shift to "Everyday Math" which teachers saw as more back to basics and less different from their previous practice than the textbook that preceded it. The administration that began just before fieldwork in Sandyfield introduced new textbooks and a new approach to instruction that changed content coverage as well.

In sum, all three districts had centrally selected curricula and monitored the use of those curricula, but they differed in the way the monitoring took place. Victorian was the most directive in its requirements that the curriculum be followed and Sandyfield was the most collegial. In fact the curriculum selected in Sandyfield had originally been identified by a group of teachers. Riverside had the longest history of professional development to educate teachers about constructivist approaches to math and science teaching, and this professional development was least explicitly linked to textbook implementation. Sandyfield had started most recently, and tied its professional development most explicitly to the textbook. The coherence of district efforts in both Riverside and Victorian had been interrupted by the departure of a superintendent and his team, but that departure appeared more voluntary in Riverside than in Victorian, and teachers actively sought to change the district's decision about which math text to use only in the latter district. While there were differences among these districts, it should be noted that all three actively sought to influence teachers' approaches to teaching math and science. These were not loosely coupled districts.

Teacher Leaders' Influence on Teachers

Teacher leaders engaged in three tasks that influenced teachers. They provided materials, and monitored and supported the growth and development of people, most notably teachers. The latter was the key task, but teacher leaders' capacity to do it depended on a fragile set of relationships. Monitoring, for instance, might work against the trust necessary to support growth. As we describe how teacher leaders carried out each task, we attend to the conditions that facilitated supporting growth and development. Table 4.2 indicates how many teachers from each school reported teacher leaders engaging each type of activity.

Table 4.2 Teacher Leaders' Tasks as Perceived by Teachers

Number of Interviewed Teachers per School	Lopez N = 10	Kahlo N = 7	Marti N = 11	Madera N = 7
Number of Teachers Saying Teacher Leaders:				
Provide Materials	8	6	10	1
Monitor	1	3	4	0
Coach	7	6	9	2
Are Supportive				1
Turn Key Other Teachers After Attending a Workshop				1
They are Available, But we Have Not Needed Them				2

Providing Materials

All the teacher leaders in the schools we visited provided materials. Most teachers perceived this was helpful. A Riverside teacher mentioned, "She will make the practice easier. That's very important." Teacher leaders were the direct sources of such supplies as calculators and manipulatives as well as science kits.

At Lopez School, the science teacher leader focused primarily on providing materials. She coordinated the use of the science kits (because schools shared the same materials) and ordered supplies. One teacher mentioned, "She makes sure that we have all the resources and that our kits are refurbished with all that we need." Coordinating the use of materials in this case also implied determining and pacing the curriculum. Another teacher reported: "She coordinates all science activities. She determines what you're gonna teach and try, the idea is to get uniformity across the district." As part of this role, she assisted teachers with their planning.

The teacher leader at Marti School provided copies of workbook activities during the year teachers were using the math "Investigations" to supplement the curriculum with basic skills practices. The next year, when she could no longer provide extra material since the district prohibited using materials other than the new textbook, the teacher leader provided copies of the assessments that teachers could use after each content unit. Providing these assessments helped the district control curriculum pacing and monitor the implementation of the textbook. Since the teacher leader's role changed from school-based to district-based in Victorian, teachers had more difficulties accessing materials through the teacher leader so teachers had to go to friends instead.

Because the district supervisor provided most of the materials at Madera School, only one teacher said that the teacher leader distributed materials. Since the teacher leader role was new and ambiguous, teachers rarely asked the teacher leader for materials. But, if the teacher leader found out that a teacher needed materials, she would call the math supervisor and order them. One teacher said the teacher leader is "a point of contact people for math in the building who could contact the supervisor, so they just went to a work-shop with the math supervisor last week and they sent us a little letter about what's going on."

While most teachers saw providing materials as very useful, its influence was limited. One Marti School teacher said, "They [the teacher leaders] don't really help us with teaching it. The math coaches tell us what we need to have and they have a math folder and a portfolio folder and they help us with what needs to be contained in that." Still, teacher leaders could use providing materials to build relationships. A teacher leader in Sandyfield impressed a colleague by quickly getting a special set of manipulatives for her from the central office, for instance.

Monitoring

Eight teachers (of the 35 teachers interviewed) mentioned that the teacher leader monitored the implementation of the program. Monitoring can be intrusive and, if done inappropriately, can undermine the trust teacher leaders need to coach well. Monitoring was most prevalent at Marti School and to a lesser degree at Kahlo School.

Teachers said that teacher leaders monitored the pace of the curriculum. A teacher at Lopez in Riverside said that the teacher leader was "usually asking me questions, like where am I in the 'Foss' kits." Similar statements were made in Victorian (Marti) where the teacher leader asked teachers what chapter they were teaching.

The Victorian teacher leader also checked teachers' anecdotal notes. One teacher said, "[She] makes sure that we're basically up to date, that we're definitely taking notes and trying to keep on top of things." In this respect, the teacher leader said that although she was not supposed to supervise, "I have to turn in reports or my logs, which may have notes and things that go on between the teacher and I. Then I feel that that is a supervisory type position." Since many teachers objected to this curriculum, her monitoring put her at odds with them. She also tracked portfolios of student work and the bulletin boards. To ease some of the friction, when teachers did not have mandated materials on bulletin boards, she would put them up for the teachers.

Kahlo teacher leaders also reported monitoring curriculum implementation. A teacher leader said, "My job is pretty much to make sure that they stick to their script." She also mentioned that some teachers resisted change or had more problems than others to change their practices. In these cases she tried to approach the teachers by herself first, and then maybe ask the principal to intervene. Teacher leaders also participated in indirect monitoring through analyzing test scores and feeding back results to teachers.

Growth and Development of People

Teacher leaders' main mode of helping teachers grow and develop was through individual coaching both in the classroom and during one-on-one and small-group meetings. The same interactions that provided the information for monitoring also provided the opportunities for coaching. Twenty-four out of 35 teachers said that coaching was one of the main tasks teacher leaders performed. Unlike providing materials, coaching clearly influenced teaching, but coaching was different in each school. Most teachers reported that they had learned new teaching strategies as a result of teacher leader coaching.

At Lopez School, the math coach did not have much time because he taught in a bilingual classroom. Nevertheless, as time permitted, he would model some strategies or provide time for teachers to visit other teachers' classrooms. In addition, the teacher leader helped teachers with strategies to address a particular area that the teachers had difficulties with. He worked exclusively with the tested grades, emphasizing topics that needed coverage because they were on the state test. The Lopez science teacher leader worked with several schools so she was only there a few days a week and thus only reached a few teachers. Nevertheless, she modeled lessons and strategies and demonstrated how to use the new science kits.

The Kahlo coaches helped with teaching strategies. One saw and met all fourth grade teachers five periods a week:

> My whole afternoon is teaching fourth grade. I'm actually in their room. They tell me either before I come into their room or right after what [the lesson is about] or what they would like me to do. I might just go around working with a small group, helping them through the lesson.

She helped teachers in their classrooms with children who had difficulty in math or by "team teaching as needed." In addition to helping in the classroom, the teacher leader worked with teachers as a group, or individually, discussing and reflecting on teaching strategies. She said, "At the end of a lesson, I'll stay and I'll talk with them. I make suggestions to them. I tell them ideas that they might want to try out, or if children are having trouble, I try to model ways of rephrasing...." Teachers reported gaining more confidence, especially with new materials, as a result of working with the leaders.

In Victorian, teachers reported that they met once a month in a half-day workshop with the teacher leader. During these workshops they would "troubleshoot" and also discuss the implementation of the curriculum. A teacher said:

> We all talk about what problems, trials, and tribulations of teaching first year of "Everyday Math." And that's been very helpful because you never want to be in a boat alone, especially if you think your boat's sinking. But in our case, we were all pretty much swimming and we were doing OK. You always want to monitor well: "I'm only on chapter 6, where is somebody else?" "We're on chapter 8." So that all was taken care of by going to these meetings.

Teachers also reported that the teacher leaders helped them to ask higher order questions, explained each unit and how to use the materials that came with it, presented games, reflection activities, and math messages of the day. Teacher leaders modeled lessons as well. Most teachers saw explaining how to use the new textbook as being very helpful. They said that the teacher leaders discussed individual units, assessment, and the teaching strategies that went with them.

At Madera School, teacher leaders were assigned to a grade level group. Only two teachers, who referred to the same teacher leader, said that the teacher leader assisted them with teaching strategies or "little suggestions."

Two factors affected how influential teacher leaders were. One was the knowledge they brought to their work, including both their content knowledge and their general experience as teachers. Martha was an especially influential teacher leader with 30 years of teaching experience and two years as a math coach. With a major in math education and credits in a master's program toward math education, she has worked as a teacher and as consultant for a private testing company in teacher to teacher mentoring. Martha believed she established her legitimacy with other teachers not only because she had knowledge of math, but most importantly, because of her experience. As she put it: "I teach for some of the teachers because I've taught it a lot of years. That's probably why I was assigned. I've taught math a long time so I pretty much can do a lesson pretty spontaneously."

Furthermore, Martha clearly expressed that her deep understanding of the math program allowed her to intervene in the classrooms as a team teacher and to effectively perform the coaching tasks. She said:

[If] teachers are new to the [math program], I've gone through the lessons already so I know the general idea and I know where they're headed. And I'll help them out or I'll get them started. I might model something for them if they're not that sure or if they're a little nervous.

In contrast, Britney in Sandyfield was the least experienced teacher leader in our sample. Although she has been teaching for ten years, she had only been teaching math to the fifth grade for two years. With a major in elementary education and sociology, Britney did not feel very knowledgeable about the new curriculum. The initiative to adopt the math curriculum had started with other teachers who had piloted the program earlier. According to Britney they had more experience than she did with the program. Britney often asked one of these teachers to help her prepare a lesson. Thus, although she had the title of teacher leader, she was still learning from her peers and not in a position to help others.

The other factor was teacher leaders' modes of interaction as they worked with teachers in ways that combined both monitoring and coaching. Teacher leaders sought to share what they knew without positioning themselves as authorities, either in the sense of formal authority or more knowledgeable authority. Martha explained that she was not

A supervisor that's coming in and bossing them around or observing them where we all feel tense when we're being reported or observed or written up. But it's much more informal, my going in. And I know I don't see myself as going in as a disruption. If anything, it's like an extra set of hands or another pair of eyes observing, or another experienced teacher helping.

Sometimes this meant finding ways to suggest teachers do things differently without being negative. Another teacher leader described situations where

I'll hear the teacher doing it. And I will walk up to them, pull them aside and I'll say, "OK. Wait. Don't put the answers up so fast. Let's give them another ten minutes." And again, just try to nudge them in that direction without saying, "No! No! You're doing it wrong." I'm not trying to criticize anyone. I'm trying to get them to move in a new direction.

Occasionally, teacher leaders would find that formal changes, like reassignments, would sunder the fabric of relationships they had developed. Then they would have to allow time for new relationships to develop. In the process, they might have to take special steps to build relationships. One teacher leader said:

What we were asked to do was to select, after we had [provided training to teachers he did not know before] ... for a while, to select maybe one or two in that building that we felt would benefit from our support. But going into a building, I didn't want to slight anyone, so I would always try to see everybody and not make that one teacher feel that they were in need of me.

These statements by teacher leaders describe their modes of interaction negatively. More positively, what they have in common is respecting the autonomy and knowledge of the individual teacher, indicating that the teacher leader respects the value of that person in his or her interactions with that person.

In sum, teacher leaders provided materials to teachers and monitored their progress through the curriculum. While the latter could have been a point of tension with teachers, it was only mentioned as an issue by the teacher leader in Victorian – the district where there was already some friction over the choice of math materials. Teacher leaders' capacity to help teachers improve in the classroom depended on two factors. The first was teacher leaders' knowledge both of the content taught and the materials used. The second was the quality of relationships developed with teachers. Teacher leaders were careful to keep these positive, another indication that too much emphasis on monitoring could have created issues. There are also some indications that teacher leaders faced time constraints that inhibited the one-on-one coaching that appeared to be the most effective means of working with teachers. This may have been the reason why teacher leaders in Sandyfield appeared to be less active than their peers in the other two districts as the next section will suggest.

The District and Teacher Leaders

These teacher leaders were largely the creatures of the districts. They occupied formal positions created by the districts to work with other teachers. The most important resource these positions provided was time, and the amount of time varied substantially across districts. Victorian's math coaches were full time while Sandyfield's teacher leaders had no release time but apparently much less expectation that they would help other teachers. Riverside's math coaches were expected to teach at least one algebra class or work in several buildings.

The other constraints on teacher leaders' time point to crucial ambiguities in the teacher leadership role about both authority and purpose. Particularly in Riverside and Victorian, teacher leaders saw their general mission in much the same terms as the curriculum staff, as supporting the development of a particular approach to teaching mathematics and science. In Riverside, a math specialist said, "My goal is to try to get them to understand the deeper mathematics behind what they're teaching and also to get them to let the kids do more. To get them used to using manipulatives, get them off of drill and kill sheets." And a Victorian math coach said, "I would have to say some of the most effective [teaching strategies] would probably be actually having the students do the hands-on, using the manipulatives, getting them to explore and get deeper into the math."

Yet, on a daily basis, they took orders from their principals. In both districts, teacher leaders were originally assigned to one building. In Victorian, the math coach reported to the principal and was initially quite loyal to that individual. He followed the principal's guidance about who needed his help, but complained that he was assigned to monitoring lunch hour and other duties that had no relationship to improving mathematics teaching in the building. Apparently, to keep principals from making such assignments, the central office assigned math coaches to grade levels across buildings in the second year of fieldwork. These reassignments had mixed results. They undermined the fabric of relationships that had developed with teachers and required more driving time.

In Riverside, too, math specialists were assigned to buildings, and many of their day-to-day assignments came from principals. While the assignments described to us were more closely related to math and science teaching, they often got in the way of working with teachers. One specialist had to stop working with teachers at one point because, at the principal's request, she was spending a lot of time designing practice materials to prepare for the state test and coaching students after school. Thus, administrators gave teachers time to work with other teachers but often also gave assignments that constrained such work.

Besides providing time, district leaders attended to the professional development of teacher leaders. The district helped teacher leaders become experts to whom teachers could turn and who would have knowledge to offer teachers. Describing the math supervisor in one district, a teacher leader said:

> I love her professional development activities always, she always presents some interesting, engaging problems and it kind of gives you the ideas where you can direct your questioning. New ways to look at old materials, old styles. And generally, when I see her, when she comes in for observations, we meet in the teachers' room or I'll catch her in the hall and discuss my experiences with the teachers. It's always positive.

Teacher leaders described three kinds of professional development, two of which were most prevalent in Riverside and Victorian. The first was monthly meetings that might average as long as one day a month. These were often group-sharing and problem-solving sessions led by the district math or science curriculum supervisor. As described by teacher leaders, they covered three topics:

- Working with difficult teachers – "Do we have teachers who are fighting us on it? The kind of teacher where, when we go in there to help them, they'll do 'Trailblazers,' but as soon as you're not there for two or three days, they go back to handing out drill sheets."
- Learning about content and instruction – "A favorite lesson. Each week, somebody would bring in something that they've taught in a specific way, using a specific manipulative that they thought went very well."
- Issues related to testing – "We deal with test data."

The second was summer workshops. These were often week-long workshops. The Victorian coaches reported that two summers in a row, they spent five days, often in conjunction with teachers, learning about new curricula the district was implementing. Finally, teacher leaders would go to out-of-district events. Most teacher leaders went to some "Math Science Partnership" events. In Riverside, teacher leaders went to some national conferences as well. These activities helped teachers develop an understanding of their content area and the process of working with teachers that was deeper than that of other teachers and would help them both be of assistance to teachers and develop some legitimacy with them.

In sum, the district provided key resources for teacher leaders that affected their work with teachers. These included time and access to knowledge. The districts tried to reinforce the teacher leader position, but some of their decisions may have actually undermined it. This was because teacher leaders faced some difficult dilemmas. In order to build relationships with teachers, it was helpful to remain within a building. However, sometimes that meant working with principals who did not appreciate the instructional nature of their work and assigned them to tasks that took them away from working with teachers.

Conclusion

This chapter describes how leadership is distributed in three districts engaging in mathematics and science reform. These districts represent somewhat special cases because of their participation in a university partnership. Moreover, our perspective is somewhat peculiar because of our focus on four schools. Nevertheless, we believe we offer two useful insights into how leadership is distributed between districts and teacher leaders.

The first is that ideas about distributed leadership suggest ways that teacher leaders can be integrated into an overall district reform effort. In these districts, teacher leaders complemented district leadership efforts. They participated in some of the same leadership tasks as the district (i.e. procuring and distributing resources, monitoring progress, and developing people) but did so in a different way. The district often operated at a distance by setting rules and mandates and by procuring materials. It tended to be impersonal and distant, using formal authority and dispassionate substitutes for leadership like the curriculum and testing to exercise influence. Teacher leaders moderated that distance by being more personal and closer and they deliberatively did so, in part to compensate the lack of formal authority. Some district level supervisors also sought to cultivate personal relationships too, but even more than teacher leaders, they lacked the time to do so.

Teacher leaders' capacity to play their complementary roles depended on a variety of factors. One was the amount of time they had. Teacher leaders who spent all their time teaching or tied up in other responsibilities, whether monitoring the lunch room or developing test preparation materials, could not work with other teachers. This was a cost factor for the district (and for principals). Freeing teacher leaders to work with teachers kept them from doing other things that might seem to have greater short-term benefits. Another was their own knowledge and expertise. They had to know more about teaching their subject matter and about the curriculum teachers were using in order to have something to offer teachers. A third was the relative emphasis on the tension between personal development versus monitoring. Teacher leaders needed to be in a position where teachers could know they were to be trusted. When they were doing too much monitoring, teachers were unlikely to trust them. Here the district had a conflict of interest, because it appeared to sometimes need teacher leaders to do both. Whether district leaders appreciated this conflict is unclear.

The second insight is that districts may be able to have more influence over teaching than had been thought in the past. There are indications that these districts were not only able to get teachers to comply with curriculum mandates – the sort of policy enforcement that Rowan and Miskel (1999) suggest is possible. At least one district – Riverside – may have been able to shape teaching practice through a long-term program of professional development. The key here is that it was a program lasting several years and combining several leadership tasks and other elements. On the other hand, while teacher leaders can complement district leadership, the specific role of the teacher leader did not appear to be necessary to district leadership. What was important and necessary was in-class support to implement changes (Veenman et al., 2001). In Riverside, that in-class support came from the district supervisor and the teacher leaders. In Sandyfield, it came from the district supervisor and from a math consultant who visited the schools often. While the teacher leaders lacked time and experience to influence teachers, teachers seemed to gradually change because of other sources of leadership. In Victorian, teachers depended largely on the teacher leader for everyday support since the district had a strong focus on monitoring and setting demands. The teacher leader seemed almost necessary at Victorian because teachers did not have direct communication with their supervisors.

This exploratory study analyzed the relationship between district and teacher leaders. We need research that goes farther to operationalize different leadership tasks from different actors and link them to changes in teaching practice. Ultimately, research is needed across more districts to ascertain the possibilities of distributed leadership that includes districts, schools, and teacher leaders and the implications of such leadership for the improvement of teaching and learning.

Acknowledgments

The work of writing this chapter was supported by grant #EHR-0226989 from the National Science Foundation with additional support coming from the Laboratory for Student Success.

An earlier version of this chapter was published in *Leadership and Policy in Schools*, 6(1).

Note

1 Districts also supported individual course taking, but that was not part of the subject of this inquiry.

References

Bidwell, C.E. (1965). The school as a formal organization. In J.G. March (ed.), *Handbook of organizations* (pp. 972–1019). Chicago, IL: Rand McNalley.

Bryk, A.S. & Schneider, B. (2002). *Trust in schools: A core resource for improvement.* New York, NY: Russell Sage Foundation.

Bulkley, K., Fairman, J., Martinez, C., & Hicks, J. (2004). The district and test preparation. In W.A. Firestone & R.Y. Schorr (eds), *The ambiguity of test preparation.* Mahwah, NJ: Lawrence Erlbaum and Associates.

Cawelti, G. & Protheroe, N. (2001). *High student achievement: How six school districts changed into high-performance systems.* Philadelphia, PA: Laboratory for Student Success.

Creswell, J. (1998). *Qualitative inquiry and research design. Choosing among five traditions.* Thousand Oaks, CA: SAGE.

Elmore, R.F. & Burney, D. (1999). Investing in teacher learning: Staff development and instructional improvement. In L. Darling-Hammond & G. Sykes (eds), *Teaching as the learning profession: Handbook of policy and practice* (pp. 263–291). San Francisco: Jossey-Bass.

Fairman, J. & Firestone, W.A. (2001). The district role in state assessment policy: An exploratory study. In S.H. Fuhrman (ed.), *From the capitol to the classroom: Standards-based reform in the states* (pp. 124–147). Chicago, IL: University of Chicago Press.

Firestone, W.A. & Shipps, D. (2005). How do leaders interpret conflicting accountabilities to improve student learning? In W.A. Firestone & C.J. Riehl (eds), *A new agenda: Directions for research on educational leadership.* New York, NY: Teachers College Press.

Floden, R.E., Porter, A.C., Alford, L.E., Freeman, D.J., Susan, I., Schmidt, W.H., & Schwille, J.R. (1988). Instructional leadership at the district level: A closer look at autonomy and control. *Educational Administration Quarterly, 24*(2), 96–124.

Gigante, N. (2006). *Teacher leadership in context: Its relationship with social, material, and human resources in schools implementing reform.* Unpublished Doctoral Dissertation, Rutgers University, New Brunswick, NJ.

Gronn, P. & Hamilton, A. (2004). A bit more life in leadership: Co-principalship as distributed leadership practice. *Leadership and Policy in Schools, 3*(1), 3–35.

Harris, A. & Muijs, D. (2005). *Improving schools through teacher leadership* Berkshire, UK: Open University Press.

Hatcher, R. (2005). The distribution of leadership and power in schools. *British Journal of Sociology of Education, 26*(2), 253–267.

Heller, M. & Firestone, W.A. (1995). Who's in charge here? Sources of leadership for change in eight schools. *The Elementary School Journal, 96*(1), 65–86.

Kerr, S. & Jermier, J. (1978). Substitutes for leadership: Their meaning and measurement. *Organizational Behavior and Human Performance, 22*, 374–403.

Leithwood, K., Jantzi, D., & Steinbach, R. (1999). *Changing leadership for changing times.* Buckingham, UK: Open University Press.

Leithwood, K., Louis, K.S., Anderson, S.E., & Wahlstrom, K. (2004). *Review of research: How leadership influences student learning.* New York, NY: Wallace Foundation.

Leithwood, K., Mascall, B., Strauss, T., Sacks, R., Memon, N., & Yashkina, A. (2007). Distributing leadership to make schools smarter: Taking the ego out of the system. *Leadership and Policy in Schools, 6*(1), 37–67.

Lichtenstein, G., McLaughlin, M.W., & Knudsen, J. (1992). Teacher empowerment and professional knowledge. In A. Lieberman (ed.), *The changing contexts of teaching. Ninety-first yearbook of the National Society for the Study of Education, Part I* (pp. 37–58). Chicago, IL: NSSE.

Lortie, D.C. (1975). *Schoolteacher: A sociological analysis.* Chicago, IL: University of Chicago Press.

Louis, K.S. & Kruse, S.D. (1995). *Professionalism and community: Perspectives on reforming urban schools.* Thousand Oaks, CA: Corwin.

McLaughlin, M.W. & Talbert, J.E. (2002). Reforming districts. In A. Hightower, M. S. Knapp, J.A. Marsh, & M.W. McLaughlin (eds), *School districts and instructional renewal* (pp. 173–192). New York: Teachers College Press.

Manno, C.M. (2005). *Teacher leadership in mathematics and science: Subject content knowledge and the improvement of instruction*. Unpublished Doctoral Dissertation, Rutgers University, New Brunswick, NJ.

Marsh, J.A. (2002). How districts relate to states, schools, and communities. In A. Hightower, M.S. Knapp, J.A. Marsh, & M.W. McLaughlin (eds), *School districts and instructional renewal* (pp. 25–40). New York, NY: Teachers College Press.

Meyer, J.H. & Rowan, B. (1977). Institutionalized organizations: Formal structure as myth and ceremony. *American Journal of Sociology, 83*, 340–363.

Ouchi, W.G. (2003). *Making schools work: A revolutionary plan to get your children the education they need*. New York, NY: Simon & Schuster.

Patton, M.Q. (1990). *Qualitative evaluation and research methods* (2nd edn). Newbury Park, NJ: Sage.

Pearce, C.L. & Conger, J.A. (2003). *Shared leadership: Reframing the hows and whys of leadership*. Thousand Oaks, CA: Sage Publications.

Reid, A.O. (1992). Computer management strategies for text data. In B. Crabtree & W. Mill (eds), *Doing qualitative research, 3*, 125–145.

Rowan, B. & Miskel, C.G. (1999). Institutional theory and the study of educational organizations. In K.S. Louis & J. Murphy (eds), *Handbook of research on organizations* (2nd edn, pp. 359–384). San Francisco, CA: Jossey-Bass.

Silva, D.Y., Gimbert, B., & Nolan, J. (2000). Sliding the doors: Locking and unlocking possibilities for teacher leadership. *Teachers College Record, 102*(4), 779–804.

Smylie, M., Conley, S., & Marks, H.M. (2002). Building leadership into the roles of teachers. In J. Murphy (ed.), *The educational leadership challenge: Redefining leadership for the 21st century* (pp. 162–188). Chicago, IL: University of Chicago Press.

Spillane, J.P., Halverson, R., & Diamond, J. (2004). Theory of leadership practice: A distributed perspective. *Journal of Curriculum Studies, 36*(1), 3–34.

Stecher, B.M. & Barron, S. (1999, April 21). *Test-based accountability: The perverse consequences of milepost testing*. Paper presented at the Annual Meeting of the American Education Association, Montreal, Canada.

Stein, M. K. & D'Amico, L. (2002). The district as a professional learning laboratory. In A. Hightower, M.S. Knapp, J.A. Marsh, & M.W. McLaughlin (eds), *School districts and instructional renewal* (pp. 61–75). New York: Teachers College Press.

Timperley, H. (2005). Distributed leadership: Developing theory from practice. *Journal of Curriculum Studies, 37*(4), 395–420.

Togneri, W. & Anderson, S.E. (2003). *Beyond islands of excellence: What districts can do to improve instruction and achievement in all schools – a leadership brief*. Baltimore, MD: Association for Supervision and Curriculum Development and the Learning First Alliance.

Veenman, S., Denessen, E., Gerrits, J., & Kenter, J. (2001). Evaluation of a coaching programme for cooperating teachers. *Educational Studies, 27*(3), 317–340.

York-Barr, J. & Duke, K. (2004). What do we know about teacher leadership? Findings from two decades of scholarship. *Review of Educational Research, 74*(3), 255–316.

5

School Principals at Work

A Distributed Perspective

JAMES P. SPILLANE, ERIC M. CAMBURN, AND
AMBER STITZIEL PAREJA

Focusing on the school principal's day-to-day work, we examine who leads curriculum- and instruction-related and administration-related activities when the school principal is not leading but participating in the activity. We also explore the prevalence of co-performance of management and leadership activities in the school principal's workday. Looking across a range of administration-related and curriculum- and instruction-related activities school principals participate in, we show that who takes responsibility for leading and managing the schoolhouse varies considerably from activity to activity and from one school to the next.

Recent work suggests that viewing school leadership from a distributed perspective has the potential to provide new and useful insight into how management and leadership unfolds in the daily life of schools. Writing about school leadership and management from a distributed perspective has identified numerous individuals – both positional and informal leaders – in the school across whom the work of leadership and management can be distributed (Camburn et al., 2003; Heller & Firestone, 1995; Spillane, 2006). While there have been advances in articulating a distributed conceptual framework on school leadership (Gronn, 2000; Spillane, 2006), the empirical research base in this area is less developed. Most empirical work has involved small samples of schools and work on larger samples has tended to focus on the designed organization as reflected in formal leadership/management positions as distinct from informal leaders who might not appear on a formal organization chart.

In this chapter, we take a distributed perspective to examine how school principals in one mid-sized urban school district in the United States tackled the challenge of managing and leading their schools. We examine the distribution of leadership across people from the perspective of the school principal's workday. This is important in that some commentators propose or construe a distributed perspective on leadership as downplaying the school principal's role in managing and leading the schoolhouse. We do not subscribe to this view. As an analytical framework for studying the practice of leading and managing schools, a distributed perspective is not intended to negate or undermine the role of the school principal, but rather to extend our understanding of how leading and managing practice involves more than the actions of the school principal. We believe that school principals' workdays can provide an informative window through which to view school leadership and management practice. In the research reported here, we take a distributed perspective to investigate the workday of the school principal.

At the outset it is important to say something about what we mean by leadership and management – leading and managing. We turn here to the distinction Cuban draws between managing and leading – "maintaining what is rather than moving to what can be" (1988, p. xxi). Managing refers to efforts to maintain current arrangements whereas leading refers to moving to new arrangements. In this way leadership or management can refer to the administration, instructional, and political aspects of the school principal's work. (It is important to note, as Cuban points out, that leading or leadership can sometimes be about preserving the status quo in the face of pressure for change.) Hence, leading and managing or leadership and management can be used to refer to both administration type activities (e.g. budgeting, personnel) or instruction and curriculum type activities (e.g. what is taught, how it is taught). The current organization of schools presses a "managerial imperative" (Cuban, 1988).

In this chapter, we refer to management and leadership or managing and leading activities throughout because we do not know if the activities school principals reported participating in were intended (or indeed understood) by organizational members to manage or maintain existing arrangements or to lead change in existing arrangements. Although leadership has consumed the bulk of the writing in education over the past decade or so, we believe that management is also critical; it is difficult to lead without managing. Based on earlier work, we believe that while the distinction between leadership and management is helpful analytically, in the daily work of schools the same activities or organizational routines can involve both leadership and management. In practice, leading and managing happen in tandem and are often intertwined; pulling them apart is difficult. We do know, based on the principals' reports, whether the activity was administration-focused, or instruction- and curriculum-focused. We focus chiefly on those activities that school principals identified as having to do with administration and with curriculum and instruction.

One additional distinction is important. When we refer to school principals or others leading an administration or curriculum and instruction activity we do not mean that this was an activity designed or understood by organizational members to bring about change in existing arrangements; it could have been about maintaining existing arrangements, or changing them, or both together. Instead, when we refer to the principal or someone else leading an activity we mean that they had responsibility (either alone or with someone else) for the performance or execution of the activity. In this way, we attempt to distinguish between leaders and followers in a particular situation.

We begin by describing the study on which this paper is based, and then turn to an outline of the core elements of a distributed perspective. Turning our attention to findings, we examine which school actors perform leadership and management work when the school principal is present but not leading the work. Next, we analyze the prevalence of co-performance of leadership and management activities when the school principal is in a leadership role, identifying the co-performers by position. Comparing and contrasting different types of leadership/management activities, our results suggest that the distribution of responsibility for the work in which school principals participate varies considerably depending on the activity at hand. Our results indicate that the co-performance of leading and managing activities, as measured from the perspective of the school principal's practice, is commonplace in elementary, middle, and high schools in the district studied.

Data and Methods

We draw on data from a mixed method longitudinal study funded by the Institute for Education Sciences (ISL), designed to evaluate a leadership development program called "the National Institute for School Leadership" (NISL). The research was conducted in a mid-sized urban school district in the Southeastern United States that we will call Cloverville.[1] This evaluation study involves a randomized treatment design where half of Cloverville's school principals were assigned to participate in NISL in the first year of the study and the other half were assigned to a control group.

Data Collection and Instruments

Baseline data for the study was collected from 52 school principals in the spring of 2005. The sample included elementary, middle, high, and special schools. The mixed methods research design included experience sampling method (ESM) logs, an end of day (EOD) principal log, a principal questionnaire, a school staff questionnaire, observations of school principals and of the NISL treatment, in-depth interviews with school principals, and school principals' responses to open-ended scenarios.

This chapter reports on data collected in the spring of 2005 from the ESM log. Experience sampling is a technique in which respondents complete an instrument at multiple randomly selected times during the day after being alerted by researchers. One of the strengths of ESM instruments is that they capture behavior and affect in real time as they occur in a natural setting. For the ESM log used for this study, principals were beeped at random intervals throughout the school day alerting them to fill out a brief questionnaire (see Appendix 5.1) programmed on a hand-held computer (PDA). Among other things, principals reported on where they were and what they were working on. The principals reported on which of the following four types of activities they were engaged in: administrative (i.e. managing school personnel), curriculum and instruction (i.e. observing classroom instruction), professional growth (i.e. participating in a professional development session), and fostering relationships (i.e. interacting socially). Table 5.1 displays the various types of activities in which principals reported participating. The principals also reported whether they were leading or co-leading the activity, and with whom they were co-leading – administrators, teacher leaders, specialists, regular

Table 5.1 Activities Principal was Engaged in According to ESM

Activity	Number of Times	Percent of Times
All	*2066*	*100.0*
Administrative	1309	63.4
Managing Budgets, Resources	144	7.0
Managing Personnel	324	15.7
Managing Schedules	54	2.6
Managing Campus	115	5.6
Managing Students	423	20.5
Engaging in School Improvement Planning	66	3.2
Other	183	8.9
Instruction and Curriculum	458	22.2
Provide Student Instruction	21	1.0
Review Student Classroom Work	21	1.0
Review Lesson Plans	7	0.3
Review Instructional Materials, Textbooks	23	1.1
Plan Curricula	49	2.4
Discuss Teaching Practices, Curricula	82	4.0
Observe Classroom Instruction	136	6.6
Model a Lesson	13	0.6
Plan, Implement Professional Development	27	1.3
Review Data	33	1.6
Prepare, Implement Standardized Tests	19	0.9
Other	27	1.3
Professional Growth	120	5.8
Formal Professional Development Session	65	3.1
Working with Professional Development Materials	6	0.3
Receiving Coaching, Training	11	0.5
Studying Effective Practices	25	1.2
Other	13	0.6
Fostering Relationships	179	8.7
Interacting Socially	85	4.1
Other	94	4.6

classroom teachers, etc. If they were not leading the activity, school principals reported on who was leading. The random samples of principal practice yielded representative estimates of the percentage of time the principals in the study spend leading alone and leading with co-leaders for the days of the study.

In this study principals were beeped approximately fifteen times a day for six consecutive days. Forty-two participating principals provided data for multiple school days. Overall, these 42 principals filled out the ESM log 66 percent of the time they were beeped.[2] According to the principals' self-reports in EOD logs completed at the same time as the ESM log, 73 percent of their days were "typical days." We suspect that there are seasonal patterns in school principals' work practices and we are currently exploring these patterns using EOD data from our 52 school principals taken from different time points (e.g. Fall, Winter, Spring) in the school year.

Log Validity

Self-report data collection methods like the ESM, which reduce the amount of lag time between the performance and subsequent reporting of a behavior, have been found to be quite accurate. While much of the early empirical work on principal practice used structured observations, self-report annual surveys have gained increasing use in the field. However, studies have uncovered inaccuracies in annual survey reports of complex behaviors like principal practice, mainly because it is hard for people to remember such behaviors after a long period of time has elapsed (Camburn & Han, 2006; Hilton, 1989; Lemmens et al., 1988; Lemmens et al., 1992). When respondents provide a report of a behavior soon after they engage in it, their reports tend to be more accurate. Data collection instruments that are completed once per day or even more frequently have been shown to reduce reporting inaccuracy associated with recall difficulty. Among these kinds of data collection methods, the experience sampling method used for this study is thought to be one of the most accurate because it eliminates bias associated with retrospective recall (Schwartz & Stone, 1998; Stone & Shiffman, 1994).

The validity of ESM instruments has been established in studies spanning a variety of disciplines. For example, Robinson (1985) found that reports of activities from an ESM instrument correlated highly with data from concurrently conducted observations of those activities. ESM reports have been found to correlate well with a number of biological markers and other self-reports of behaviors, to reliably discriminate between key populations, and to reliably discriminate between different kinds of events in people's lives (Stone et al., 1998).

In this study, we validated principals' responses to the ESM instrument against observation data. During the spring of 2005, a researcher "shadowed" five principals by following them throughout the school day and keeping a

Table 5.2 Percent Agreement Between ESM and Shadower Data

ESM Item	Number of Agreements[a]	Percent Agreement
Are You LEADING This Activity? (yes/no)	50/53	94
Indicate Who is CO-LEADING This Activity With You		
Leading Alone[b]	16/22	73
Student(s)	20/22	91
Teacher Leader(s)	21/22	95
Classroom Teacher(s)	19/22	86
Principal(s)	21/22	95
Subject Area Specialist	21/22	95
Other Professional Staff	18/22	82
Non-Teaching Staff	18/22	82
District Staff	20/22	91
Parent(s)	22/22[c]	100
Community Member(s)	22/22[c]	100
Other	20/22	91

Notes

a Agreement occurred when the same answer was recorded in the ESM for both the principal and the observer (i.e. both recorded yes or both recorded no).

b In relation to leading alone, all six disagreements concerned administrative matters. In five of the six cases, the principal attributed co-leadership to another person, while the shadower thought that the principal was leading alone.

c Perfect agreement occurred for these items because neither principals nor the observer recorded parents or community members as co-leaders.

narrative record of everything the principals did. On the days on which they were shadowed, principals completed the ESM instrument when they were beeped at random times. When principals were beeped, the researcher independently filled out a portion of the same ESM questionnaire that the principal filled out. Table 5.2 shows the rates of agreement between principals and the observer on ESM items asking whether the principal is leading the activity, and with whom the principal is co-leading. As Table 5.2 illustrates, principals' and the observers' answers to the ESM instrument were very consistent with each other, with agreement rates ranging from 73 to 95 percent. While our validation data are limited to five elementary school principals, our data suggest that principals' ESM reports are quite accurate.

Analytical Framework: A Distributed Perspective

The distributed perspective offers an analytical framework for thinking about and analyzing school leadership and management (Spillane, 2006). It involves two aspects: the *leader-plus* and the *practice* aspect.

The leader-plus aspect recognizes that leading and managing schools can involve multiple individuals, not just those at the top of the organization or those with formal leadership designations. School leadership and management do not reside exclusively in the actions of the school principal nor in the actions of other formally designated leadership and management positions that are commonplace in schools. From a distributed perspective, school leadership and management potentially involve more than the work of individuals in formal leadership/management positions – principal, assistant principal, and specialists. Individuals who are not formally designated leaders may also take responsibility for organizational routines and provide leadership and management. If school administrators do not have a monopoly on leadership and management work, then it behooves us to examine who takes on this work. Prior studies, using various research methodologies, examines the leader-plus aspect by analyzing individuals with formally designated leadership/management positions, who perform key organizational routines (e.g. faculty meetings, grade level meetings), who take responsibility for key organizational functions (e.g. building a vision, monitoring instruction), and who school staff turn to for guidance about different aspects of the core work of schooling (Camburn et al., 2006; Heller & Firestone, 1995; Spillane, 2006). In this chapter we take a different approach, analyzing who has responsibility for those activities school principals engage in during their workday.

The practice aspect of the distributed framework foregrounds the day-to-day work of leadership and management. It refers to what is done in a particular time and place to act in response to what Bourdieu terms "the urgency of practice" (1981, p. 310). The urgency of practice limits reflection and the weighing of options, reinforcing the importance of individual dispositions to act in one way rather than another in particular situations, what Bourdieu terms "habitus" (1990). We exercise these dispositions to act in one way or another in particular situations and these dispositions may not be at the level of conscious decisions (Bourdieu, 1990; Foucault, 1977). Habitus underscores that how we engage in the world is in part a function of our own past and the pasts of the groups and institutions to which we belong (see Parker, 2000). Something happens, people act, but only in relation to others. Hence, getting to interactions is critical.

A distributed perspective then, frames practice as a product of the interactions of school leaders, followers, and their situations (Spillane, 2006). Practice takes shape at the intersection of these three elements. This latter point is especially important and one that is frequently glossed over in discussions and studies taking a distributed perspective. Rather than viewing leadership practice through a narrow psychological lens where it is equated chiefly with the actions of an individual and cast as the product of an individual's knowledge and skill, the distributed perspective draws attention to the interactions of people and their situations. Such an acknowledgment does not suggest that individual knowledge and actions are irrelevant to understanding practice; it suggests that they are insufficient in that they fail to adequately capture the nature and urgency of practice. The leadership practice aspect moves the focus from an exclusive concern with the actions of individual leaders to an analysis of the interactions among leaders, followers, and their situations. Our research approach reflects this conception of practice by capturing management and leadership in schools through principals' interactions with others in particular places and times during a school day.

In the results section below we begin with the leader-plus aspect of a distributed perspective by identifying who is performing or executing those activities where the school principal is participating, but may or may not be responsible for their execution; that is, Who does the school principal report is performing or executing the activity? We then turn our attention to the practice aspect: specifically, we examine those situations that involve the school principal co-performing or co-executing activities with one or more others. Our focus in this analysis is entirely on those who have responsibility for executing the activity – the leader(s) of the activity; we do not analyze the follower dimension in this chapter.

Results

In this section we take up two research questions motivated by the leader-plus and practice aspects of the distributed perspective:

- To what extent is responsibility for administration and curriculum spread across multiple individuals in schools?
- To what extent do administration and curriculum and instruction related activities involve co-performing with one or more other individuals?

In examining these questions, we provide evidence supporting three assertions about the practice of leading and managing schools. First, we show that the school principal's work in leading and managing schools involves multiple individuals – some with formally designated leadership positions, others lacking such positions. Second, we show that the co-performance of leading and managing activities, as measured from the perspective of the school principal's practice, is relatively commonplace, though it varies from one school to the next. Third, going beyond the distribution of responsibility, we examine how distributed practice unfolds in schools and show that the mix of school actors who are involved in the co-performance of different leadership and management activities varies from activity to activity. We remind the reader that our focus in this chapter comes exclusively from the vantage point of the school principal's workday.

The Distribution of Responsibility for Leading and Managing

Various studies have shown that school administrators do not have a monopoly on leadership and management work (Camburn et al., 2003; Heller &

Firestone, 1995). Research that has focused on the designed organization as represented in formally designated leadership positions indicates that a range of school staff takes responsibility for leadership and management work including principals, assistant principals, subject area specialists, mentor teachers, and other professional staff (i.e. family outreach personnel). A recent study of more than 100 US elementary schools estimated that the responsibility for leadership and management functions was typically distributed across three to seven formally designated leadership positions per elementary school (Camburn et al., 2003).

By casting nets that go beyond the designed organization and focusing on the lived organization, some studies show that individuals with no formal leadership position – mostly classroom teachers – also take responsibility for school leadership and management (Heller & Firestone, 1995; Spillane 2006; Spillane et al., 2003). Teachers have been found to contribute to an array of leadership functions, including sustaining an instructional vision and informally monitoring program implementation (Firestone, 1989).

Building on these earlier findings, we examined the extent to which responsibility for those administration- and curriculum-related and instruction-related activities that the school principal participated in were distributed in Cloverville schools. Viewing leadership and management work related to curriculum- and instruction-type and administration-type activities through the window of principals' workdays, we consider how responsibility for such work is distributed among people. We do not attempt to generalize to these school principals' work practices for an entire school year as we anticipate seasonal variations in their work. We are currently exploring this issue using EOD log data. Still, we argue that the distribution of responsibility captured by these six work days gives us a glimpse of who is involved in the work of leading and managing schools. Analyzing data from the ESM log completed by Cloverville's principals, we get a sense of how responsibility for leadership and management work is distributed across people in the day-to-day life of the school. Of course, relying only on those activities that the school principal participates in to examine who takes responsibility for leadership and management work obscures our view of such work that is carried out independently of the principal. Other staff members – including assistant principals, reform coaches, and others – lead activities independent of the principal, but we have not directly measured these efforts in our study. However, given the centrality of school principals' efforts, this approach should yield useful insight into the practice of leadership and management in Cloverville schools.

The ESM log asked principals whether or not they were leading the activity in which they were participating. Perhaps our most direct piece of evidence of distributed leadership and management is the percentage of times principals reported that someone besides themselves was leading the activity. Table 5.3

Table 5.3 Principal Time According to ESM

Activity	Percent of Times Leading	Percent of Times Leading Alone	Percent of Times Co-Leading	Percent of Times Not Leading
All (N = 2066)	68.6	35.6	33.0	31.4
Administration (n = 1309)	77.8	42.9	34.8	22.2
Instruction and Curriculum (n = 458)	55.2	25.1	30.1	44.8
Fostering Relationships (n = 179)	65.9	25.1	40.8	34.1
Professional Growth (n = 120)	23.3	10.8	12.5	76.7

shows the percent of times when the principal was beeped that s/he reported s/he was leading – including leading alone versus co-leading – and not leading. Principals reported that they were not leading on nearly one-third (31 percent) of the occasions they were beeped (see Table 5.3). As we will discuss below, this differed depending on the activity, with school principals more likely to be leading administration type activities and less likely to be leading instruction and curriculum related activities (see Table 5.3). Hence, even when viewed exclusively from the window of principals' daily practice, other individuals emerge as important actors in the work of managing and leading the school. (The mere presence of the principal in an activity, even though the principal reported not leading the activity, may be construed by some as leading the activity in that the presence of the principal suggests to participants the importance of the activity.)

When these school principals reported someone else was leading an administration or curriculum and instruction activity, the categories of individuals they identified as leaders included classroom teachers (with no formal leadership designation), other professional staff, subject area specialists, teacher leaders, and assistant principals, among others (see Table 5.4). Our analysis of how school principals in Cloverville spend their day suggests that the actual work of leading and managing the school involves multiple others. Even more striking is the finding that individuals with no formal leadership designation tend to lead over one-quarter of all the activities that school principals reported participating in but not leading. We found that classroom teachers with no formal leadership designations led over 25 percent of the activities that Cloverville's principals were involved in over a six-day period. Thus, we argue that in addition to formal leaders, many staff members with no formal leadership/management designation are key players in the daily leadership and management of the school.

As we might expect, there was considerable variation between schools in Cloverville in the proportion of time the principal was leading the activity. Excluding outliers, some principals lead 44 percent of the activities they participated in while others lead 90 percent of the activities, with the large

Table 5.4 Who Led Activities When Principal Was Not Leading[a]

Leader	Percent of Times Leading
Classroom Teacher	32.1
Other Professional Staff	25.4
Subject Area Specialist	16.7
Teacher Leader	16.7
Assistant Principal	14.3
Other	13.4
Non-Teaching Staff	12.1
Not Specified	10.9
Student	4.6
District Staff	4.4
Parent	3.8
Community Member	1.2

Note

a The percentages listed in this table indicate the percent of times the principal reported each type of person leading when the principal was engaged in administrative or instruction and curriculum related activities and was not leading. Principals could identify more than one type of leader for any one activity. Hence, the numbers in the table add up to more than 100 percent.

majority of principals leading between 60 and 74 percent of the time. In other words, while some principals reported that someone else was leading over 50 percent of the activities they participated in over the six-day period, others reported that someone else was leading only 10 percent of the time. Given that our data is entirely based on school principals' reports of how they spend their time, it is difficult to gauge if this variation reflects differences in the extent to which others are engaged in the actual practice of leading and managing the school or if school principals are selective with respect to those activities they participate in when someone else is leading the activity. It could be, for example, that some school principals are less likely to participate in activities where other formally designated leaders, such as the assistant principal, are leading or managing, and in some cases this might constitute an effective use of the principal's time. Regardless, these data suggest that even when the practice of leading and managing the schools is analyzed exclusively from the perspective of the school principal's practice, other leaders emerge as important players.

The Co-Performance of Leadership and Management

We contend that understanding how responsibility for the performance of leadership and management is distributed across multiple individuals provides only one representation of the distribution of leadership in schools – the leader-plus aspect. Beyond identifying the players across whom leadership and management is distributed, it is also important to understand the social arrangements for the distribution of leadership and management work. Based on their work in the Distributed Leadership Studies, Spillane and colleagues have identified three arrangements by which the work of leadership and management is distributed across people (Spillane, 2006; Spillane et al., 2003). *Collaborated distribution* characterizes practice that is stretched over the work of two or more leaders who work together in place and time to co-perform the same leadership routine. *Collective distribution* characterizes practice that is stretched over the work of two or more leaders who co-perform a leadership routine by working separately but interdependently. *Coordinated distribution* refers to situations where a leadership routine involves activities that have to be performed in a particular sequence. Our ESM log data on Cloverville school principals enables us to estimate the prevalence of the first type of arrangement – collaborated distribution – in the school principal's workday. (We have no data on situations involving collective or coordinated distribution.)

Using the school principals' ESM log data, we analyzed those situations where school principals reported co-performing a leadership or management task with one or more individuals in the same place and at the same time. In this way, the ESM log allows us to capture how frequently school principals engage in situations of collaborated distribution. (We draw a distinction here between individuals who were present and co-leading with the school principal and individuals who were present but not co-leading the activity. School principals reported on both types of individuals.) Again, it is important to remember that our data is based entirely on school principals' self-reports of their practice and only captures situations involving collaborated distribution. The inclusion of log data from other formally designated leaders would undoubtedly complicate the picture.

Even when school principals in Cloverville reported leading the activity in which they were participating, they were not always performing solo. Overall, school principals reported co-performing almost half (47 percent) of the administration- and instruction-related and curriculum-related activities which they led. Principals reported co-leading with just one other individual 63 percent of the time, while they reported co-leading with two or more individuals 37 per cent of the time. When school principals in Cloverville reported they were co-leading an activity, they identified classroom teachers most frequently as their co-leaders (see Table 5.5). Specifically, school principals' identified classroom teachers among their co-leaders for over 30 percent of the activities involving co-performance. Indeed, actors with no formal leadership designations including classroom teachers, students, and parents, figure prominently in co-performing leadership and management activities with the school principal. For 44 percent of all co-leading situations, school principals identified at least one of the following as their co-performers: students, parents, and/or teachers. Again, this analysis underscores the theory that actors with no formal leadership designations are important in attempt-

Table 5.5 Principal's Co-Leaders[a]

Co-Leader	Percent of Times Leading
Classroom Teacher	30.1
Other Professional Staff	24.2
Teacher Leader	22.9
Assistant Principal	20.9
Non-Teaching Staff	16.0
Student	14.3
Subject Area Specialist	10.9
Other	4.7
Parent	4.5
District Staff	3.5
Community Members	1.7

Note

a The percentages listed in this table indicate the percent of times the principal reported each type of person co-leading with the principal when s/he was engaged in administrative or instruction and curriculum related activities and was co-leading. Principals could identify more than one type of co-leader for any one activity. Hence, the numbers in the table add up to more than 100 percent.

ing to understand how the work of leadership and management is distributed over people in schools. Others identified by school principals as co-leaders included other professional staff, teacher leaders, and assistant principals (see Table 5.5).

As one might expect, the prevalence of the co-performance of leadership and management activities differed according to the school. To begin with, the solo performance of leadership and management activities by the school principal was more prevalent in some schools than others. Some principals reported co-performing with at least one other actor over 60 percent of the time, while others reported co-performing fewer than 10 percent of these activities. Hence, overall figures for the Cloverville school principals obscure considerable variability between schools. There was also considerable variability between Cloverville principals with respect to whom they reported as co-performers. We will examine this in the next section when we consider how the distribution of responsibility for leadership and management work differs by activity-type.

The Co-Performance of Leadership and Management Activities by Activity Type

The evidence presented thus far indicates that leadership and management work in schools is distributed among individuals with formally designated leadership/management positions and individuals without such designations. Evidence from other research indicates that the set of school staff across whom leadership is distributed varies from activity to activity. For example, a number of studies have found that the parties across whom responsibility for leading and managing the school is distributed differs depending on the organizational function or leadership routine (Camburn et al., 2003; Heller & Firestone, 1995; Spillane, 2006), and the subject matter (Spillane, 2006). The performance of some leadership and management routines (e.g. monitoring classroom instruction) tends to be distributed across fewer actors than other routines (e.g. providing professional development on language arts instruction) (Spillane, 2006).

We found that the manner in which the leadership and management work that the school principal participates in is distributed across people differs depending on the particular activity. First, the extent to which school principals co-performed an activity with someone else versus performing the activity on their own varied from one activity to the next. Second, the set of individuals who co-performed an activity with principals varied depending on the type of activity.

For leadership and management activities in which they participated, school principals were more likely to report leading those related to administration than leading those related to instruction and curriculum (see Table 5.3). Overall Cloverville school principals reported leading over three-quarters (78 percent) of all administration related activities in which they participated. In contrast, principals reported leading just over half (55 percent) of instruction- and curriculum-related activities. For those activities in which the principal participated, other leaders were more likely to be leading an instruction- and curriculum-related activity than an administration-related activity. Among the instruction- and curriculum-related activities principals did report leading, they generally did not provide student instruction but rather observed classroom instruction and discussed teaching practices and/or curricula. Our data also indicate that the degree to which responsibility for curriculum- and instruction-related activities involves other leaders varies much more from school to school than the degree to which responsibility for administration-related activities involves other leaders (Figure 5.1).

The distribution of responsibility for instruction- and curriculum-related activities also differed depending on the school subject. School principals were most likely to be leading instruction and curriculum activities that had to do with science (73 percent) and least likely to be leading those related to mathematics (39 percent) (see Table 5.6). Moreover, instruction- and curriculum-related activities about writing or social studies were more likely to involve the principal leading alone than activities related to reading or mathematics. This evidence, though limited by the small sample size, suggests that situations that involved the principal co-performing differed depending on the school subject.

Examining situations in which the principal co-performed with different categories of others (e.g. assistant principal, teacher leader) by different types of leadership and management activities sheds light on the practice aspect. Figure 5.1 plots the percentage of time principals engaged in co-leadership with teacher leaders, classroom teachers, assistant principals, and other staff

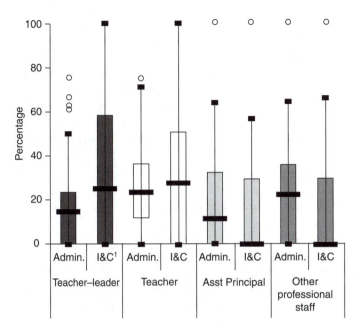

Figure 5.1 Variance in Principal's Co-Leaders by Activity Type

Note
1   I&C = Instruction and Curriculum

Table 5.6 Percent of Time Principal Leading and Leading Alone Instruction and Curriculum Activities by Subject[a]

Subject	Percent of Times Leading	Percent of Times Leading Alone	Leading Alone as Percent of Times Leading
Science (n = 15)	73.3	33.3	45.5
Multiple Subjects (n = 132)	62.9	23.5	37.4
English/Language/Arts (n = 34)	61.8	38.2	61.9
Not Subject Specific (n = 58)	60.3	20.7	34.3
Social Studies (n = 24)	58.3	45.8	78.6
Reading (n = 37)	54.1	18.9	35.0
Special Education (n = 40)	47.5	27.5	57.9
Other Subject (n = 42)	45.2	26.2	57.9
Writing (n = 5)	40.0	40.0	100.0
Math (n = 66)	39.4	16.7	42.3

Note
a Number of observations does not sum to total reported in Table 5.3 due to missing observations. There were 453 observations where the principal recorded the subject area when engaged in instruction and curriculum activities.

members, comparing administration-type activities with curriculum- and instruction-type activities. We found that teacher leaders and classroom teachers are more likely than assistant principals and other professional staff to co-perform with principals on matters of curriculum or instruction. Moreover, teacher leaders and classroom teachers are more likely to engage in co-performing on curriculum and instruction matters than on administrative matters. There is considerably more variation between schools in the frequency with which principals co-perform with teachers on curriculum- and instruction-related activities than in the frequency with which principals co-perform with teachers on administration-related activities.

The pattern of results for the assistant principals is a reverse image of the results for teachers. Not surprisingly, our results indicate that principals and assistant principals do not regularly co-perform activities on matters of curriculum and instruction. Instead, principals are more likely to engage in co-performing with assistant principals around administration issues.

The evidence from Cloverville suggests that the way in which leadership is distributed across people and the amount of variation between schools depends on the particular type of leadership and management activity in question. The results have intuitive appeal and suggest a sort of task specialization in the performance of leadership and management work. Principals are more likely to report co-performing with teachers in the area of curriculum and instruction than in administration. However, principals are only slightly more likely to report that they are co-leading with assistant principals in the area of administration (20 percent) than in the area of curriculum and instruction (18 percent). Despite the general patterns we observed, we also saw substantial variation from one school to the next, particularly in the area of curriculum and instruction. This suggests that schools in Cloverville employ a wide range of approaches in involving school staff members, both formally designated leaders and individuals with no formal designations, in the work of leadership and management.

Discussion and Conclusion

Taking a distributed perspective, we examined how the work of leading and managing the schoolhouse is distributed across people by focusing exclusively on the work of the school principal. While for some this may be the antithesis of taking a distributed perspective to studying school leadership and management practice, for us it is a natural approach. Extending our earlier theory-building work undertaken as part of the Distributed Leadership Study (Spillane, 2006), we analyzed data from Cloverville, a mid-sized Southeastern school district in the US, to explore whether and how leadership was distributed across people as explored from the vantage point of the school principal's actual practice. Our analyses centered on the lived organization as measured through the work practices of school principals.

Overall, our analyses support a number of hypotheses generated in prior research. The work of managing and leading the schoolhouse is distributed over multiple actors; some occupying formally designated leadership positions, others without such formal designations. Looking at the lived organization as captured by a log of the school principal's day, we found that the work of leading and managing schools was also distributed over actors with no formal leadership positions. Classroom teachers (with no formal leadership positions) figured prominently in taking responsibility for administration and curriculum and instruction related activities that school principals in Cloverville participated in during the six school days we studied. Other actors with no formal leadership positions, such as students, also figured (though less prominently). Along with the school principal, actors with formal leadership designations, as well as actors with no formal leadership designations, take responsibility for school leadership and management activities.

Examining school principals' practice more closely and looking at situations where school principals reported co-performing an activity with one or more others – situations involving collaborated distribution – we showed that co-performance was relatively commonplace in Cloverville schools. Overall, school principals co-performed almost half (47 percent) of the activities they reported having responsibility for, or a third (33 percent) of all work-related activities over a six-day period. Again, both individuals with formal leadership/management designations and individuals without such designations figured prominently as co-performers with Cloverville's principals. Indeed, classroom teachers with no formal leadership/management positions figured more prominently than individuals with such designations.

The extent to which the work of leading and managing the schoolhouse was distributed across two or more actors, however, differed depending on the type of leadership and management activity (e.g. administration-related activities versus instruction and curriculum-related activities). While school principals reported taking responsibility for over three-quarters of all administration type activities in which they participated, they reported taking responsibility for just over half of the instruction and curriculum activities. For instruction- and curriculum-related activities in which the school principal was engaged, other leaders were more likely to have responsibility for the activity compared to administration type activities. Overall the prominence of co-performance (as distinct from solo performance by the school principal) was roughly the same for administrative activities as it was for instructional- and curriculum-related activities (35 percent and 30 percent respectively).

The extent to which the work of leading and managing the schoolhouse was distributed across people also differed depending on the school. There was considerable between-school variation in both the extent to which others had responsibility for the activities that principals were participating in and the extent to which principals were co-performing activities that they reported taking responsibility for. In summary, the distribution of responsibility for leading and managing differed from one school to the next.

Our analysis adds to a body of empirical research indicating that the work of leading and managing the schoolhouse is indeed distributed (Camburn et al., 2003; Heller & Firestone, 1995; Spillane, 2006). In this study, this is demonstrated not only by the involvement of multiple formally designated leaders and informal leaders (i.e. leader-plus aspect), but also by the prevalence of the principal co-performing (practice aspect) administration-related and curriculum- and instruction-related activities.

Our effort to take a distributed perspective to the principal's workday using ESM logs has limitations. First, our ESM log sheds no light on whether the activities the school principal engaged in were designed to lead change or maintain the status quo. Second, with respect to the practice aspect, our analysis only manages to identify situations involving collaborated distribution, telling us nothing about situations involving collective or coordinated distribution. Third, with respect to collaborated distribution, our analysis in this chapter simply tells us about its prominence in the principal's workday and who the co-performers are, but tells us nothing about the nature of these interactions. For example, we are unable to examine from these data the roles that different co-performers play in situations involving collaborated distribution – how they play off one another in minute-by-minute interactions. Getting at these minute-by-minute interactions requires more intense ethnographic approaches using analytical approaches such as discourse analysis.

While the ESM log data has limitations, it also has strengths. Specifically, it enables us to capture practice when it occurs with others in a particular place and time. We are able to sample practice as it unfolds in the school principal's day. In this way, it more authentically represents the phenomenon as we define it compared to annual or seasonal survey methods that rely heavily on recall. Moreover, we can do this across larger populations of schools and days than is typically possible with more labor intensive ethnographic and shadowing techniques. In this way, we can begin to identify patterns in practice that may be associated with macro-structures such as school type, student population, and school principal characteristics such as gender and career stage. These sorts of analyses can in turn inform micro-analyses of particular instances of practice. Indeed, we believe that combining different approaches is essential if we are to generate robust empirical knowledge about the practice of leading and managing.

Appendix 5.1

Experience Sampling Form

1. Are you engaging in a SCHOOL-RELATED activity?
   ❑ Yes
   ❑ No (terminates questionnaire)

2. a Using the scale below, indicate how TIRED or ENERGETIC you feel.

   _____

   Tired   Energetic

   b Using the scale below, indicate how DISTRACTED or FOCUSED you feel.

   _____

   Distracted   Focused

   c Using the scale below, indicate how IRRITABLE or CHEERFUL you feel.

   _____

   Irritable   Cheerful

   d Using the scale below, indicate how DETACHED or INVOLVED you feel.

   _____

   Detached   Involved

   e Using the scale below, indicate how BORED or EXCITED you feel.

   _____

   Bored   Excited

3. WHERE are you?
   ❑ My Office
   ❑ Main Office
   ❑ Classroom
   ❑ Conference Room
   ❑ Hallway
   ❑ Other On Site Location
   ❑ District Office
   ❑ Other Off Site Location

4. WHAT are you doing? (select one)
   ❑ ADMINISTRATION
      ❑ Manage BUDGET, RESOURCES
      ❑ Manage PERSONNEL

❏ Manage SCHEDULES
❏ Manage CAMPUS
❏ Manage STUDENTS
❏ SCHOOL IMPROVEMENT PLAN
❏ Other
❏ INSTRUCTION and CURRICULUM
   ❏ Provide STUDENT INSTRUCTION
   ❏ Review STUDENT CLASSROOM WORK
   ❏ Review LESSON PLANS
   ❏ Review INSTRUCTION MATERIALS
   ❏ Plan CURRICULA
   ❏ Discuss TEACHING/CURRICULA
   ❏ Observe CLASSROOM INSTRUCT
   ❏ Model a LESSON
   ❏ Plan/Implement PROF DEVEL
   ❏ Review DATA
   ❏ STANDARDIZED TESTING
   ❏ Other

If you selected INSTRUCTION and CURRICULUM, what is your PRIMARY intention? (select one)
   ❏ Increase KNOWLEDGE of TEACH
   ❏ Monitor CURRICULA IMPLEMENT
   ❏ Monitor INSTRUCTION PRACTICE
   ❏ Devel/Commun SCHOOL GOALS
   ❏ Motivate TEACHERS/STUDENTS
   ❏ Develop TEACHER'S CAPACITY
   ❏ Develop INSTRUCTIONAL POLICY
   ❏ Redesign TEACHING/LEARNING
   ❏ Other
❏ OWN PROFESSIONAL GROWTH
   ❏ Formal PROF DEVEL SESSION
   ❏ Work w/PROF DEVEL MATERIALS
   ❏ Receiving COACHING/TRAINING
   ❏ Studying EFFECTIVE PRACTICES
   ❏ Other
❏ FOSTERING RELATIONSHIPS
   ❏ Interacting SOCIALLY
   ❏ Other

5. **Are you LEADING this activity?**
   ❏ Yes
   ❏ No

If yes, indicate who is CO-LEADING this activity with you. (select all that apply)
- ❑ Working Alone
- ❑ Student(s)
- ❑ Teacher Leader(s)
- ❑ Regular Classroom Teacher(s)
- ❑ Principal(s)
- ❑ Subject Area Specialist
- ❑ Other Professional Staff
- ❑ Non-Teaching Staff
- ❑ District Staff
- ❑ Parent(s)
- ❑ Community Members
- ❑ Other

If no, indicate who is LEADING this activity. (select all that apply)
- ❑ Student(s)
- ❑ Teacher Leader(s)
- ❑ Regular Classroom Teacher(s)
- ❑ Principal(s)
- ❑ Subject Area Specialist
- ❑ Other Professional Staff
- ❑ Non-Teaching Staff
- ❑ District Staff
- ❑ Parent(s)
- ❑ Community Members
- ❑ Other

6. Who is the INTENDED AUDIENCE for this task? (select all that apply)
- ❑ No One
- ❑ Student(s)
- ❑ Teacher Leader(s)
- ❑ Regular Classroom Teacher(s)
- ❑ Principal(s)
- ❑ Subject Area Specialist
- ❑ Other Professional Staff
- ❑ Non-Teaching Staff
- ❑ District Staff
- ❑ Parent(s)
- ❑ Community Members
- ❑ Other

7. **What SUBJECT is this for?** (select one)
   ❑ Not Subject Specific
   ❑ Multiple Subjects
   ❑ Special Education
   ❑ Math
   ❑ English/Language Arts
   ❑ Reading
   ❑ Writing
   ❑ Science
   ❑ Social Studies
   ❑ Other Subject

8. **HOW are you doing this?** (select one)
   ❑ Face-to-Face Interaction
       ❑ One on one
       ❑ 2 to 5 people
       ❑ 6 to 10 people
       ❑ 11 to 50 people
       ❑ More than 50 people
   ❑ Paperwork or Books
   ❑ Phone
   ❑ Looking or Observing
   ❑ Electronic Media
   ❑ Other

9. **What is the DURATION of this activity from start to anticipated finish?**
   ❑ Less than 1 minute
   ❑ 1 to 15 minutes
   ❑ 15 to 30 minutes
   ❑ 30 to 45 minutes
   ❑ 45 minutes to 1 hour
   ❑ More than 1 hour

10. **On the scale below, indicate how CONFIDENT you feel in performing this task.**

Not   Very

Questionnaire completed. Thank you.

Acknowledgments

An earlier draft of this chapter was presented at the Annual Meeting of the American Educational Research Association, San Francisco, April 7–11, 2006.

An earlier version of this chapter was published in *Leadership and Policy in Schools*, 6(1).

Work on this chapter was supported by the National Institute for School Leadership Evaluation Study funded by the Institute for Education Sciences (Grant # R305E040085) and the Distributed Leadership Studies funded by the National Science Foundation (RETA Grant # EHR – 0412510).

Notes

1 Cloverville is a pseudonym as are all other names used in this chapter to refer to participants, their schools and their town.
2 Response rates were calculated for principals that participated for a majority (i.e. four days) of the six-day sampling period. Non-responses seem to have occurred mostly after the principals' school days had ended, when the principals were not participating in school-related activities (e.g. on their lunch breaks), or when they were in meetings where they presumably could not be interrupted. The percentage of beeps where there was no response is fairly constant at around 30 percent between the hours of 9 am and 3 pm. The earlier the hour before 9 am, or the later the hour after 3 pm, the higher was the non-response rate. We are exploring the non-response issue in ongoing work.

References

Bourdieu, P. (1981). Men and machines. In K. Knorr-Cetina & A.V. Cicourel (eds), *Advances in social theory and methodology* (pp. 304–317). London, UK: Routledge.

Bourdieu, P. (1990). *The logic of practice*. Stanford, CA: Stanford University Press (R. Nice Trans; original work published 1980).

Camburn, E. & Han, S.W. (2006). *Factors affecting the validity of teachers' reports of instructional practice on annual surveys* (Working paper of the Consortium for Policy Research in Education). Madison, WI: Wisconsin Center for Education Research.

Camburn, E., Rowan, B., & Taylor, J. (2003). Distributed leadership in schools: The case of elementary schools adopting comprehensive school reform models. *Educational Evaluation and Policy Analysis*, 25(4), 347–373.

Cuban, L. (1988). *The managerial imperative and the practice of leadership in schools*. Albany, NY: State University of New York Press.

Firestone, W.A. (1989) Using reform: Conceptualizing district initiative. *Educational Evaluation and Policy Analysis*, 11(2), 151–165.

Foucault, M. (1977). *Discipline and punish: The birth of the prison*. London, UK: Allen Lane.

Gronn, P. (2000). Distributed properties: A new architecture for leadership. *Educational Management and Administration*, 28(3), 317–338.

Heller, M.F. & Firestone, W.A. (1995) Who's in charge here? Sources of leadership for change in eight schools. *Elementary School Journal*, 96(1), 65–86.

Hilton, M. (1989). A comparison of a prospective diary and two summary recall techniques for recording alcohol consumption. *British Journal of Addiction*, 84, 1085–1092.

Lemmens, P., Knibbe, R., & Tan, F. (1988). Weekly recall and diary estimates of alcohol consumption in a general population survey. *Journal of Studies on Alcohol*, 49, 131–135.

Lemmens, P., Tan, E., & Knibbe, R. (1992). Measuring quantity and frequency of drinking in a general population survey: A comparison of five indices. *Journal of Studies on Alcohol*, 53, 476–486.

Parker, J. (2000). *Structuration*. Philadelphia, PA: Open University Press.

Robinson, J.P. (1985). The validity and reliability of diaries versus alternative time use measures. In F.T. Juster & F.P. Stafford (eds), *Time, goods, and well-being* (pp. 63–92). Ann Arbor, MI: Institute for Social Research.

Schwartz, J.F., & Stone, A.A. (1998). Strategies for analyzing ecological momentary data. *Health Psychology, 17*, 6–16.

Spillane, J.P. (2006). *Distributed leadership*. San Francisco, CA: Jossey-Bass.

Spillane, J.P., Diamond, J.B., & Jita, L. (2003). Leading instruction: The distribution of leadership for instruction. *Journal of Curriculum Studies, 35*(5), 533–543.

Stone, A. & Shiffman, S. (1994). Ecological momentary assessment (EMA) in behavioral medicine. *Annals of Behavioral Medicine, 16*, 199–202.

Stone, A.A., Schwartz, J.E., Neale, J.M., Shiffman, S., Marco, C.A., Hickcox, M., & Paty, J. (1998). A comparison of coping assessed by ecological momentary assessment and recall. *Journal of Personality and Social Psychology, 74*(6), 1670–1680.

6

Positioning the Principals in Patterns of School Leadership Distribution

STEPHEN E. ANDERSON, SHAWN MOORE, AND
JINGPING SUN

This chapter presents an analysis of how leadership for school improvement was distributed in five schools in varying state and district contexts, with an emphasis on understanding the principal's role in the distribution of leadership. The analysis integrates concepts from research on core leadership practices (setting directions, developing people, redesigning the workplace, managing the instructional program) and on alternative patterns of leadership distribution in organizational settings. The findings highlight the need to distinguish between school-wide and goal-specific patterns of leadership distribution in schools, and to recognize that how principals interact with other sources of leadership may vary for different focuses of improvement in the same school. The principals' orientation toward state and district influences on school goal setting, and toward the use of professional expertise (their own, teachers, external sources) in the pursuit of school improvement goals were key factors shaping leadership distribution.

Leadership can be conceptualized and studied as both an individual phenomenon and as an organizational phenomenon. The former orients us toward an analysis of the beliefs, actions, personal traits, and influence of individuals recognized by others as leaders within particular organizational contexts. The organizational perspective suggests that leadership in any particular setting is unlikely to be constituted in the actions and influence of a solitary individual. Consequently, an understanding of leadership requires us to examine the variety of leadership sources, beliefs, actions, interactions, and influences recognized by participants in those settings. Therein lies the conceptual rationale for interest in the distribution of leadership practice and influence in schools. The findings reported and discussed here are based on a multi-site case study analysis of patterns of leadership distribution and their relationship to student learning in schools.[1] The aim was to describe the distribution of leadership in a set of schools selected for variability on a survey measure of overall leadership distribution, to analyze the distribution patterns observed in relation to concepts of leadership distribution proposed in the literature, and to consider how our findings affirm, contradict, or provide additional insight into current conceptualizations of distributed leadership. We also aimed to explore the relationship between the leadership distribution patterns in these schools and student learning processes and outcomes. In this chapter we orient our analysis and discussion of the findings to the roles that principals play in the patterns of leadership distribution examined from varied vantage points: school leadership overall, school goals, and core leadership practices – setting directions, developing people, structuring the workplace, managing the instructional program (Leithwood et al., 2006a). Our findings highlight the prominence of principals in determining alternative patterns of leadership distribution at the school level and in relation to specific improvement goals and initiatives. Formal organizational structures were not necessarily congruent with the actual distribution of leadership sources and influence reported by school personnel. The findings also reveal that variable patterns of distributed leadership may be enacted in the same school. This variation is associated with the principal's use of their own and other sources of professional expertise for key focuses for improvement, and with the principal's approach to school goal setting in the context of state and school district policies and processes. The analysis suggests that school goals that target student learning provide more scope for leadership distribution and coordination than goals that focus on implementation of specific programs and practices. The links between distinct patterns of leadership distribution and student achievement, however, appear to be more indirect than direct.

Conceptual Background

Educational leadership researchers have begun to investigate and theorize about the properties and complexities of leadership distribution in educational institutions such as schools and school districts – sources, focuses, functions, interactions, contexts, outcomes (e.g. *Educational Evaluation and Policy Analysis*, 2003; Gronn, 2002; Leithwood et al., 2006b; MacBeath, 2005; Spillane 2006; Spillane et al., 2004). We know now that a variety of leadership distribution patterns are possible, though consensus on a typology and terms remains elusive, and the implications and consequences of different forms of leadership distribution for the accomplishment of organizational goals, climate, and so forth, are unknown.

Gronn (2002) refers to *holistic* and *additive* models of leadership distribution. Distributed leadership from an additive point of view refers to a dispersed pattern of leadership, whereby leadership behaviors are associated with multiple members of an organization for varying goals and/or tasks but without a sense of rational and strategic alignment in who provides leadership for what. Different members can be identified as providing leadership for different things, but without a coordinated and concerted focus. A holistic pattern of leadership distribution, however, suggests greater interdependency and coordination among varied sources of leadership focused on shared goals and tasks.

At a more micro-level, Spillane (2006) identifies three arrangements for distributing leadership responsibilities – *division of labor* (different leaders separately perform different tasks), *co-performance* (multiple leaders jointly perform interdependent tasks), and *parallel performance* (multiple leaders perform the same tasks but in different contexts). Gronn (2002) and Goldstein (2003) similarly distinguish between situations in which leadership for specific tasks is enacted by multiple leaders together or separately. Spillane (2006) expands upon this formulation by defining three types of co-performance: *collaborated distribution* (two or more leaders jointly enact the same leadership practice in the same context); *collective distribution* (two or more leaders perform interdependent tasks in different contexts in support of the same goal); and *coordinated distribution* (interdependent actions of two or more leaders performed in a particular sequence).

More recently, Leithwood and his colleagues (Leithwood et al., 2006b) conceptualized a typology that offers a more general theoretical framework for exploring the distribution of leadership in organizations, rather than focusing narrowly on an idealized image and practice of distributed leadership. The framework is grounded in a research-based definition of leadership and core leadership functions in school systems (e.g. setting directions, developing people, redesigning the organization, managing the instructional programs – Leithwood & Riehl, 2005; Leithwood et al., 2004, 2006a). This typology emphasizes variability in the alignment of leadership functions, and in beliefs associated with different forms of alignment – *planful alignment, spontaneous alignment, spontaneous misalignment, anarchic misalignment.*

The analysis in this paper builds upon past theory and research to explore the nature and patterns of leadership distribution in schools as it relates to school-level indicators of sources of leadership influence and of student performance. Particular attention is given to the role that principals play in the distribution of leadership.

Methodology

The data for this analysis were drawn from interviews with school personnel in a sub-sample of schools participating in a larger five-year multi-method study of leadership and student learning, funded by the Wallace Foundation. The larger study involves approximately 180 schools (elementary, middle, and high) located in 44 school districts (three to five schools per district) across nine states (four to five districts per state). All schools participated in the principal and teacher survey components of the study. Thirty-six schools from 18 school districts (two per state) took part in site visits that involved interviews with district and school personnel and classroom observations. School interviews included principals and assistant principals, five classroom teachers, teachers acting in formal leadership roles, and parent and community representatives. School performance data (student results and school ratings on state mandated tests over time) were also collected from available school, school district, and state reports and websites.

A teacher survey administered during the first round of data collection included a set of items designed to measure the relative influence of multiple categories of actors on school decision-making. Respondents scored the direct influence on school decisions of the following individuals or groups on a six-point scale (*none, very little, little, some, great, very great*): Students, Parent Advisory Groups, Some Individual Parents, School Teams (departments, grade levels, other teacher groups), Teachers with Designated Leadership Roles, Some Individual Teachers, Principal, Other Building-level Administrators, District-level Administrators. From these items, we derived a measure of "collective leadership" (the sum of the ratings) that combines and compares schools in terms of the range of sources of leadership influence and the strength of that influence on teachers (Mascall & Leithwood, 2007).

We pulled a purposive sample of the site visit schools for this analysis. We classified the site visit schools as high, medium, or low on the collective leadership and on the student performance measures. From the resulting matrix, we selected five schools for variation in collective leadership score and student performance for qualitative analysis of leadership distribution at the school level. The sample (Table 6.1) included elementary and middle schools; schools in high and low SES settings; and schools in inner city, suburban, and rural settings across four states (Texas, Missouri, Oregon, and New Jersey).

The database for each school consisted of all interviews conducted during the first site visit (about eight to ten interviews per school). For the larger study, all site visit interviews were tape recorded, transcribed, and entered into an NVIVO project database. We employed a three-stage process of analysis for each case. In stage one we created descriptions of leadership activities in each school based on the NVIVO data queries. We developed a findings template that drew upon Spillane's conceptualization of leadership practice as constituted in the activities of administrators, teachers, and other sources in specific situations that are designed to influence others in the service of the core work and goals of the school (Spillane, 2006). The template allowed us to construct descriptions of (1) sources of leadership linked to (2) specific actions and (3) goals in (4) specific contexts, the (5) co-participants in those situations, reported (6) effects of those actions, and any (7) factors directly or indirectly influencing those leadership variables. This analysis generated from 15–25 leadership scenario templates per school. In stage two of the case analy-

Table 6.1 Sample School Characteristics

School	Total Leadership	Student Achievement[a]	Setting[b]
London Elementary	High	High	Size: 546 Pupils Diversity: High Poverty: High
Overton Elementary	High	Low	Size: 250 Pupils Diversity: Medium Poverty: Medium
Gregory Elementary	High	High	Size: 536 Pupils Diversity: Medium Poverty: High
Playa Junior High	Low	Middle	Size: 586 Pupils Diversity: High Poverty: High
Forest Elementary	Low	Low	Size: 398 Pupils Diversity: High Poverty: Medium

Notes

a Student achievement rankings calculated by comparing the percentage of students scoring at or above minimum state proficiency standards on state mandated assessments in reading and mathematics (2002–2005) relative to other schools in the states where these schools are located.

b Diversity (Low = 66% + White; Medium = 18–65% White; High = 0–17% White; Poverty (Low = 0–17% F/R Lunch; Medium = 18–65% F/R Lunch; High = 66%+ F/R Lunch).

sis we coded each scenario according to the core leadership practices exemplified in that scenario (using definitions for *setting directions, developing people, redesigning the organization,* and *managing instruction* derived from Leithwood et al., 2006a). Then we wrote an analysis of the leadership distribution patterns that we discerned in the scenarios, applying concepts from research on leadership distribution as appropriate (Gronn 2002; Leithwood et al., 2006b; Spillane 2006). The final stage consisted of writing a case report for each school, integrating findings from the scenario analysis and was structured according to the research questions for this analysis, as follows:

What are the sources of leadership for student learning?
What are the focus and goals of leadership beliefs and actions?
What actions are associated with leadership for student learning?
How is leadership for student learning distributed?
How do leadership distribution patterns and actions relate to student learning?

The school case reports were treated as the database for cross-case analysis.

Teacher Survey Findings (see Table 6.2)

Comparisons of the teacher survey responses concerning sources of leadership influence in the five case study schools were suggestive of certain patterns of leadership distribution distinguishing schools that scored higher or lower on collective leadership. First, teachers rated their principals highest in terms of their influence on school decisions in four of the five schools (district administrators were scored slightly higher in Gregory Elementary). District level influences on school decisions were consistently rated the second highest (first in the case of Gregory). Thus, teacher attributions of strong leadership influence to principals and to district administrators applied to all schools, regardless of differences in their collective leadership scores. This finding, while not surprising, suggests that an analysis of leadership sources in schools should be sensitive to the presence and strength of external influences from district, and potentially, other external sources.

What can be gleaned from the survey data about the lateral distribution of leadership influence to sources in the school beyond the principal? In relative terms, neither students nor parents (advisory groups or individuals) are highlighted as salient sources of influence on school decision making. Among the professional staff, assistant principals are influential in schools where they are present (Overton had no assistant principal), although the ratings assigned to Other Building Administrators are relative to the strength of the overall collective leadership scores. The most intriguing finding is that school teams and teachers with designated leadership roles are consistently rated more highly as sources of influence on school decisions in the three high collective leadership schools (London, Overton, Gregory) than in the lower (Playa, Forest) collective leadership schools, although the formal leadership structures in all these schools were quite similar.

The survey findings indicate variations in degree of influence of potential

Table 6.2 Collective Leadership Scores from Teacher Survey

Sources	London Elementary	Overton Elementary	Gregory Elementary	Playa Junior High	Forest Elementary
Students	4.10	3.64	4.00	3.20	2.87
Parent Advisory Groups	4.10	4.46	4.16	3.32	3.37
Some Individual Parents	4.29	3.92	4.07	3.64	4.07
School Teams	5.10	5.31	5.06	4.16	3.43
Teachers w/Designated Leadership Role	5.03	5.43	4.68	4.08	4.13
Some Individual Teachers	4.45	4.64	4.35	4.17	4.40
Principal	5.61	5.86	5.23	5.40	4.93
Other Building Administrators	5.13	4.07	4.97	4.68	3.93
District Level Administrators	5.26	5.50	5.55	5.12	4.73
Collective Leadership Score	43.06	42.84	42.07	37.77	35.77

sources of leadership in the schools, but provide little insight into the distribution of leadership practices and interactions among individuals or groups exercising that influence. For that, we turn to the qualitative data from our interviews with school personnel. Here we highlight findings particular to the role of principals in the distribution of leadership at the school level and in relation to school goals and to the enactment of core leadership tasks.

Principals and Distribution in the Sources of Leadership

Pervasiveness of Principal Leadership Across Multiple Leadership Scenarios

Consistent with the findings of other investigations of leadership distribution and influence on teaching and learning, school personnel in our case studies did not attribute leadership actions and influence to only one source, and not always to the principal (Camburn et al., 2003; Hall, 1992; Heller & Firestone, 1995; Leithwood et al., 2006a; Spillane, 2006). Depending on prevailing organizational district and school cultures, school goals, leadership tasks, perceived expertise, bureaucratic authority, and a variety of other factors (e.g. collegial relations, newness to the school or role), the array of individuals or groups identified as providing leadership included a mix of principals, assistant principals, teachers in formal leadership roles (e.g. grade or subject team leaders), teachers with specialist positions (e.g. literacy specialists, technology specialists, counselors), teachers informally recognized by peers as acting in leadership capacities, school leadership or management committees, school program teams or committees (e.g. Special Education, Gifted and Talented, Limited English Proficiency), parent involvement personnel, district administrators and professional staff, and external consultants linked to particular areas of curriculum, program, and teacher development priorities at the school level. Mere identification of the number and variety of individuals and groups contributing to school leadership, however, provides scant insight into the actual distribution of leadership. Overall, principals were more likely than any other source of leadership in these schools to be implicated in multiple leadership scenarios.

Our comparative analysis of the overall distribution of leadership sources in these five schools reveals three relatively distinct patterns. In pattern one (London, Overton, and Gregory Elementary) the leadership influence of the principal is overtly evident across multiple focuses of school improvement activity in planful collaboration with influential school-based teacher leaders (individuals and groups) and with outside sources (district specialists, external consultants) associated with particular goal-oriented initiatives. In these schools we also found a strong emphasis on professional collaboration among teachers, and teachers in instructional leadership roles that crossed curriculum and grade boundaries. Not surprisingly, these schools were rated as high collective leadership on the survey measure. In pattern two (Playa Junior

High), the leadership influence of the principal also extends across multiple focuses of school improvement activity, but the evidence of influential sources of and principal collaboration with teacher leadership and/or external change agents is less robust. Teacher leadership is more limited to traditional grade level or program specific structures, and there is less active emphasis on teacher collaboration school-wide. In pattern three (Forest Elementary), the principal interacts administratively with multiple focuses of school improvement activity, but exerts little influence on implementation. Key teachers or external agents are identified with support for different improvement initiatives, yet teachers attribute little influence to the enactment of those roles. Teachers do not report an emphasis on or culture of teacher collaboration within and across traditional or non-traditional organizational structures. The findings for Playa and Forest are consistent with the lower collective leadership scores for these schools.

Analysts of leadership sometimes conceptualize leadership distribution as a school-level phenomenon and sometimes at the micro-level of a specific focus of goal-oriented activity. Gronn (2002) distinguishes between additive and holistic leadership at the organizational level. Additive distribution refers to situations in which multiple people engage in leadership practices with little coordination in action or goals, and with isolated rather than combined effects on goal accomplishment. Holistic distribution refers to a pattern of interdependent actions among multiple sources of leadership that exerts a combined influence on the accomplishment of shared organizational goals. Among our cases, Forest Elementary provides the clearest example of a school where the overall pattern of leadership distribution reported by school personnel corresponded to an additive pattern, at least in a formal bureaucratic sense (since teachers attributed little actual influence to those in formal positions of management/leadership responsibility). The distribution of leadership sources in London, Overton and Gregory Elementary conformed more to the holistic pattern of leadership distribution overall, and this was clearly a function of the extension of the principal's leadership influence across multiple focuses of school improvement. Playa Junior High did not clearly fit either an additive or holistic pattern of distribution in leadership sources, in part because of the absence of a strong teacher leader presence. The case reports suggest strong correlations between the principal's management style and the overall patterns of leadership distribution reported in the schools (cf., Hall, 1992; Hall & Hord, 2001; Hord et al., 1984).

Finally, we note that teachers in several of the case study schools talked about the collective influence of teachers on school decisions in general and on decisions concerning directions and plans for school improvement. This was typically framed as function of whether the principal and district authorities invited, valued, and acted upon input from teachers. In London Elementary, for example, teachers reported that a previous principal rarely solicited teacher input, and that when she did she rarely acted in ways that acknowledged the value of that input. As a result, they felt unsupported and increasingly kept their opinions and ideas to themselves, thereby decreasing the potential for significant teacher influence more broadly on setting directions and other decisions in the school. That changed when the new principal came in and was perceived as genuinely seeking, listening to, and respecting teacher input and influence on school decisions. Teachers and principals in Overton and Gregory Elementary also affirmed the presence of a strong collective voice and influence of teachers, facilitated by the principal's orientation to teacher input and to organizational structures that enabled that input. Thus, in our conceptions of distributed leadership at the school level, we need to account for the presence and strength of teacher leadership that is embodied in norms, structures and processes that enable collective teacher input and influence, and not just focus on those individuals identified as teacher leaders. This is not equivalent to the anarchic leadership scenarios associated with clichés that "everyone is a leader in this school."

Bureaucratic Structures and Variability in Leadership Sources and Influence

It is tempting to associate the bureaucratic distribution of roles, responsibilities and authority as specified in formal organizational charts and policies with the distribution of leadership sources and influence. Our findings indicate that the relationship between the formal organizational structure and school leadership is more problematic than predictable in two ways. First, the bureaucratic allocation of responsibility to perform certain functions and tasks does not necessarily mean that the persons or groups exercising those functions and tasks will be perceived as influencing what others think and do. Spillane (2006) argues that leadership sources and acts can be recognized as such even if they do not yield their intended effects. That argument is conceptually compelling, but difficult to sustain in the face of evidence of people in leadership positions whose actions are not seen or felt by school personnel to make much difference (Forest Elementary). Second, alternative patterns of leadership distribution can be enacted through the same formal bureaucratic structures. All the case study schools had multi-stakeholder school management/leadership committees and special program committees (e.g. Special Education, Bilingual Education). They all had a similar array of formal teacher leader positions, including subject and grade team leaders. Some had teachers assigned to coach-like instructional leadership roles associated with priorities for improvement in program and instruction (e.g. literacy, mathematics). The patterns of leadership influence, however, varied.

Even in single schools, we found examples of variation over time in how leadership influence was enacted and distributed through the same bureaucratic structures. Principal succession was a factor in each of these situations (Hargreaves et al., 2003). In London Elementary School the current principal and her predecessor both worked with the organizational structure of a School Based Management Team, grade level teams, cross-grade subject teams, special program committees (gifted education, bilingual education, etc.) and specialist roles (counselor, literacy teacher, parent involvement coordinator, etc.). Under the previous principal the leadership distribution pattern was highly additive. The principal was uninvolved with school improvement initiatives. These were mandated by the district and were proceeding in an uncoordinated way guided and managed by grade team leaders, specialists, and external consultants. The new principal took on a proactive leadership role and influence within the existing governance structures in a way that spanned multiple focuses of school improvement activity. That shifted things toward a holistic pattern of leadership distribution. In Gregory Elementary School a previous principal led the implementation of the Accelerated Schools (AS) comprehensive school reform model, including the formation of five curriculum cadres, a school site council, and the AS school improvement planning process. While the cadres and council were formally chaired by teachers, and teacher influence on school directions, improvement plans, and professional development was reportedly strong, school personnel reported that the previous principal played a more overt co-leadership role within those structures than the current principal. The present principal and assistant principal talked about deliberately stepping back from a formal co-performance role to a more indirect advisory role in the cadres and site council (though the principal also described his micro-political efforts to get teachers to "buy in" to his goals and ideas for change). Teachers also reported that adherence to the AS school improvement needs assessment and planning processes became less stringent under the new principal. These two cases illustrate that while formal organizational structures create an institutional landscape for the distribution and enactment of leadership, they do not necessarily determine how it plays out over time.

In sum, it seems important to distinguish the formal allocation of leadership roles and responsibilities from what Leithwood et al. (2006b) define as the planful alignment of multiple leadership sources, practices and influence. Their emphasis is on strategic alignment and coordination in the goals and actions of those in leader roles in ways that yield a collective influence. Formal bureaucratic structures may or may not require or facilitate the kind of consensus building, communication, interaction, and collaboration that we would associate with the planful alignment of leadership in their terms.

All the schools had externally mandated multi-stakeholder site-based management committees made up of school administrators, teacher representatives from grade levels and program areas (e.g. Bilingual, Gifted, and Talented), resource teachers (e.g. counselor, literacy coordinator, special education), parent representatives, and representatives from the broader community (e.g. business, community services). The committees went by different names – School-Based Decision-Making Committee (London and Playa), School Site Council (Gregory), Principal's Leadership Committee (Overton), School Leadership Committee (Forest). These committees met on a regular basis (e.g. monthly) and had formal mandates and authority to make decisions and advise on school goals and plans, school budget allocation, the management of the curriculum and instructional programs, school activities, and so on. Some committees were chaired by principals (London, Overton, Playa), and some were not (Gregory, Forest). Formal mandates notwithstanding, how these committees and decision processes actually work and their actual influence on school decisions and on teaching and learning is quite uncertain. Teachers in Forest Elementary, for example, claimed that most school decisions were controlled by the principal and a small group of teachers known informally as the principal's cabinet. They did not attribute much leadership and influence over important matters in the school to the School Leadership Committee. By contrast, the principals at London and Gregory Elementary Schools provided detailed anecdotes to illustrate how they facilitated discussions and group decisions by questioning the consequences of alternative proposals from committee members, keeping people aware of policy and financial constraints, inviting broader input, and contributing their own perspectives and expertise depending on the circumstances of the decision. Lack of clarity about the leadership role of school management committees stems in part from the fact that while as a group they may exert influence through their collective decision making and advisory powers on school directions, organizational arrangements, professional development, and instructional program management, they are also micropolitical contexts in which multiple sources of leadership interact in unpredictable ways. To fully understand this one would need to account for the role of the committee in the distribution of leadership practice in the school, and for the sources and patterns of leadership activity within the committees.

Principals, Leadership Functions, and Patterns of Leadership Distribution

Whereas the concepts presented by Gronn (2002) and Leithwood et al. (2006b) highlight key underlying dimensions of leadership distribution patterns (e.g. planned versus unplanned, formalized in organizational structure versus informal and temporary, more and less aligned), Spillane et al. (2004) (cf., Spillane, 2006) provide more explicit conceptualizations of different ways of distributing leadership practices – collaborated, collective, coordinated, parallel. These concepts were useful in our analysis of leadership scenarios associated with specific leadership functions and goals. Our analysis of leadership scenarios in the schools revealed variable patterns of leadership distribution and the principal's role associated with the core leadership practices (setting directions, developing people, workplace redesign, and managing the instructional program) and particular directions of goals for improvement (e.g. reading, math, teacher teamwork).

There are two ways of examining the distribution of leadership influence from a functional/task perspective. One is to look for distribution patterns within a particular core leadership practice. For example, what is the distribution of leadership sources, actions and influence in the setting of directions or goals for school improvement? A second way is to consider the distribution of leadership sources and influences across the different core practices with respect to a specific goal focused domain of activity. For example, how is leadership for improvement in reading instruction distributed in terms of goal setting, professional development, organizational arrangements, and program management, and how does that compare with other focuses of improvement activity? Here we illustrate and examine variability in leadership distribution and the role of principals for two core leadership functions: developing people and setting directions. Then we consider examples of leadership distribution of associated with specific goals.

Developing People: Principals' Use of Expertise

Availability and access to sources of professional expertise, as well as organizational norms concerning legitimate sources of professional expertise, affected the distribution of leadership sources and roles in the case study schools (most particularly in regards to professional development and managing the instructional program). The principal's professional expertise in specific areas of curriculum and teaching, in interpreting student assessment data, in school management practices (e.g. vision setting, collaborative decision making), and so forth, shaped the linkages of their leadership practices to other leadership sources. Variability in the principal's claim to expertise and orientation toward the use of expertise from other sources figured not only into between school differences in the overall patterns of leadership distribution, but also to variation in the distribution patterns for different focuses of school improvement in some schools.

The principal in London Elementary was known in the district for her expertise in reading. She collaborated strategically with an independent reading consultant to introduce and to reinforce the use of specific methods of teaching reading. In a coordinated pattern of leadership influence, the consultant introduced alternative teaching methods in a series of professional development sessions during the schools year, and the principal monitored implementation and provided follow-up support during her classroom walkthroughs. She had also acquired expertise in the interpretation and use of student assessment data while working as a district reading grant coordinator and instructional facilitator. The principal delivered training in data use to teachers and followed that up by sitting in on grade team meetings every six weeks to coach teachers in the interpretation and use of formative assessment data to plan for tutoring and other interventions. In contrast, she did not claim expertise in mathematics content and teaching. Her leadership for in-school development of a mathematics curriculum guide and for implementation of an externally developed mathematics program consisted mainly in facilitating and coordinating the leadership activities (in-service training and follow-up assistance, curriculum and assessment development) of grade level and subject leaders and external program trainers. She also arranged for training for the parent coordinator to enable her to help parents support their children's learning in math.

The principal of Playa Junior High also presented herself as a master teacher. She personally encouraged, modeled and coached teachers in the use of general instructional strategies aligned with her goal of getting teachers to adopt more active and interactive teaching and learning strategies focused on higher order learning objectives. The school was located in a small district (about 2500 students) without a stable of subject area consultants, so the principal and teachers relied on subject specific professional development from a variety of external sources (regional education service center, commercial programs, neighboring district, state conferences). The principal strategically screened these opportunities and controlled the use of school professional development resources to ensure alignment of those inputs with her vision for instruction.

The principals in Overton and Gregory Elementary Schools did not claim general or subject specific expertise in curriculum and teaching (though they both performed regular walk-throughs and conversations with teachers about the implementation of school wide programs and expectations). They emphasized and described their roles as leaders in the interpretation and use of student performance data for school improvement planning, and in creating time and opportunities for teachers to develop in-house expertise, and to share, problem solve, plan, and learn from one another. In both situations the principals facilitated linkages between external sources of professional expertise and key teachers who were expected to take leadership in diffusing external knowledge and skills to other teachers in the school. These two schools differed, however, in the relative emphasis given to external knowledge dissemination versus internal knowledge creation and diffusion. At Gregory Elementary the principal, teachers, and district authorities had adopted a strategy of identifying and adopting external programs aligned with locally determined student learning needs (e.g. expository writing, early reading), sponsoring the training of selected teachers as resident experts, and then arranging for those teachers to provide in-service training and consultative assistance to other teachers implicated in implementing those programs. At Overton Elementary the major emphasis was on a lesson study approach to improvement, whereby teachers jointly developed, piloted, assessed and critiqued lessons aligned with state curriculum and accountability expectations.

The principal referred to the strategic use of external consultants more to stimulate teacher thinking and innovation in areas identified in the school as directions for improvement than to support the implementation of specific programs. In contrast to the other schools, the principal in Forest Elementary relied on external experts from the district and on designated specialists in the school for expert input related to school initiatives. She did not claim nor did teachers attribute to her any special professional expertise. While she accommodated the work of the designated experts as required by the district and state, she did nothing to promote and enable more general development and sharing of expertise among teachers in the school.

To summarize, leadership distribution in the case study schools was shaped in part by access to and norms concerning the use of various sources of professional expertise: the principal's expertise, the expertise of teachers in the building, and expertise from the district office and other external sources (regional service centers, universities, commercial program developers, state education agencies, other districts). How this played out was influenced by the principal's personal claims to expertise as an instructional leader, the principal (and district office) orientation to use of professional expertise, and by district office size and professional resources available to the school. In schools where the principal laid claim to expertise within a particular curriculum area identified as a priority for improvement, the principal was likely to take a direct but shared role in leadership for teacher development with external and/or internal sources of expertise. This shared responsibility for teacher development was enacted in various collective and coordinated arrangements, though we did not encounter situations in which these principals co-trained teachers with other sources of expertise in the same venue.

Setting Directions: Principals' Orientations Toward Goals for Improvement

The influence of state and federal curriculum policies, standards, and accountability systems (curriculum expectations, performance standards, school rating systems, Adequate Yearly Progress targets) on direction setting was pervasive in the improvement priorities of all the schools, districts and states sampled in our cases. School-based improvement initiatives in all the schools mirrored district and state priorities in core academic areas (e.g. reading, writing, mathematics, science). Government policies created a context for the enactment of local leadership at the district and school levels, but were also a major source of influence of local directions for school improvement. In that sense, those policies can be regarded as a source of leadership. Alternatively, these policies and related procedures can be viewed more as tools that leaders actively utilize to shape local directions for action (Spillane, 2006).

The distribution of leadership for direction setting at the school level is strongly shaped by how the principals view and enact their influence on school goal setting in the context of state and district policies, priorities, and leadership traditions. This varied remarkably across the five case study schools. The principal and teachers in Forest Elementary, for example, portrayed themselves as complying with state and district mandated programs (e.g. reading, mathematics) and procedures (e.g. computerized curriculum mapping, developing student data reports). No one identified any current school goals beyond these externally mandated initiatives. In that sense, the principal presented herself and the School Leadership Committee as managing the implementation of externally mandated directions, not as setting directions per se. This orientation to change mirrored the highly centralized, directive, and seemingly uncoordinated approaches to school improvement attributed to the state and district levels of the education system (e.g. the district mandated a new language arts program without clear directions as to the ongoing status of the existing Success for All program and facilitator).

The state and district did not mandate commercial or locally developed programs at Overton Elementary. While district authorities defined system priorities for improvement in accordance with school scores on state tests (e.g. mathematics), the principal's actions were directed more toward influencing and supporting teachers' individually required professional development plans through the development of organizational structures, processes, and norms intended to build and support an effective professional learning community. She held teachers accountable for addressing annual school goals set with the Principal Leadership Committee (writing, multiple intelligences) and enacted through book study teams and curriculum cadres. She moderated teacher accountability for district improvement expectations in mathematics that she felt were unrealistic given the student demographics, current performance levels, and the quality of available assessment tools. Direction setting in the school was led collectively by the principal, the Leadership Committee, and teacher leaders. It was quite decentralized in its effects. Outside the Committee, direction setting was carried out in a planfully aligned parallel practice by teacher leaders in the cadres and study groups, and by the principal in her classroom walk-throughs and consultations with teachers about their professional development plans and classroom practices. In sum, the principal in Overton Elementary School focused her leadership influence less on setting or enforcing program or achievement targets for improvement than on structuring the workplace (the Leadership Committee, the curriculum cadres and coaches), facilitating teacher learning (lesson study, book study teams), and managing the instructional program (monitoring teaching and professional development plans) in ways that guided teachers to collegially define their own directions for improvement mindfully and transparently in the context of state standards, student results, and district and school-wide priorities for improvement.

The distribution of leadership sources and influence on direction setting in

London, Gregory, and Playa schools were marked by the principal's overt advocacy for certain school goals for improvement in teaching and learning, while adopting a more collaborative and facilitative stance toward others. At London Elementary the principal decided that reading instruction and outcomes could be enhanced if teachers were to adopt and implement a wider variety of teaching strategies. She communicated this goal to teachers, provided training herself and with an external expert, and monitored teacher implementation in the classroom and grade team meetings. At the same time, she facilitated ongoing improvement activities mandated at the district level prior to her appointment (curriculum writing, use of a commercial mathematics program, technology integration), in collaboration with grade team and subject leaders and specialist teachers who were traditionally responsible for follow through with district improvement decisions. The principal exerted an influence on these directions for improvement, however, by shifting the emphasis from implementation of programs and practices to analyzing and responding to their effects on student learning, and by ensuring program and lesson alignment with the state curriculum expectations. She did this by insisting that in-school curriculum development include common assessments, by training teachers in the interpretation of student test data, and by monitoring and coaching teacher use of student performance data in grade team meetings in collaboration with grade team leaders and specialists (e.g. literacy teacher, counselor) to plan tutoring and evaluate programs. While the principal autocratically set a focus on reading, her approach to (re)shaping directions for change, including those mandated by the district, was to collectively engage teachers in the analysis of student learning needs using teacher made assessments aligned with state curriculum expectations and accountability tests. At least during her first year, she co-performed this leadership role and influence with existing teacher leaders in contexts such as grade team and school management committee meetings.

The principal in Gregory Elementary inherited a tradition of decentralized decision making about directions for school improvement, albeit attuned to broad priorities set by the state and by district authorities. State and district sources gave priority to improvement in student performance in reading, for example, but neither the district nor the state mandated the implementation of a particular reading program. District officials expected and supported (e.g. funding for professional development) principals and teachers to clarify the specific learning needs of students in their school in relation to these priorities, and to identify and implement appropriate solutions. The adoption of the Accelerated Schools comprehensive school reform model at Gregory Elementary, which employs a school improvement needs assessment and planning process that relies heavily on teacher-led cadres responsible for inquiry, action planning, and implementation facilitation, was consistent with this ethos. The common game plan for improvement once a need was defined by a curriculum cadre at Gregory and endorsed by the School Site Council, was to search for programs to fit the need, to get one or two teachers trained as experts, and to arrange for those teachers to train and assist their peers during summer institutes, weekly early release days, and formally scheduled professional development days. The process, as designed, was largely teacher led, with the principal acting more in a consultative role and in accessing resources to support the professional learning needs of teachers. School personnel described how this had worked as designed with the adoption and ongoing implementation of an early reading program. As a second year administrator new to the district, however, the principal at Gregory Elementary took it upon himself to undertake his own analysis of student test results, and described some initiatives that he was instigating, rather than waiting to follow the teachers' lead (e.g. the adoption and implementation of an expository writing program, reteaching and retesting students whose results were marginally below state standards for acceptable and for exceptional performance). In terms of setting school directions, these initiatives appeared to be largely occurring as a result of the principal's influence, though he was successful in securing district level endorsement for the writing program. Perhaps not surprisingly, he also reported that teacher take up of these directions was less enthusiastic than for those that had genuinely been developed through the teacher-led cadre process.

At Playa Junior High the major current direction for school improvement reflected the principal's intent to get teachers to be less didactic in their teaching, to broaden their repertoires of instructional strategies, and to focus on higher order learning expectations for students (beyond knowledge recall and test preparation). There was little indication of more widely distributed leadership sources and influence on the setting of this goal. The principal explained her initiative as a strategy to motivate and help teachers move student performance beyond the predominantly "acceptable" current ratings on the state accountability system. Teachers were also involved in school-based curriculum writing in response to a district mandate decentralized to all schools in this small district. The principal and teachers reported that she had delegated responsibility for managing the curriculum development work to traditional subject department heads and teams.

The general point of the preceding illustrations and analyses is that patterns of leadership distribution and influence can vary by core leadership practice not only between schools and districts, but also for different focuses of improvement within the same school. Principal beliefs about their own and other sources of professional expertise both inside and outside the school were a key factor shaping the distribution of leadership for professional development. In all the cases state and district defined priorities for improvement exerted a strong influence on direction setting within the school. In this sense, in-school leadership for setting directions for improvement typically occurred in a context of what Waters and Marzano (2006) refer to as defined autonomy. The flexibility for principals and teachers to determine their own directions was affected in part by whether state or district authorities tended to mandate programs or to enable schools to choose or develop their own programs. In all the schools we found a strong emphasis on the analysis of student performance data as a tool for direction setting. The extent to which data analysis processes and products appeared to genuinely influence school goals was dependent upon the principal's engagement and leadership with the use of student data, often in collaboration with key teacher leaders in the school. Principal involvement in data use tended to be generalized, whereas teacher involvement tended to be specialized within particular curriculum areas. In those instances, the principal's leadership stretched across multiple teacher leaders and focuses of improvement. Our cases highlight two circumstances in which principals may be more prone to act directly and less collaboratively to influence school directions for improvement. First, is when the principal is acknowledged as having specific expertise in curriculum and/or instruction (London Elementary, Playa Junior High). Second, is when student performance is comparatively high relative to other schools and to state prescribed standards, and the principal perceives that teachers may be feeling and acting complacent about the success of all students, or about setting goals for learning that exceed minimum public standards of performance adequacy (London and Gregory Elementary Schools, Playa Junior High).

Complexity of Leadership Distribution as a Function of Goal Type and Breadth

Leadership distribution patterns are affected by the kinds of goals that school personnel associate with leadership activities. Some goals (e.g. improving student performance in mathematics, strengthening professional community) are more encompassing than others (e.g. implementing a specific mathematics program, standardizing student discipline policy and practices). The more encompassing the goal, the greater the likelihood that multiple sources of leadership will be involved, and the greater the range of goal-related activities to which leadership might be attributed.

Contrasting illustrations from Forest Elementary and London Elementary will help to clarify this point. Both schools were involved in the first couple of years of implementing new district mandated externally developed mathematics programs. While student performance in mathematics in Forest Elementary was below state averages on state mandated standards and tests and the school was not currently satisfying Adequate Yearly Progress expectations, school personnel did not identify improvement in student math performance as an explicit school goal. The goal (one of many program specific goals in the school) was simply to implement the district mandated Grade 6–8 mathematics program. A district math consultant visited the school weekly to assist math teachers with implementation. Two potentially related initiatives were also underway. The school counselor was responsible for compiling and preparing student assessment data reports at the beginning of the year to assist teachers with lesson planning and with tracking student progress, and a few weeks prior to state test dates to help teachers identify student needs for additional coaching. The principal was reportedly keenly interested in student performance data, though no one could identify any actions that she was taking to influence the use of student data. The school technology coordinator had been trained by district staff to facilitate the implementation of a state computerized curriculum mapping and lesson planning tool. The school interview data did not indicate that these strands of activity and the leadership sources and actions associated with them were consciously connected. The result, from a teacher perspective, was a leadership distribution pattern of anarchic misalignment in Leithwood et al.'s (2006b) terms.

In London Elementary the principal's explicit vision and goals for the school included improving student success (including but not limited to mathematics), greater coherence in curriculum and teaching, and greater teamwork focused on student among teachers and with other stakeholders (e.g. parents). Although the percentage of students performing at or above state standards on the state's testing program in mathematics was acceptable and high relative to similar schools in neighboring districts, the principal's goals emphasized the success of all students and learning outcomes beyond those touched on by the tests. Consultants working for the commercially developed mathematics program dropped in every six weeks to provide implementation training and assistance to the teachers. Not unlike Forest Elementary, the school faculty was also engaged in a school curriculum writing project (mandated by district but organized by school) that involved developing curriculum guides and assessments keyed to the state curriculum in core subject areas. The principal arranged for the school curriculum guide writers to get input from the external program consultants on the program fit to the school guide and state curriculum. She also relocated the curriculum writers' classrooms to ensure that all teachers had convenient informal access to them for advice. Not only was the principal committed to the use of assessment data as a tool for identifying and addressing student learning needs, she delivered data use training for teachers and she sat in on grade level team meetings to facilitate teacher analysis and use of assessment data to plan six week tutoring cycles. She also arranged for the parent coordinator to get trained in the math program so that she could prepare ways to show parents how to help their children with math homework. With the exception of the parent involvement piece, the activities related to implementation of the mathematics program in London were similar to Forest (external program with in-service training, curriculum mapping aligned to state standards, assistance with data use). At London, however, these activities and varied sources of leadership were linked in a collective pattern through the principal's actions.

The pattern of leadership distribution was more complex. It encompassed multiple core leadership practices (setting directions, developing capacity, workplace arrangements, managing instructional program) and multiple leadership sources. This pattern is clearly associated with the focus on a shared learning goal. The pattern seems more likely to produce a combined and greater impact on student learning in math than in Forest, where the focus was limited basically to program implementation. This leadership distribution scenario corresponds well to Leithwood et al.'s (2006b) concept of planful alignment across core leadership practices.

Student Learning and School Leadership Distribution

We can make no general claims about the relationship between student learning and school leadership distribution with only a five-school sample. We did examine our data to explore and reflect upon that relationship within each school. Our qualitative data consisted of the interviews with school personnel. Our quantitative data consisted of public records of student performance on standardized tests from 2002/3 to 2005/6 (obtained from school, district and state websites). We reviewed the test result data in terms of the percentages of students scoring at or above acceptable state proficiency standards in reading/language arts and mathematics for schools and districts (Table 6.1).

We did not detect any clear correlation between the patterns of leadership distribution revealed in the qualitative data and the student test results evidence. This is not a surprise for several reasons, beginning with the inherent difficulties of controlling for other variables that likely affect school performance results on standardized tests. The student mobility rate in Forest Elementary, for example, was 25 percent. Student enrolment in Overton Elementary declined from 330 to 220 between 2002 and 2006, with a simultaneous shift in demographic mix (the percent of African American pupils remained at about 42 percent, while the Hispanic population grew from 1 percent to 10 percent and the percent of White students declined). The possible effects of changing student demographics on test results confound attempts to attribute those results to leader actions or to other education inputs.

Some additional features of the achievement data from these schools complicate efforts to analyze relationships between student performance and leadership. First, the test result data from each of the case study schools were either stable over time or fluctuated within a modest range from year to year (the turnaround in student performance at Gregory predated our data). From 2002/3 to 2005/6 we did not see evidence of consistent trends upward or downward in the percentages of students performing at or above acceptable state standards in any of the schools. Second, while the percentage of students performing at or above acceptable state standards varied across our research sample, and we used these differences to aid with sample selection, all five schools were actually performing about average relative to other schools in their respective states. These two features make it logically difficult with a small sample to associate specific leadership distribution patterns and the principal's leadership role with higher or lower student performance, or with improving or declining performance.

Any attempt to associate school leadership with student learning processes and outcomes also needs to take into account the potential consequences of changes in personnel in key leadership positions. The principal in London Elementary was in her first year. Among the other schools, the principal in Forest Elementary was the only one in our sample who had been in her school for more than two or three years. Teachers in London, Overton and Gregory Elementary Schools alluded to differences in the leadership styles and in leadership distribution and practices between the previous and current principals. The impact that these changes in leadership might have on student learning outcomes would not necessarily show up in the first year or two of their tenure (Hargreaves et al., 2003).

Our case study findings highlight the need to be sensitive to the focus and scale of leadership distribution and action as they relate to student learning outcomes. At the micro-level of specific goals and leadership tasks, different patterns of distribution across leadership sources and actions can co-exist in a school (e.g. improvement in mathematics and reading performance in London Elementary). It would be a logical error to infer that the way leadership is distributed and practiced for one leadership scenario necessarily applies to all leadership scenarios in a school, and to generalize the influence on student learning of leadership patterns associated with only one focus of improvement.

If we are to think about school-level patterns of leadership distribution and practice, we need to be clear about what indicators of student learning might be associated with those patterns. Students in London Elementary, for example, were performing at or above state averages in reading, language arts and mathematics, but below the state averages in science. It would be misleading then to assert a consistent relationship between student learning outcomes and an additive or a holistic pattern of leadership distribution at the school level. We could, however, begin to hypothesize that variability in student performance by program area might be greater where additive patterns prevail, and that greater consistency in the quality of student performance across programs might be found where more holistic patterns of school-wide leadership distribution prevail over sustained periods of time. This would be an interesting avenue for further research. At present, however, the conceptual tools for theorizing and analyzing leadership distribution as a school-level phenomenon remain relatively undeveloped, and not clearly distinguishable from related concepts associated with other streams of leadership and school improvement discourse. Is a holistic pattern of school leadership distribution, for example, fundamentally different from the characteristics of a vibrant collaborative culture (Rosenholtz, 1989), a professional community (Louis & Kruse, 1995), or a professional learning community (Dufour et al., 2005)?

Ultimately, the search for direct measurable correlations between indicators of academic achievement and patterns in the distribution and enactment of leadership may be less productive than to explore how leadership distribution interacts with other variables that can be shown to bear a more direct relationship to student learning. For example, using the teacher and school administrator survey data from our project, other members of our research team identified a classroom-level factor they call "focused instruction" that is positively correlated with student achievement in mathematics. Focused instruction, in turn, is positively correlated with teachers' sense of professional community in the school (Louis et al., 2007). It may be more fruitful to investigate what patterns of leadership distribution contribute most to professional community, particularly those elements of professional community that have been shown through other studies to contribute most to student learning processes and outcomes, than to try to isolate direct links between leadership and teaching and learning.

With that example in mind, we are faced with an intriguing finding from our case study analysis of leadership distribution. The reported leadership patterns in London Elementary led us to characterize the school as an example of additive distributed leadership under a previous principal, in contrast to the holistic pattern that was emerging under the new principal who was openly and proactively working to develop greater unity of purpose and teamwork focused on student success. Yet the percentages of students performing at or above state proficiency standards in mathematics, reading, and writing were already at or above state averages when she arrived. For mathematics the school results were actually about 10 percent higher than the state average for elementary schools, and this is a school with a socio-economically challenged student population of the type often associated with low performance (e.g. 84 percent on free/reduced lunch, 84 percent Hispanic). Evidently, it is possible to achieve acceptable levels of student performance on conventional indicators of student achievement, at least in this state, without a strong professional community led by the principal. We can speculate that an effective program in the hands of competent teachers with adequate in-service training can yield acceptable results in some contexts despite the absence of a cohesive professional community. This leads us to question under what conditions more holistic and coordinated patterns of leadership distribution associated with strengthening teachers' professional community can be linked to improvements in student learning outcomes beyond minimum standards.

In this regard, we found that leadership for the implementation of the commercially developed mathematics program at London was limited under the previous principal to periodic teacher training by a team of external consultants. Under the new principal, the focus shifted from implementing the program to improving student learning in mathematics. Various strands of activity (school curriculum writing with common lessons and formative assessments, training and use of student assessment data for tracking student progress and planning interventions, parent involvement activities) and sources of leadership (principal, grade team and subject leaders, external consultants, parent coordinator) were pulled together in a coordinated effort to this end. It was too soon to tell how all this might affect the learning levels of the small percentage of students whose performance was not already acceptable, or the quality of student learning beyond those expectations assessed on the state's standardized tests. It is clear, however, that the range of coordinated interventions, leadership sources and actions focused on student success in mathematics expanded under the new principal, and that the potential for further growth in student success in this curriculum area was greater. Comparatively, the collective leadership survey measures among our case study schools were strongest in the three schools where the principals and teachers provided the most explicit accounts of direction setting grounded in collective analysis of student performance data.

Concluding Comments

In this study we described and analyzed how leadership associated with school improvement goals and initiatives was distributed in five schools in varying state and district contexts, with an emphasis on understanding the principal's role in the distribution of leadership practice and influence. In our analysis we drew upon some key concepts from past research and discussion of leadership and leadership distribution. These included Gronn's (2002) distinction between holistic and additive forms of leadership distribution; Leithwood and his colleagues' conception of core leadership practices (Leithwood & Reihl, 2005; Leithwood et al., 2006a); of variability in leadership distribution based on the degree of planfulness and alignment in leadership sources, actions and influence (Leithwood et al., 2006b); and Spillane's (2006) explanations of different distribution patterns in the enactment of leadership (collaborated, coordinated, collective, parallel). We conclude by highlighting what we see as some of the key findings and points of discussion from our analysis.

We see a need both analytically and practically to distinguish between school level and goal- or initiative-specific patterns of leadership distribution in schools. Among our cases we were able to distinguish between schools where the overall patterns of leadership sources, actions, and influences were more holistic or collective across multiple focuses of improvement, and those where the overall distribution of leadership was more additive and less planfully aligned across and within specific focuses of improvement. These patterns were clearly associated with the principals' beliefs and orientations toward external and internal influences on school direction setting, toward sources and uses of professional expertise (their own, teachers', external), and toward participatory or shared leadership. These findings resonate with prior research on principal management styles as it relates to school improvement goals and teamwork.

On the other hand, we found that principals did not always interact and collaborate with other sources of leadership in the same ways for different school improvement goals and initiatives in the same school. This differentiation in the principal's role in leadership distribution was most likely where the principal claimed expertise in areas of teaching and learning that were targeted for improvement, or in situations where the principal believed that teacher motivation to undertake improvement in student learning needed to be pushed. Overall, however, principals are more likely than other sources of leadership to be implicated in multiple leadership scenarios in their school. Leadership from teacher leaders and external sources is more likely to be goal or initiative specific. Principals perform a boundary spanning role not typically performed by others, nor picked up by others in the absence of active principal leadership.

The formal bureaucratic allocation of roles, duties, and authority is not necessarily congruent with the distribution of leadership sources and influence as attributed by school personnel. Institutionalized structures do not predict leadership actions and influence. Leadership is micro-political in its enactment, though it can transpire in a more or less planful and formally arranged organizational context. To really understand the distribution of leadership one needs to explore evidence of actual behaviors and influence associated with core leadership practices and specific focuses of school improvement activity. In sum, principals working in the context of similar organizational structures may enact their leadership roles and engage in shared leadership in alternative ways.

The search for normative links between specific leadership distribution patterns and student achievement results is a noble cause, but our findings suggest that it is not likely to yield clear guidelines for practice. Some of the reasons are quite pragmatic, such as the confounding effects of frequent principal turnover (and the unpredictable consequences on leadership patterns) and student mobility on attributions of school input effects on student learning outcomes. Another challenge is sorting out the effects of leadership on student learning from the effects of well-implemented good programs. Effective school leadership certainly enhances the likelihood that good programs will be selected or developed and well implemented by teachers, but the extent to which or the conditions under which program choice and the quality of program implementation are dependent on the nature of leadership distribution in a school remains a mystery yet to be unraveled.

Other reasons that confound the search for causal relations between particular patterns of leadership distribution and student achievement relate to the kinds of within school variability in distribution patterns by school improvement focus and/or core leadership tasks that we have illustrated in the preceding analysis. Different leadership distribution patterns may be correlated with similar levels of student achievement in different areas of school program, or the same pattern of distribution across multiple program areas may be associated with varying levels of student performance. In effect, knowing that the goal and/or task specific leadership distribution arrangements between principals and other sources of leadership is collaborated, collective, coordinated or parallel may be useful in terms of describing and explaining the grammar of leadership in a school (Spillane, 2006). The planful or spontaneous choice of those arrangements, however, is likely contingent on a variety of local factors, including state policy influences, district office leadership traditions and influence, the principal's management style, and available sources of professional expertise, that are not simply transferable between settings and leadership scenarios. Even if we could convincingly demonstrate that a specific pattern of leadership distribution and the principal's role made a difference in student achievement in a specific scenario, it would be unreasonable to expect that pattern to be replicated in all improvement scenarios in the same and different schools.

We conclude on a more positive note, positive in the sense of arguing that principals sharing leadership with others in planful yet alternative patterns of leadership distribution is probably a worthwhile way to approach improvement in student learning. Our findings, albeit tentative and small scale, suggest that the potential for more widely and collectively distributed leadership action and influence increases when principals and teachers derive school priorities for improvement from shared investigation and consensus on student performance results and needs, rather than defining improvement needs mainly as the implementation of new programs and instructional practices.

Acknowledgment

This research was undertaken as part of the Learning from Leadership Project funded by the Wallace Foundation.

References

Camburn, E., Rowan, B., & Taylor, J. (2003). Distributed leadership in schools: The case of elementary schools adopting comprehensive school reform models. *Educational Evaluation and Policy Analysis, 25*(4), 347–373.

DuFour, Richard, Eaker, Robert, & DuFour, Rebecca (eds) (2005). *On common ground: The power of professional learning communities.* Bloomington, IN: National Education Service.

Educational Evaluation and Policy Analysis. (2003). Special Issue on Educational Leadership, *25*(4).

Goldstein, J. (2003). Making sense of distributed leadership: The case of peer assistance and review. *Educational Evaluation and Policy Analysis, 25*(4), 397–422.

Gronn, P. (2002). Distributed leadership. In K. Leithwood & P. Hallinger (eds) *Second inter-*

national handbook of educational leadership and administration (pp 653–696). Dordrecht, The Netherlands: Kluwer.

Hall, G. (1992). Characteristics of change facilitator teams: Keys to implementation success. *Educational Research and Perspectives, 19*(1), 95–110.

Hall, G. & Hord, S. (2001). Expanding views of change leadership: The change facilitator team. *Implementing change: Patterns, principles and potholes* (pp. 148–167). Boston, MA: Allyn & Bacon.

Hargreaves, A., Moore, S., Fink, D., Brayman, C., & White, R. (2003). *Succeeding leaders? A study of principal succession and sustainability.* Toronto, ON: Ontario Principals' Council.

Heller, M.F. & Firestone, W.A. (1995). Who's in charge here? Sources of leadership for change in eight schools. *Elementary School Journal, 96*(1), 65–86.

Hord, S., Stiegelbauer, S., & Hall, G. (1984). How principals work with other change facilitators. *Education and Urban Society, 17*(1), 89–109.

Leithwood, K. & Riehl, C. (2005). What we know about successful leadership. In W. Firestone & C. Riehl (eds), *A new agenda: Directions for research on educational leadership* (pp. 22–47). New York, NY: Teachers College Press.

Leithwood, K., Day, C., Sammons, P., Harris, A., & Hopkins, D. (2006a). *Successful school leadership: What it is and how it influences pupil learning* (Research Report 800). Nottingham, UK: National College for School Leadership, University of Nottingham, Department for Education and Skills.

Leithwood, K., Mascall, B., Strauss, T., Sacks, R., Memon, N., & Yashkina, A. (2006b). Distributing leadership to make schools smarter: Taking the ego out of the system. *Leadership and Policy in Schools, 6*(1), 37–67.

Leithwood, K., Seashore Louis, K., Anderson, S., & Wahlstrom, K. (2004). *Review of research: How leadership influences student learning.* New York, NY: The Wallace Foundation.

Louis, K.S. & Kruse, S. (1995). *Professionalism and community: Perspectives on reforming urban schools.* Newbury Park, CA: Corwin Press.

Louis, K.S., Wahlstrom, K., Michlin, M., & Dretzke, B.J. (2007, April). *Principal leadership for classroom practice.* Paper presented at the Annual Meeting of the American Educational Research Association, Chicago, IL.

MacBeath, J. (2005). Leadership as distributed: A matter of practice. *School Leadership and Management, 25*(4), 349–366.

Mascall, B. & Leithwood, K. (2007, April). *The effects of total leadership on student achievement.* Paper presented at the Annual Meeting of the American Educational Research Association, Chicago, IL.

Rosenholtz, S. (1989). *Teachers' workplace: The social organization of schools.* New York, NY: Longman.

Spillane, J. (2006). *Distributed leadership.* San Francisco, CA: Jossey-Bass.

Spillane, J.P., Halverson, R., & Diamond, J. (2004). Towards a theory of school leadership practice: Implications of a distributed perspective. *Journal of Curriculum Studies, 36*(1), 3–34.

Waters, J.T. & Marzano, R. (2006). *School district leadership that works: The effect of superintendent leadership on student achievement* (A working paper). Denver, CO: Mid-continent Research for Education and Learning (McREL).

7

"A Job Too Big For One"

Multiple Principals and Other Non-Traditional Approaches to School Leadership[1]

W. NORTON GRUBB AND JOSEPH J. FLESSA

The job is just too big for one person, with all the different programs and all the needs of the students and the parents. And we could see that it was too much for a human being to do. We really needed two – at least two full-time human beings to do that job.

A teacher at a school with dual principals

This chapter examines ten schools that have adopted alternative structures: two principals working together, three principals working together, rotating principals, and one school with the principal's duties distributed among teachers. These ten sites provide examples of alternative ways of organizing formal school leadership, with varying benefits and challenges. We observed the idiosyncratic ways in which schools and districts approached the policy dilemmas associated with attempts to change the default administrative structure of principal and assistant principal (AP). Where alternatives were imposed without school input, implementation floundered. The findings analyze the origins of the reforms; school site roles; costs and benefits; the role of the district; and the long-term stability of the approach. We offer questions for consideration of the possibilities of distributing formal school leadership.

The job of the school principal has become increasingly complex (see Institute for Educational Leadership, 2000; Krüger et al., 2005, for an international comparison). He or she is responsible for hiring and perhaps firing teachers, coordinating bus schedules, mollifying angry parents, disciplining children, overseeing the cafeteria, supervising special education and other categorical programs, and responding to all the "stuff that walks in the door." In addition to the managerial and political tasks that have historically engaged principals (Cuban, 1988), reformers have demanded that principals become instructional leaders as well (Leithwood et al., 2004; Stein & Nelson, 2003). Particularly in urban schools, the initiative for developing support services to help low-income students usually falls on principals (National Research Council, 2003, Ch. 6). In an era of accountability, policy makers have imposed new requirements, and the principal is responsible for enhancing progress on multiple (and often conflicting) measures of educational achievement. The frustrations with the lack of time, the lack of resources, and the pressures of external requirements have grown substantially (Valentine et al., 2003). As one co-principal in our study commented about her current position: "There were days where we looked at each other and said, 'How could one person do this job?'."[1] Partly as a result of the job's myriad demands (Pounder & Merrill, 2001a), there has come to be high turnover in the position, a shortage of teachers wanting to become principals,[2] and a general sense of urgency in school leadership – particularly in urban districts (Gilman & Lanman-Givens, 2001). The multiple demands on the principal, and the related image of the strong principal carrying all the burdens of running and improving a school (see, for example, Kantrowitz & Mathews, 2007), comes in part from conventional rational models of organizations, relying on a hierarchical division of labor with the principal at the apex. This structure, a legacy of the administrative progressives' "one best system" and now part of the "grammar of schooling" (Tyack & Cuban, 1995), continues to permeate policy discussions about leadership. The literature on effective schools has also contributed to this conception because of its conclusion that all effective schools have strong leaders (Carter, 1999; Edmonds, 1979). From this perspective, there is little wrong with the nature of the principal's job that increased authority could not solve (e.g. Institute for Educational Leadership, 2000, p. 13).

Current school leadership policies emphasize recruiting strong individuals capable of fulfilling the job's demands (Institute for Educational Leadership, 2000). Another response recommends strengthening principal preparation and finding ways of preparing principals in different ways. Efforts that focus on recruitment, selection, and preparation of school site leaders share the perspective that a super-principal or hero-principal (Copland, 2001) is necessary to run a high-quality school, and that this person can be found and trained for the job. Of course, efforts to improve principal recruitment preparation are laudable. But these efforts remove from discussion the possibility that school reformers might also usefully focus on alternatives to the principalship as it is traditionally structured (Pounder & Merrill, 2001b); distributing formal leadership in non-traditional ways has received relatively little attention from researchers or reformers.

There are several reasons to think that solely preparing principals in different ways might not work well. Given the complexity of schools, principals cannot simply order their teachers to teach better. Instead they must work indirectly, by creating a culture of internal accountability, in which teachers improve their teaching in concert with others (Carnoy et al., 2003; Leithwood et al., 1998). This approach, the subject of institutional and neo-institutional theory, segues into the perception that even if the rational bureaucratic approach were effective, it would still not be a desirable model. It denies the expertise of teachers, and therefore fails to capitalize on important resources; it is undemocratic for teachers and other staff (see Ingersoll, 2003); it creates an impossible job for the person at the top, one that is often isolating; it often prevents principals from tackling instructional issues; and it does not address the principal's limited span of control in a complex organization (Flessa, 2003). Models of professional or collegial organizations, with less hierarchical arrangements and a greater role for shared decision making, provide us with a different image of schools (Bryk & Schneider, 2002; Meier, 1995). Similarly, Spillane's (2001) conception of distributed leadership clarifies that leadership in practice is almost always distributed among administrators, teachers, and staff, rather than held solely by the principal.

Purposes and Methodology

An alternative approach to finding hero-principals would be to restructure the position itself. While this might be done by imagining alternative arrangements, the approach in this chapter is empirical – examining schools that have experimented with distributing formal leadership roles via non-traditional approaches to the principalship, especially multiple principals.

To analyze schools with non-traditional principalships, we sent out notices of interest to several web sites, interrogated the schools we knew, to see if they were familiar with others, and scoured both the practitioner and the research literature. In the end we visited nine schools in California. In addition, Michael Chirichello (2003) adapted our methodology, and provided transcripts from one school in Massachusetts. Seven of these ten schools proved to have many of the characteristics of urban schools, including a heterogeneous racial and ethnic mix of students, and many low-income and immigrant students. This chapter, therefore, describes what is largely a California sample of schools. Table 7.1 describes aspects of the ten schools we observed, labeled by the pseudonyms we use throughout the chapter.[3]

In the end we observed three alternative models:

1. Schools with two co-principals – three co-principals, in one case – that in turn fall into two sub-categories: divided schools, in which two co-principals each operate a school that is largely independent of the other; and integrated schools, in which two co-principals operate one integrated school.
2. An approach involving a rotating principalship, in which an individual serves as principal for three years, training an in-coming principal during this period and staying a fourth year to serve as a mentor.

Table 7.1 Summary of Schools Examined

School Pseudonym	Level and Size	Type of Principalship	Racial/Ethnic Composition (%)	Special Features
Calvin Charter	K–8 730	Three Co-Principals, Integrated	0.1 Asian 93.7 Latino 1.2 Black	Bi-literacy for all Students; Support Services
Hillside	9–12 1030	Dual Principals, Integrated	0.8 Asian 35.1 Latino 0.6 Black	District Initiation and Full Support
Lookout Circle	K–6 720	Dual Principals, Integrated	1.1 Asian 80.0 Latino 5.0 Black	Family Resource Center, Special Ed, LEP, After-School Programs
Manzir	9–12 350	Four Co-Leaders, Integrated	1.4 Asian 39.6 Latino 1.2 Black	Reverted to a Conventional Model When Two Leaders Left
Maricopa	K–5 660	Dual Pprincipals, Divided (K–2, 3–5)	0.7 Asian 29.5 Latino 0.6 Black	Initiated Because of Size; Complex Bilingual Programs
Munson	K–8 1190	Dual Principals, Divided (K–4 and 5–8)	63.2 Asian 29.5 Latino 1.2 Black	Initiated Because of Size Problems
Onofrio	K–8 930	Dual Principals, Divided (K–4 and 5–8)	69.2 Asian 24.7 Latino 0.4 Black	Initiated Because of Size Problems
Riverside	K–6 170	Eight Teachers Share Leadership	0.6 Asian 2.4 Latino 1.2 Black	Small School, Originating as a Professional Community
Robinson	K–6 2500	Dual Principals, Integrated	2.0 Asian 1.1 Latino 2.0 Black	Initiated by District Because of Size; District Support
San Sebastian	K–8 300	Rotating Head Teachers	0.1 Asian 93.7 Latino 1.2 Black	Teacher-Led School; School Decisions Made by Teachers

3. A small school with no principal, where the teachers have divided the principals' tasks among themselves.

While the first of these is most common, there is much to be learned from the other two. This is admittedly a limited sample of non-traditional approaches, but it is sufficient to clarify both their limits and possibilities.

Data Collection

In preparation for site visits, the research team collaborated on the development of interview and observation protocols. We designed one interview protocol for school site administrators and district supervisors; we designed another parallel protocol for teachers. Because we were interested in understanding how leadership responsibilities were distributed among adults at the various schools, we adapted protocols from the Distributed Leadership Study at Northwestern University, made available by its director, James Spillane. Our purpose in conducting semi-structured interviews was to elicit what Mishler (1986) calls "respondents' worlds of meaning" and to use those responses for analysis and interpretation of the various forms and effectiveness of the administrative changes. Our team used the same protocols at each of the different sites, thereby providing us with a basis for cross-site comparisons.

In addition to the interview protocols, the research team adapted an observational protocol for use during faculty meetings or grade level team meetings. Researchers' fieldnotes tracked interactions with a selective-verbatim note-taking strategy that also included impressions of moments of tension or consensus.

We typically spent four person-days in each school, with two people spending two days. We observed staff meetings and interviewed those who served in leadership positions as well as teachers. At Lookout Circle we interviewed the building's union representative as well as a focus group of parents. We also sought to interview district personnel for all sites, to get their perspectives about these innovations, though we succeeded in only half of these schools; our conclusions about district support are therefore based on limited information. We taped and transcribed interviews, approximately 50 overall, in all but one school (Calvin), and quotations in this chapter are verbatim.

The evidence from interview transcripts, site visits, and observational fieldnotes fell into four categories, and the remainder of this chapter is organized according to those issues: (1) the origins of the alternatives (decisions to depart from the "default model" of a single principal are crucial to understanding the limits of the conventional approach); (2) the nature of distributed leadership in these schools, both among individuals in principal positions and between principals and teachers; (3) the benefits and costs of these alternatives, including the financial costs; (4) the roles of districts, since districts can encourage or discourage non-traditional approaches. We conclude the chapter with a summary of the conditions necessary to make these models work well, as well as some recommendations for both practice and subsequent research.

The Origins of Alternative Approaches: Multiple Goals, Multiple Forms

In the ten schools we examined, alternative ways of restructuring the principals' positions arose in several ways. These origins continued to influence how schools operate, so that superficially similar innovations – co-principals, for example – in practice work in different ways. In the most common pattern, a school simply became too large for a single principal. In Munson, Onofrio (both in the same district), and Maricopa, the school grew to about 1200 students. At the initiative of the district, Munson and Onofrio were divided into two schools, one K-4 and the other Grade 5–8, each with its own co-principal, on the same site. Maricopa also a K-5 school, split into a K-2 and a Grade 3–5 school, each with its own co-principal and AP. This is a "small school" rationale, a notion that the numbers of teachers and students becomes too great and the complexity too overwhelming when a school becomes a certain size.

Since these co-principalships were instituted to respond to size problems, they tended to operate as principals of independent (though co-located) schools, rather than as joint principals of a single integrated school. The co-principals at these three schools worked with one another on issues of joint interest – for example, the timing and content of assemblies, the timing of Parent Nights, the transition from the lower school to the upper school, partnerships with outside service providers, and communication with parents and the public. The extent of cooperation was more substantial in Maricopa because of a complex bilingual education program, with four or five options coordinated across grade levels. But in all three cases the communication between the two schools came largely through the co-principals and their two assistant principals. Teachers from the two schools hardly ever mingled; one said, "The Cinco de Mayo celebration is about it!" They reported to and were evaluated by their own principal and AP; parents go to the principal of the school in which their child is enrolled, and the district communicates with the principal of the grade levels they are concerned with.

In Mansfield, MA, a similar story explains the emergence of two schools with dual principals. At Robinson Elementary, a size of almost 2500 students precluded parental access to the principal. The superintendent suggested that Robinson have two co-principals, and has since extended this model to the other elementary school in town. But these schools act as integrated schools rather than two independent schools, with principals sharing responsibilities rather than dividing the school.

Lookout Circle illustrates a very different origin. The original principal (call her Mary) seems to have been a super-principal, instigating many different programs – a Family Resource Center, programs for the special education and LEP (Limited English Proficient) students – which stretched her to the limit. She then asked her assistant principal (call her Monica) to become a co-principal, and Mary took a pay cut to increase Monica's pay to the principal's level so that the change would cost the district nothing. Monica reported that "Mary's quote to me was, I'd rather have my health back and take a small reduction in pay." This change was a direct response to the workload of the principal's position; as Monica commented:

> Before the change I never saw Mary. And she was just always so frantic, and you never know when you could catch her on a good day, because she had the whole role on her shoulders. Whereas now, she has like half the role on her shoulders.

The transition of Monica into the co-principal position – what we call the problem of succession – was facilitated by Monica's long history with the school. The two tend to divide the principal's duties: Mary has taken on instructional issues and teacher observations, while Monica is largely responsible for the after-school program, the Family Resource Center and the gardening program. They are jointly responsible for hiring and teacher evaluations; staff meetings are held with both co-principals present; and parents and the district have learned that they can go to either co-principal.

Another school with co-principals, Hillside, is a high school.[4] When a long-established principal left, the district approached one of the two assistant principals (call her Kathleen) to take the principal's position, but she refused. Teachers, concerned that they would lose both assistant principals, suggested co-principals. The district still ran a conventional search for a principal, but none of the candidates was fully qualified. The committee then initiated a co-principalship with both Kathleen and the other assistant principal (Robert), as teachers had originally suggested. The two have complementary strengths – Kathleen is described as more direct, while Robert is more collaborative – and they operate the school jointly.

A sixth school, Calvin Charter School, has three co-principals. Because the school had been founded as an administrator-teacher collaborative, the notion of collaborative principals seemed natural. Of the three, one is in charge of K-4, the other of Grade 5–8, and the third (the organizational director) has special responsibility for coordination. There are other specializations too: the head of K-4 handles communications with the district, plans professional development, and completes reports on English learners; the head of Grade 5–8 is concerned with bilingual education, student behavior, contacts with community agencies, staffing and new teachers; and the organizational director is the "bottom-line" person most responsible for finances, often represents the school in public, and facilitates the organization of the school. While this structure appears to assign two APs to different grade levels, each is engaged with teachers and students in many different grades, not merely their own; all three principals make important decisions about hiring, the curriculum, and direction of the school jointly; all three are keepers of the vision, including bi-literacy for all students, a full range of supportive services, and knowing all students well. The school meets as a whole, not as two separate schools, and all committees are staffed with individuals from all parts of the school. The organizational director may be first among equals because of her greater experience, but they have worked consistently to make themselves a trio of equal partners.

An obvious question is whether schools with co-principals are just minor variants of the conventional principal/AP model. Unanimously, teachers and co-principals responded that a co-principal is different from an assistant principal. Each co-principal has the power of decision making. Anyone wanting to see the head of the school can go to a co-principal, whereas many would bypass an assistant principal. As a teacher at Lookout Circle noted,

> [The difference is] it's because they have equal – in everybody's eyes, including the parents, the students and the teachers – both of them are equal. And they both have the same amount of say and one doesn't override the other.

The responsibilities of co-principals are structured differently from those of APs:

> Vice principals in our district just stay for a year and then they're traded and they go on to be principals.... It's really different this year. It changed from the first year when she [the co-principal] was a vice-principal, when she was doing very specific things. And this way they're both responsible for everything.

So both the authority and the tasks of co-principals are different from those of APs.

Other Alternatives: A Rotating Principal and No Principal

The two remaining schools in our sample are quite different. San Sebastian Community School grew out of a parent-participation nursery school, and then developed into a teacher-run school in which the idea of a rotating leader was established as one of the early commitments. The head of the school is called a head teacher, not a principal:

> Our head teacher is a teacher first and not a representative of the, I'm not going to say not an administrator, but not a representative of the

district. Peter [a former head teacher] used to say that the head teacher is just a teacher in the office. And he also used to say that the most important job is in the classroom.

Most decisions in the school are made by teacher committees, though the head teacher makes the quick decisions necessary "on a dime." The head teacher is on the district's personnel roster as a teacher, causing problems that we examine below; but this means that she has tenure, is not subject to the whims of the district, and has the same formal status as other teachers (though she is paid for 17 extra days a year). The idea underlying rotating head teachers is that an individual emerges from various committees as a natural leader; she or he then spends the year before assuming the head teacher position working with the current head teacher; then he or she steps into the position of the head teacher for three years, and for at least the first year the former head teacher is still at the school to provide support and counsel. During the third year the head teacher begins mentoring their successor. This is a well-developed approach to the problem of succession, though it requires active participation by teachers in decisions since this process generates new candidates for head teacher.

The final school is the most radical. Riverside School emerged from a reform effort as a professional community, with one individual (call her Katrina) serving as both principal and a full-time kindergarten teacher. This resulted in overload for Katrina; as one of the other teachers said, "The very first year Katrina basically was doing principal and teacher at the same time, and it was just overwhelming. So, okay, Katrina, what parts can we take from you? What can we do to help?"

The school was also threatened by being either closed down or run by a part-time principal from the outside, without any of its collaborative principles. In response, the faculty with the support of the assistant superintendent developed a self-governing school. The tasks of a principal are divided among individuals and committees including a facilities director, a parent education coordinator, a curriculum team of five teachers, two restructuring coordinators, a Title I coordinator, two coordinators for developmentally-delayed students, a student study team coordinator, and site council representatives. Most administrative tasks have been delegated to an administrative assistant (upgraded from a secretarial position) and an office assistant. A school facilitator coordinates the system and is the nearest thing to a head, but everyone views him as a coordinator rather than the principal. Formal authority in this school is negligible, unlike the positional authority in hierarchical organizations; authority is conferred collegially. As one teacher mentioned, "People don't have to have formal authority – well, clearly they don't have the formal authority to ask you to do things. You do things because you've almost distributed that authority among each other and you honor that." This model of a self-governing school run by professional norms can arise only under special conditions, including teachers with adequate leadership competencies, a small and cohesive faculty, a culture of collaboration, and relative stability among the faculty. But even if it is unlikely to be a widespread solution, it illustrates crucial elements of restructuring the principalship.

In addition, we visited a school we call Manzir, with a leadership team of four individuals. By the time we visited, two of the original four had left the school for personal reasons, and no experienced teachers were willing to fill their positions. The school then reverted to a more conventional model, of a principal with two assistant principals. This case illustrates that, without the district or the school itself confronting the problem of succession, a school with non-traditional leadership is likely to backslide into the default position of a conventional hierarchy.

One other motivation should be mentioned. The only school to turn down our request for a visit was one where a co-principal hinted that the district had installed him to oversee the original principal, whom the district did not trust. Similarly, at Onofrio School, one of the two co-principals (call her Lynetta) was known as a difficult individual; the other co-principal noted:

> I don't know about [hiring a co-principal] to keep an eye on her, but I think it was to neutralize her. They put her here to get neutralized. In fact, there was a single principal and they put her in a co-principal [position] … because parents were complaining about her and her style.

Perhaps the hope was that a strong co-principal could not only moderate the influence of an abrasive principal, but might also teach her to be less difficult. In practice Lynetta's influence was limited to Grades 4–6 and to providing consistent headaches for her co-principal. By failing to confront the underlying problem, the district undermined any possibility that co-principals could work smoothly in the interests of the school.

So several distinct reasons explain the creation of alternative approaches: size, principal exhaustion, the effort to keep valuable people, and the need to "neutralize" abrasive individuals. These tend to continue influencing how these schools operate.

The Nature of Distributed Leadership: The Roles of Administrators and Teachers

The concept of distributed leaderships clarifies that patterns of leadership can take many forms. This concept has been used largely to describe the relative balance of decision-making power between administrators on the one hand and teachers on the other. However, with non-traditional principals, the more relevant question is the distribution of decision making among those serving in principal roles.

Dilemmas of Interchangeability and Specialization

In divided schools with co-principals – Onofrio, Munson, and Maricopa – each co-principal retains all the responsibilities of a conventional principal, though with a smaller number of teachers and students. The benefits of small scale include the ability to respond more quickly to teachers, parents, and students, and more time for instructional responsibilities including visiting classrooms. Teachers in these schools perceive their principals as more accessible and more available to help them with administrative and pedagogical tasks than they were before the division of the school. In addition, while many conventional principals speak of their jobs as lonely, particularly because they often have to leave the community of teachers (Loder & Spillane, 2005; Yee, 1999), co-principals in these divided schools have the benefit of another person to turn to. They can often defer decisions with the rationale that one principal must consult another; this prevents decisions from being made too quickly, under pressure from distraught parents or insistent teachers. There are also some simple logistical benefits: One principal can leave, for personal or professional reasons, and be sure that the school is covered; it's easier for one principal to take care of the emergency while the other continues with normal operations.

However, many benefits of distributing leadership responsibilities emerge only in schools that are integrated. In developing the co-principal position at Lookout Circle, Mary and Monica specifically rejected the notion of dividing schools by grades or programs because, as Monica mentioned, "Everything was so integrated, each of us needs to have that cross-section of every program. We need to have a view of what's going on in the whole school." In part, this is a statement of efficiency versus effectiveness: If dual principalships are a route to efficiency, then they reduce the burden per person, valuable in its own right, but it does not transform the principalship. If they are viewed as a way to become more effective because two people understand the school, they transform the job.

One benefit is what we call interchangeability: Where teachers, parents, and students have learned that they can go to either principal, they always have another avenue for help if one principal is busy or away. It's easier to schedule meetings where a principal must be present, like Individual Education Plan meetings for special education students. The endless series of parent meetings, district meetings, and community meetings – many in the evening – can be rotated among principals. Of course, real interchangeability requires that co-principals share information so that both are fully informed; typically these co-principals share one office and consult several times throughout the day. In addition, co-principals must learn to provide a united voice so that no faction can play one off against the other; in general these co-principals either delay decisions so they can harmonize their responses, or have worked together so long that they "just know" what the other would do. The coordination between two principals is not automatic, however, so schools restructuring the principalship need to consider it explicitly.

A second benefit in integrated schools is that co-principals can begin to specialize according to their interests. As examples, Monica at Lookout Circle has taken responsibility for extended-day programs, parent support programs, a discussion group called Tuesday Parent Talks, and the gardening program; she focuses more on math than on reading. At Calvin Charter School one co-principal specializes in relations with the district, while another has taken more responsibility for the bilingual program. The most extreme case of specialization occurred in Riverside, where teachers divided the responsibilities of a principal and a maintenance supervisor. Where co-principals specialize, this means that such functions receive more attention, since an overburdened principal will pay less attention to those practices that she dislikes. To be sure, specialization works against interchangeability: if one co-principal is responsible for after-school programs, then most issues about after-school programs must await her presence. But neither one is possible in conventional schools with a single principal, or in divided schools, and so the expanded possibilities of specialization and interchangeability are unambiguous benefits however the two are balanced.

Opportunities for Teacher Leadership

The second and more conventional dimension of distributed leadership involves the allocation of responsibilities between principals and teachers. In the case of Riverside, where teachers and principals are one and the same, conflicts are minimal because of the consensus on the school's vision, and because teachers have worked together for a long time. As one teacher commented,

> Because we're such a small staff, we all have a fairly cohesive view of what we want it to look like ... how the children are going to behave, how we're going to behave, what we expect from parents, what we expect from each other, how you treat each other, how you treat the site.

Similarly, the rotating principalship at the San Sebastian Community School is another way of distributing leadership among the teachers in a school. Teachers are consistently involved in leadership roles on various committees; every three years one of them steps up to the lead teacher's position, with the mentoring of the outgoing lead teacher.

However, schools with dual principals vary substantially in responsibilities of teachers. At one extreme, Onofrio and Munson are essentially separate schools under one roof, and the co-principals have made little effort to distribute much authority to teachers. At the other extreme, Lookout Circle is a school where the co-principals want teachers to participate fully in the operation of the school, and they have delegated a great deal to teacher-led committees. Similarly at Robinson, the co-principals have engaged teachers actively in the school's operation; as one said, "This is a profession where if you don't talk to one another, if you don't problem-solve together, and if you don't put your creative minds together, you get nowhere." Somewhere in the middle, Maricopa is a divided school, where teachers know only about their school, either the Grade 3–5 school under a co-principal (we will call Roberto) or the K-2 school under Cynthia. Roberto was widely praised by his teachers for putting teachers on important committees and giving them a say in the school. On the other hand, Cynthia's teachers mentioned very little of this; one teacher noted that Cynthia was more "authoritarian" while Roberto was more consultative and egalitarian. In a divided school, evidently, each school may follow a different pattern.

The two forms that distributed leadership can take – between principals, or between principals and teachers – are potentially linked, because of the ability of co-principals to model collaboration. At Riverside, one of the co-principals mentioned that

> people see us modeling, working together … I think it's made some people who were hesitant perhaps to have partner teachers, so they can – I don't know, I think it's just helped this spirit of collaboration and kind of coaching and mentoring.

A teacher confirmed the value of their modeling:

> You know, to see two people interact as peers, as equals, I think is really beneficial for the staff and for the students. Almost like, you know, how having a two-parent family is a better model than having a single [parent].

At the schools that operated in an integrated fashion, staff meetings provided good illustrations of modeling, with co-principals usually splitting the presentation of issues and plans, sharing the management of teacher comments, and clarifying their joint roles if there are decisions taken about future actions.

So multiple principals are compatible with many different forms of distributing leadership. The division of responsibilities between several co-principals can vary, and the possibilities for interchangeability, for specialization, and for modeling collaboration vary from school to school. In the balance between administrators and teachers, co-principals can act in authoritarian ways; but they can act in more collegial ways, more as Riverside or San Sebastian Community School does. Co-principals provide additional administrative resources, but how those resources are used depends on the motives for creating dual principals and on the goals of the co-principals themselves. When schools have used non-traditional administrative structures to further their visions of teacher-led schools, then the positions of co-principals or head teachers have become very different from anything in the conventional hierarchical school.

The Benefits and Costs of Alternative Approaches

Despite the variety of approaches to the principalship, some benefits almost always emerge. One is sharing decisions with someone else, "having somebody that you can really talk to as an equal, who's in the exact same position as you, at the site who you can totally trust and throw ideas off of", as one co-principal at Munson mentioned. Mary at Lookout Circle noted similarly, the advantages of "having somebody to not just share the responsibilities, but also somebody to be able to communicate with about problems. I think the creativity is more than sharing responsibilities, but having two heads instead of one."

The benefit of two heads and different perspectives extends to working with teachers. As a co-principal at Robinson commented about observing classrooms,

> We divvy it up so that two sets of eyes see the same person, so that coming to it without a preconceived idea, so that if you saw something in a previous observation that you can't get out of your head you go back.... So we have two sets of eyes, and we send each other copies of our observations.

Other benefits include having someone at the site even if one principal has to leave, a particularly important issue in a year-round school like Maricopa, and the ability to share the burdens of endless meetings.

Another substantial benefit is the greater accessibility of teachers and parents to a principal since the teacher:principal (or parent:principal) ratio is lower. The comment of a Robinson co-principal is typical: "With this model teachers feel that there's somebody that they can go to to get their needs met. Parents feel the same way. You don't have somebody waiting for two to three days to get a response." As one teacher from Lookout Circle commented,

> Something that to me has changed in a positive manner is that I can usually at least find one principal. They're so much more accessible.... Someone's always available for [difficult] situations – e.g. a special ed student who goes out of control.... They're in the classrooms a lot more too. And that's nice because I want them to come see what I'm doing. I've worked hard on planning and I want them in my room.

Multiple principals can also share the "stuff that walks in the door" so that each gets to priorities that are ignored in conventional schools, like the improvement of instruction, often the last task to get attention (Cuban, 1988; Flessa, 2003, 2004). Co-principals or multiple principals generally get around to more tasks, particularly with specialization. At Lookout Circle, for example, dual principals allowed more time for instructional improvement, and one co-principal specialized in working with support services from community organizations. The three co-principals in Calvin Charter all spent more time observing classes than would otherwise be possible. In cases like San Sebastian, with teachers rotating into the principalship, and Riverside, with eight teacher-principals, those administering the school have deep understanding of instruction in that school. Nothing guarantees that instructional leadership will happen, of course, since co-principals still need to see instructional improvement as a priority. But at least non-traditional structures help clear away the barriers of too many things to do and too much "stuff that walks in the door."

In addition, the stress levels of co-principals are generally reduced in these schools. The clearest example was Lookout Circle, where one principal had feared for her health:

Being a principal alone in a school of 1100 children with all those parents and all those teachers was absolutely physically impossible. Physically draining – to the point where I was concerned about my health…. Whereas there's certainly still stress connected to the job, there's a lot to do, but it's much more relaxed getting it done, because you don't feel that you have to do every single thing.

The Riverside approach also alleviated the overwhelming burden on the prior principal. So developing co-principals is one way to alleviate the stress of a job that is "just too big for one person."

However, this may not always happen because of what we might call the "capacity problem," following the common observation that even new urban highways are always congested to capacity because people and businesses relocate near them. Lookout Circle provides an example: while Mary was less stressed once she had a co-principal, the demands on each have not necessarily lessened because each of them sees new reforms to initiate, new programs to create. As Monica expressed this dilemma,

The more people, the more programs you bring on campus, the more situations there are for you to have to deal with as a principal. There's the kid who has a discipline problem after school with Kids Connection and it's too big for them to handle, then I've got to handle it at five o'clock at night. So, there are good things, but then there are these other issues that I have to deal with.

Similarly, the eight co-principals at Riverside are each so busy, with administrative duties on top of full-time teaching responsibilities, that we wondered if this should be called "distributed pain" rather than distributed leadership. When administrators are active and innovative, responsibilities expand to fill all the time and resources available. New approaches to the principalship might make such schools more effective, but they might not resolve the problem of over-work.

Yet another benefit of reducing the barriers between teachers and administrators is present only in schools where teachers have taken on positions of leadership. As the superintendent of the Riverside district commented,

> Having the staff take on many of the administrative responsibilities I think has really opened their eyes to what an administrator's job is. And it's created quite a bit of respect. I don't hear staff at Riverside talking about, making comments about an administrator's life other than it's very difficult, very stressful and so I think that's helped.

In such schools teachers can benefit from the creation of cohesive communities. As one of the teacher-principals at Riverside noted,

> The morale difficulties come from a very logical question of why are we doing this? Why are we working so hard? When, if we had a principal, I could just teach and I could go home and teaching's enough.... But we get to make it the school that we want in this way. We get to decide what curriculum thrusts we're going to do, or what type of school we're going to be.

A final and powerful benefit, at least in some schools, involves the problem of succession – the problem of preparing for a change in leadership. Most schools and most districts seem not to prepare for succession. When a principal moves or retires, a search takes place and an individual is hired based on district criteria, sometimes with little collaboration from the school and little thought about how an individual fits the culture of the school. Many schools (especially urban schools) go through a great deal of starting and stopping, of having new principals unfamiliar with a school and its community come in with new priorities (Valentine et al., 2003). But the problem of succession is successfully addressed in some alternative approaches, particularly in the rotating principals of San Sebastian Community School. Both the selection process, of having an experienced teacher step into the head teacher's role, and mentoring from the outgoing lead teacher assure that the transition is relatively smooth and the priorities of the school are maintained. In other schools with co-principals, the problem of succession is potentially easier since when one leaves, the other can act as a mentor to a new co-principal – hopefully someone from the faculty who has participated in school-wide councils.

The Ambiguity and Extra Expense of Alternative Approaches

The costs of alternative approaches need to be reckoned too. From the perspective of the rational bureaucratic model, one cost might come from teachers, staff, and parents playing one principal off against another. As one principal at Onofrio noted, "It's awfully hard, it's like having a body with two heads. And if you're not careful, people will pit you against each other." The principals in every school we visited were acutely aware of this danger, and had taken steps to prevent it – usually through extensive communication. As a co-principal at Lookout Circle noted,

> We don't make decisions necessarily right at the moment that somebody approaches us, because we want to check it out with the other person. If it's something that's going to have long-term consequences or fiscal impact, we want to talk with the other. We also don't want to get into kind of the Mom-Dad split, where if I don't get my way with one, I'll go to the other.

Similarly, from the bureaucratic perspective one might expect confusion if teachers, parents, students, or the district do not know which individual to turn to. But principals have anticipated this issue, and have either clarified a division of labor between them or have worked to be interchangeable. There may be an initial period of confusion, for new parents and students, but it does not last long; even in a divided school like Onofrio,

> Just the first year, I think they [parents] were a little confused about the two offices and stuff but now it just seems part of the culture, and they understand it and sometimes if they show up at this office and really their child needs to be dismissed from the other office, no problem, and they go up there.

Where the school has become a community, responsibility for students becomes collective. One Riverside teacher noted that the students are aware not of the novel governance but about the culture of a family where "all teachers know all students." At the beginning of the year one of them said, "I don't have to listen to you. You're not my teacher." And I said, "Oh yes you do. We are all your teachers."

The personal costs of non-traditional leadership vary enormously among schools. At Onofrio and Munson, where the district had given literally no thought to the compatibility of co-principals, teachers expressed concern about how ineffective co-principals could be if they did not get along. As one co-principal said about the other:

> Theoretically it [co-principals] should work really well, but it doesn't ... she could not get along with Lynetta. But, she said it was too stressful dealing with all the jockeying that goes along because you have to be able to share and collaborate and if you work with somebody who doesn't have that style, it's very difficult. And she, Lynetta, does not like to collaborate. It's my way or no way.

At Munson a co-principal attributed the success of the model to luck:

> I think it could be very, very hard, given the mix of the two people, especially since principals that I know tend to like being in charge and they tend to not be so patient about things. But we've really lucked out that we have the same kind of background.

But luck is not the solution; paying attention to the compatibility of co-principals is the key, and schools that had addressed this issue did not worry about compatibility.

The financial costs also vary considerably, though additional costs do not seem substantial in any school. At Maricopa the co-principal cost an additional principal position, about $80,000 for 1600 students, or $50 per student. At Munson and Onofrio, the additional cost was the difference between an assistant principal's salary and a principal's salary, a cost of about $7000 in schools of 1200 students, not more that $6 per student – a trivial sum even in cash-strapped California. At Lookout Circle the first co-principal took a pay cut to promote an assistant principal, so the additional costs were zero; but even if the district had paid the new co-principal a principal's salary, the cost would have been only $9 per student. At Hillside the two co-principals share a principal's and an assistant principal's salary plus $3000 for extra days, or about $3 per student. At Robinson the alternative would have been a principal plus two assistant principals, so co-principals actually saved the district money; Riverside eliminated the need for a half-time principal so it saved the district about $135 per student. So, the financial costs are small, at least in these ten schools, and there are even savings in a few schools.

One complication is that costs (as well as benefits) take place in different currencies. Riverside provides a good example. The district wanted to consolidate three schools to save administrative costs, but the Riverside teachers would not agree; the superintendent complained that "there is a real strong sense of autonomy on the part of the school, and now that it's self-governed, it's very difficult to get the staff and the parent community to examine other options." The district views costs in terms of dollars and administrative complexity, while the school views costs in terms of autonomy lost. Similarly, in Lookout Circle, the district complained not about the money costs (since there were not any), but about the uncertainty of whom to contact and the unfairness of one school having "too much [administrative] talent." Unless districts can figure out how to weigh intangible benefits from non-traditional arrangements against both intangible costs (like district certainty) as well as dollar costs, they may oppose such changes.

Overall, then, there are potentially substantial benefits of unconventional principalships – not, to be sure, in forms that can be linked to test scores or student progress just yet, but in ways that arguably affect a school's effectiveness. The calculation of benefits and costs clarify that it may be necessary to think of administrative costs in different ways. Conventionally, administrative resources are viewed as the necessary but unproductive costs of getting the work of an organization done, often viewed as "bloat" to be kept as low as possible. But administrative resources can enhance effectiveness, especially when principals pay greater attention to the quality of instruction, or enhance the climate of a school through greater collaboration (Carnoy, Elmore, & Siskin, 2003), or find support services for low-income children. In some schools, the additional resources in administration – time as well as financial resources – have created a more stable environment where teachers can improve their teaching and where problems can be identified and solved. Innovative administration in these cases seems enormously beneficial rather than a form of bloat, even if that's difficult to prove. In other cases – Munson and Onofrio – the limited ambitions underlying co-principals and poor execution have resulted in very little benefit. So no innovation is fool-proof; as with everything else in schools, what counts is not the level of resources, but rather how resources – here, administrative time – are used at the school and classroom level (Grubb et al., 2006).

The Contradictory Roles of Districts

Schools are embedded in districts, and districts create many of the conditions that affect how principals work. Except in charter schools like Calvin, districts have the power to ban or promote alternative approaches to leadership. In several of these schools, districts initiated the practice of dual principals: in Munson, Onofrio, and Maricopa, where schools became too large for one principal; and in Mansfield, when the superintendent suggested dual principals based on his reading. It is therefore worth examining what role districts have played, a subject of increasing interest in the school reform literature (Honig, 2004; Marsh, 2000; Togneri & Anderson, 2003).

With two or three exceptions, districts in our limited sample get low marks for their policies and practices toward principals. With the conspicuous exception of Mansfield, the districts that initiated joint principals did a poor job of implementation. In Munson, Onofrio, and Maricopa, there was no thought given to the compatibility of co-principals; the existing principal was not even included on the selection team, and met his or her co-principal literally when she reported to work the first day. As one commented, "I met her [the co-principal] in the summertime. I showed up and she said, 'Here we are. We're going to work together.' Luckily we had a lot in common." In Maricopa, the district split the school in two and assigned a co-principal without any warning, without any staff input, and without worrying about the "chemistry" of the leadership team; the transition to dual principals was reportedly chaos. At Munson, the co-principals describe their good working relationship as a matter of luck, and at Onofrio one co-principal suffers silently with an abrasive peer. Developing non-standard approaches is difficult enough without such thoughtlessness.

In other cases where the idea of alternative approaches came from the school principals describe persuading districts as difficult: "It wasn't an easy sell, but the district did agree to it," said a co-principal at Lookout Circle. Most districts work within the rational bureaucratic model: the additional complexity of relating to two or three principals is an aggravation. The district supervising Calvin would clearly like a conventional principal/AP structure because it sometimes does not know whom to approach, even though the principals there have worked to be interchangeable. In Riverside, the superintendent complained about the school not being a "team player," that its non-hierarchical structure made it difficult to deal with: "It's just that there's a hierarchy with the way things are supposed to work [in the district], and it doesn't work that way over there." Both in San Sebastian Community School and in Riverside, none of the leaders has an administrative credential, and the districts sometimes leave them out of conversations where credentialed administrators participate; Riverside feels under-represented since it does not have a seat on the Superintendent's Council. In these examples, a non-hierarchical school with unconventional principals creates discomfort for district administrators accustomed to conventional hierarchies and qualifications.

Both Riverside and San Sebastian Community School provide particularly pointed illustrations of bureaucratic norms. Both are schools where students score well, and where parents are vociferously supportive and protective. In Riverside, the superintendent admitted: "If you ignore all these other [bureaucratic] issues and you just say what's good for kids, this school is wonderful." But the traditional hierarchical structure is designed to elicit performance through complex rules constraining what schools do and how they spend resources, and that structure of control is inconsistent with school-level autonomy held accountable through performance. Similarly at San Sebastian Community School, the district periodically threatens to compromise the school's operation through one rule or another, which invariably causes parents to defend the school. The head teacher described her role as a buffer between the district and parents:

So where it feels tricky is protecting the school, not me feeling torn between the district, but just not always being sure how to walk the line so that we're not – I mean I feel like we've been able to be the innovative school that we are because we've stayed off the radar screen.

So unconventional high-performing schools may have to "stay off the radar screen," lest they get caught up in the district's bureaucratic machinery.

Other conflicts with districts involved resources, in both a broad and a narrow sense. At Lookout Circle, the primary concern of the district was to find enough principals, and the district felt that the school was "getting more than your fair share of talent, there's too much talent in your school" with two capable co-principals. The district had been trying to re-assign one of the co-principals to another school with greater need; as one co-principal explained the district's practices:

A lot of times VPs are whisked off to be a principal somewhere else. It's like right when they're starting to maybe get that niche or work well together, they're whisked off. Because we've been together now almost two full years, and we're still improving, and we work very very well together, but it took us almost two years to get to this place.

The district agreed to support the co-principalship for two years, but then went back on the agreement. Evidently the district's need for more principals pre-empted the school's desire for co-principals and stability.

A different conflict over financial resources also surfaced in that district. The superintendent admitted that she would not have supported dual principals if it had cost the district additional money, because the inequity of additional resources would have created resentment in other schools: "Well, how can that school have two principals, then why can not everybody have an additional principal? And that would have been a domino into a much bigger fiscal impact." This is an example of what we call the politics of resentment: with restricted resources, any departure from equal treatment is interpreted as favoritism, even in the case of a "throwaway" school with an overworked principal that arguably needed more administrative resources (Grubb, 2006). The district could have mollified resentment with an equity argument, or by defending Lookout Circle was a pilot innovation, or by allowing school-site budgeting, but it chose to stick with a conventional equal distribution of administrative resources.

Even though our sample is limited, these actions suggest that many districts have failed to consider what their roles ought to be in enhancing school-level leadership. Aside from keeping credentialed individuals in the principal's position, there's little vision of how to improve the quality of leadership or nurture innovation, and no real effort to support schools where teachers and principals create different structures. A co-principal in Munson noted about his district:

> Districts tend to just drop you off and let you go. Then they want to know everything. This is just my fourth year being a principal, but I thought there would be a lot more, they say they want a lot of contact and to know everything that's up, but you kind of learn to just tell them everything's fine.

The district where Lookout Circle is located claims to have a theory of action about how it treats schools; the superintendent declared:

> We are very supportive of any initiatives that come from our school sites that from their perspective will help provide stronger support for student learning. Our basic philosophy is that our role in the central office is services support to the school site, not the other way around.

But one of the co-principals noted:

> This school was known as a throwaway school with the throwaway kids and the throwaway principal and the throwaway teachers. When I first came here it was deplorable, deplorable. The process of change was a slow one, in which the district wasn't particularly engaged except to find a better principal.

Evidently, then, the district's claim of supporting schools was at best overstated, and its theory of action in reality was limited to searching for a hero-principal.

Finally, no district we examined had any plan for succession. Most relied on raiding other districts, trying to lure good principals from neighboring districts. The district where Lookout Circle is located claims to have a "grow-your-own" approach; as the superintendent described it:

> Traditionally what is referred to as "vice principals," we call them associate principals because they are actually designed to be a part of our career ladder designating that role for principalship.... It is more of an internship notion to kind of create our own career ladder and our own leadership capacity.

In practice this amounts to training an assistant principal for a couple of years and then sending him or her to another school, sacrificing stability and school ties. The careful selection and mentoring practices in San Sebastian, or the effort in Lookout Circle and Calvin to elevate teachers into principal positions, is nowhere evident in district policy.

Now, we should not overstate our case against districts. The case of Mansfield, described by Chirichello (2003), provides an example where an innovative superintendent worked carefully with a school to support co-principals. In Hillside and Robinson the co-principals have the complete support of the district. But the other seven schools experienced many problems with their districts, suggesting that alternative models of leadership may be difficult to institutionalize unless districts modify their hierarchical practices and become more supportive of innovation.

Conclusions and Recommendations

The Value of Alternative Approaches to School Leadership

There are at least four reasons why these innovations in the principalship matter, even when there appear to be so few of them and when they seem to be so idiosyncratic. First and foremost, they raise explicitly a question that is usually ignored: why should we continue to have schools with traditional administrative structures, particularly a single principal who "owns" a school? The alternatives developed in these ten schools surely do not exhaust the alternatives available, but they begin to show both that different arrangements are possible, and that they have a range of potential benefits. Second, the benefits include closer attention to instructional practices, which principals complain that they often cannot get around to (Flessa, 2003); more attention to support services, neglected in a great many schools (National Research Council, 2004, Ch. 6); and greater availability to students, teachers, and parents. Third, alternative approaches have the potential for resolving the overload on principals, the impossibility of a job with increasing responsibilities, a "job too big for one person." If these alternatives could reduce the turnover in principals, or make the principalship more attractive to teachers, this alone might be worth the costs of reform.

Finally, these alternatives enable us to understand somewhat better what positions of leadership entail. The issues of specialization and interchangeability are part of the more general issue of distributed leadership. The potential for distributing responsibility among leaders as well as between leaders and teachers becomes more obvious in these alternative approaches. The problem of succession, woefully neglected in many districts, has several solutions that are clarified particularly by the cases of San Sebastian and Riverside. The emergence of many dual principalships as a result of increasing size, the small schools rationale, illustrates a leadership problem with large schools, quite different from the problems that students experience. Examining leadership in unfamiliar settings can help us better understand what problems need to be resolved even in familiar settings and even when leadership reform is impossible.

If alternative approaches to the roles of principals have substantial potential benefits, as long as they are carefully implemented in careful ways, the question is then how alternative approaches could be expanded and institutionalized. The standard hierarchy of the rational bureaucratic model is the default position. If support from participants is lacking, if resources dwindle, if teachers become unwilling to undertake leadership roles (as in Manzir), or if a supportive superintendent is replaced by an unsupportive one, then a school is likely to relapse into the standard hierarchy. One co-principal at Onofrio was sure that the school would revert to a conventional structure when the other left, because co-principals had not worked well there – after all, the district had paid no attention to the compatibility of the two – and since "the district is cooling on the idea: there's talk this year with budget cuts that it would be a little less expensive to have one principal and one AP at a site." Reversion had also taken place at another school in the district when one of the co-principals left because she wanted to run her own school. Munson is likely to lose its co-principals because both want their own schools. A couple of co-principals also saw it as natural that administrators would want their own school, as if a solo principal owns a school; as one of them at Munson said, "As much as I love [my co-principal], I really want my own school." And the other said the same thing:

> It's difficult. When you get ready to make schedules or make certain decisions, you have to go and consult this other person. And too, you might have two different styles. I'm kind of deliberate in my decision making. I like to go and get information, get input, and I think about it and let it simmer a little bit. Hers is, it's going to be this way. So it's kind of hard to run a school that way, you know, checking with each other.

The language of ownership is related to the conventional hierarchical model, where a principal "heads" or "runs" or "owns" a school; but no one in collaborative schools like Lookout Circle, Calvin, San Sebastian, or Riverside would speak of "ownership."

One requirement for non-traditional models cited by almost all co-principals and teachers in our sample, is compatible personal relationships. "It all depends on the personalities" of co-principals, one teacher declared; a superintendent stressed "anticipating the chemistry" between two people. One of the co-principals at Robinson was particularly thoughtful in her comments:

> Not anyone can do this. Their personalities must be compatible, they must have low egos, there cannot be any power struggles, and no energy can be spent on who is going to be out front. Trust-building is essential to the co-principalship – a trust in your partner and not feeling intimidated when one or the other co-principal is recognized for accomplishments.

Of course personal relationships and individual motivation are crucial, but they may not be sufficient. Other structural or bureaucratic factors may be necessary as well. One is support from the district – and, as we have seen, districts that work in a conventional bureaucratic style are at best uncomfortable with and at worst actively hostile to alternative approaches. Another is a culture in which teachers are already accustomed to sharing leadership; they can then become co-principals, or rotate into a principal's position, with a minimum of disruption to the school and its priorities. In such schools, principals or lead teachers or directors do not *own* the school; the notion of sharing leadership becomes natural, rather than abnormal. A third crucial factor is the availability of resources. Even though many of these models do not cost appreciably more than conventional schools, some of them may cost more than cash-strapped urban districts will pay, and all of them are vulnerable to the "politics of resentment."

Finally, all these approaches require stability, since an innovative approach requires some time for teachers, parents, and students to become used to it. The process of reforming the principal's role is itself developmental, where early efforts in restructuring roles lead to subsequent changes including newly-defined roles for both principals and teacher-leaders. In unstable schools, with teachers and administrators coming and going and district administrators turning over, it would be necessary to go through a period of learning over and over again, and any innovation would almost surely regress to conventional bureaucratic practices.

In some schools and districts, then, creating alternative principalships may face too many obstacles. But in other cases, schools and districts ought to consider restructuring the principal's role, as part of a broader policy toward leadership development and succession. The benefits for instruction, ancillary support services, other elements of a principal's job that are difficult to get around to, availability to parents and teachers, and reducing the overwhelming pressures of the position are substantial. And while these benefits do not automatically emerge, these case studies clarify what conditions are necessary to facilitate their development.

Similarly, these case studies indicate the need for researchers to consider a variety of alternative practices, rather than assuming that the solo- or hero-principal is the only approach. Surely there are more non-traditional practices than we have uncovered, and the conditions under which they work and fail need to be better understood. And ultimately the benefits that might improve students outcomes – the greater attention to instruction and support services, the potential for reducing the burdens and turnover among urban principals – ought to lead to improved student outcomes, though confirming this relationship will require considerably better understanding of both the types of non-traditional approaches and the conditions under which they do and do not work well.

Like every other reform that promises to enhance the effectiveness of schools, alternative approaches to the principal's position – with all their potential advantages – require considerable institutional energy to create and then to maintain. The current search for stronger leadership could lead to a series of changes – in principal preparation programs surely, but also in teacher programs, in district policies, perhaps in state funding mechanisms, and certainly in conceptions of what organizational structures might work – that support non-traditional approaches to the principalship. If not, given the pressures on schools, we can anticipate ever-worsening conditions for principals, increasing shortages of candidates, continued inattention to instructional leadership, and further domination of the rational bureaucratic model with all its flaws.

Acknowledgments

This chapter has been supported by funds from the David Garner Chair in Higher Education held by the lead author. We thank the other individuals who were involved in the field research: Lynda Tredway and Jane Stern of the Principal Leadership Institute, University of California, Berkeley; Linda Lambert and Margaret Szabo of the Department of Educational Leadership, California State University, Hayward (now East Bay); and Michael Chirichello, Department of Educational Leadership, William Patterson University.

Notes

1 The Institute for Educational Leadership (2000) reports that frustration in strikingly similar language. They state: "The job is simply not 'doable', according to many principals today.... Caught among these competing priorities and pressures principals increasingly see their charge as an impossible proposition" (p. 12).
2 Roza et al. (2003) dispute the convention of overall shortages, but acknowledge that there are genuine shortages in "troubled" districts, most of which are urban. In addition, turnover among principals is higher in schools with more minority students.
3 The exception is the Robinson School in Mansfield, MA, which Chirichello has already described under his own name.
4 When we began our search, we expected to find more elementary or middle schools, partly because high schools are often resistant to experimentation. To some extent our expectations were confirmed, and only one of the ten schools included in this chapter is a high school. However, high schools that have divided themselves into schools-within-schools, or "academies" or "majors" with distinct themes, lend themselves to co-principals in obvious ways, though we have not yet observed any. Similarly, the small schools movement has the potential for developing new formal leadership arrangements.

References

Bryk, A. & Schneider, B. (2002). *Trust in schools: A core resource for improvement.* New York, NY: Russell Sage Foundation.
Carnoy, M., Elmore, R., & Siskin, L. (eds) (2003). *The new accountability: High schools and high-stakes testing.* New York, NY: Routledge Falmer.
Carter, S. (1999). *No excuses: Seven principals of low-income schools who set the standard for high achievement.* Washington, DC: The Heritage Foundation.

Chirichello, M. (2003, March/April). Co-principals: A double dose of leadership. *Principal, 82*, 40–44.

Copland, M. (2001). The myth of the superprincipal. *Phi Delta Kappan, 82*(7), 528–533.

Cuban, L. (1988). *The managerial imperative and the practice of leadership in schools*. Albany, NY: State University of New York Press.

Edmonds, R.R. (1979). Effective schools for the urban poor. *Educational Leadership, 37*, 15–24, 37.

Flessa, J. (2003). *What's urban in the urban school principalship: Case studies of four middle school principals in one city school district*. Unpublished dissertation, Graduate School of Education, University of California, Berkeley.

Flessa, J. (2004). Principal behaviors and school outcomes. In L. Hughes (ed.). *Issues in Educational Leadership* (pp. 265–288). Mahwah, NJ: Lawrence Erlbaum Associates, Inc.

Gilman, D.A. & Lanman-Givens, B. (2001). Where have all the principals gone? *Educational Leadership, 58*(8), 72–74.

Grubb, W.N. (2006). *Multiple outcomes, multiple resources: Testing the "improved" school finance with NELS88*. Unpublished paper.

Grubb, W.N., Huerta, L., & Goe, L. (2006). Straw into gold, resources into results: Spinning out the implications of "improved" school finance. *Journal of Educational Finance, 31*, 334–359.

Honig, M. (2004). The new middle management: Intermediary organizations in educational policy implementation. *Educational Evaluation and Policy Analysis, 26*(1), 65–87.

Ingersoll, R. (2003). *Who controls teachers' work?* Cambridge, MA: Harvard University Press.

Institute for Educational Leadership (2000). *Leadership for student learning: Reinventing the principalship. School leadership for the 21st century initiative: A report of the task force on the principalship*. Retrieved April 1, 2005 from www.iel.org/programs/21st/reports/principal.pdf.

Kantrowitz, B. & Mathews, J. (2007). The role of the principal. *Newsweek*, May 28. Available at http://www.msnbc.msn.com/id/18754330/site/newsweek/.

Krüger, M.L., van Eck, E., & Vermeulen, A. (2005). Why principals leave: Risk factors for premature departure in the Netherlands compared for women and men. *School Leadership and Management, 25*, 241–261.

Leithwood, K., Lawrence, L., & Sharrett, L. (1998). Conditions fostering organizational learning in schools. *Educational Administration Quarterly, 34*, 243–276.

Leithwood, K., Louis, K.S., Anderson, S., & Wahlstrom, K. (2004). *Executive summary: How leadership influences student learning*. Minneapolis, MN: University of Minnesota, Center for Applied Research and Educational Improvement.

Loder, T. & Spillane, J. (2005). Is a principal still a teacher? US women administrators' accounts of role conflict and role discontinuity. *School Leadership and Management, 25*, 263–279.

Marsh, J. (2000). *Connecting districts to the policy dialogue: A review of literature on the relationship of districts with states, schools, and communities*. Working paper. Seattle, WA: Center for the Study of Teaching and Policy, University of Washington.

Meier, D. (1995). *The power of their ideas: Lessons for America from a small school in Harlem*. Boston, MA: Beacon Press.

Mishler, E. (1986). *Research interviewing: Context and narrative*. Cambridge, MA: Harvard University Press.

National Research Council (2003). *Engaging schools: Fostering high school students' motivation to learn*. Washington, DC: National Academies Press.

Pounder, D. & Merrill, R. (2001a). Job desirability of the high school principalship: A job choice theory perspective. *Educational Administration Quarterly, 37*, 27–57.

Pounder, D. & Merrill, R. (2001b). Lost luster. *School Administrator, 58*, 18.

Roza, M., Celio, M.B., Harvey, J., & Wishon, S. (2003). *A matter of definition: Is there truly a shortage of school principals?* Seattle, WA: Center on Reinventing Public Education, University of Washington.

Spillane, J. (2001). Investigating school leadership practice: A distributed perspective. *Educational Researcher, 30*(3), 23–28.

Stein, M. & Nelson, B. (2003). Leadership content knowledge. *Educational Evaluation and Policy Analysis, 25*, 423–448.

Togneri, W. & Anderson, S. (2003). *Beyond islands of excellence: What districts can do to improve instruction and achievement in all schools – a leadership brief. A project of the Learning First Alliance.* Washington, DC: Association for Supervision and Curriculum Development (ASCD).

Tyack, D. & Cuban, L. (1995). *Tinkering toward utopia: A century of public school reform.* Cambridge, MA: Harvard University Press.

Valentine, J., Clark, D., Hackmann, D., & Petzko, V. (2003). *A national study of leadership in middle-level schools.* Arlington, VA: National Association of Secondary School Principals.

Yee, G. (1999). *Divided loyalties: How teachers change when they become principals.* Paper presented at the American Educational Research Association, Montreal.

Part 3
Explaining the Effects of Distributed Leadership

8

Conceptualizing Distributed Leadership as a School Reform

Revisiting Job Redesign Theory

DAVID MAYROWETZ, JOSEPH MURPHY,
KAREN SEASHORE LOUIS, AND MARK A. SMYLIE

In recent years, educators have been trying to create "distributed leadership" in their schools, often with the support of influential groups in the educational leadership policy community. Generally these reforms involve groups of teachers becoming formal leaders by undertaking tasks they would not traditionally have done, including some that would be perceived as administrative. In this chapter, we revive work redesign theory, specifically Hackman and Oldham's Job Characteristics Model (JCM), as a tool to examine these distributed leadership initiatives and to predict the success or failures of these efforts. Based on our early observations of six schools engaged in distributed leadership reform and a broad review of literature, including empirical tests of work redesign theory inside and outside schools, we retrofit the JCM by: (1) adding more transition mechanisms to explain how changes in work could lead to the widespread performance of leadership functions; (2) accounting for the fact that distributed leadership reform is a group work redesign; and most important, (3) enumerating relevant contextual variables that should impact the development, shape, and success of such reforms. We conclude with suggestions for future directions in the research of distributed leadership reforms.

The "buzz" surrounding *distributed leadership* has traveled beyond a small circle of education researchers and with its spread has followed uncertainty about what the term actually means (Mayrowetz, in press). While authors of other chapters in this book conceive of distributed leadership as originally intended, a theoretical lens to examine the activity of school leadership (Gronn, 2000; Spillane et al., 2001), we have witnessed that many educators in schools consider distributed leadership to be a prescription for school reform. Generally, these reforms are characterized by groups of teachers becoming formal leaders and undertaking tasks they would not do traditionally, including some work that would be perceived as administrative.

In many schools, the impetus for distributed leadership reform can be traced to state policy makers and influential members of the educational leadership policy network like the Education Commission of the States, the Council of Chief State School Officers and the Wallace Foundation. Promoting distributed leadership as a prescription for school improvement has been a focus in the second round of State Action Education Leadership Projects, activities supported by the three organizations above and others.

Like any school reform, some of these distributed leadership initiatives will succeed and others will not. As researchers interested in the organizational change that distributed leadership projects are trying to achieve, we needed a conceptual model – distinct from the activity theory-based formulations of Spillane and colleagues (2001) – to study these reforms. The goal of this chapter is to provide readers with one framework that can help us understand the success or failure of these distributed leadership projects in different school contexts.

One, almost obvious, way to think about these distributed leadership initiatives is as work redesign. Specifically, if distributed leadership in schools is to begin, teachers must start to conceive of their roles differently and must assume responsibilities beyond their classrooms for purposes of overall school improvement. As teachers' jobs are redefined in this model, so too must administrators' jobs if they are to maintain their function as supporting teachers and setting the conditions for their success. Administrators will need to do more than delegate tasks or relinquish authority; they must manage the boundaries among several workgroups, while being active participants within them. Moreover, they must coordinate work done in these groups to maintain coherence in the building. Finally, teachers and administrators need to relate to each other in new ways, given these redefined roles and workplace responsibilities.

A few years ago, two of us first argued that if properly enacted, distributed leadership reforms are essentially a form of work redesign that holds great promise for school improvement (Mayrowetz & Smylie, 2004). Extending that work, the central premise of this chapter is that often overlooked theories of work redesign reopen a well-worn but under-utilized path for understanding the development, implementation, and success of distributed leadership reforms in schools. In this chapter, we revive work redesign theory, specifically Hackman and Oldham's (1980) JCM and customize it to the study of distributed leadership. Our retrofitting process is informed by three sources: meta-analyses of the JCM, empirical evidence drawn from other redesign efforts in schools (e.g. career ladders, participative decision making), and our initial observations from the first two rounds of data collection in six secondary schools purposefully trying to enact distributed leadership. These sources lead us to a number of additional theoretical lenses that we believe are necessary to bring to bear for understanding the development of distributed leadership in schools, their eventual success or failure, and, in turn, school improvement.

In the rest of this chapter, we refresh our readers' memories about Hackman and Oldham's theory and model. Then, we present an elaborated JCM to guide the study of distributed leadership in schools, highlighting the addition of two new transition mechanisms as well as several contextual variables that serve as moderators and antecedents to our model. We conclude with suggestions for future research in understanding distributed leadership reforms.

The Original JCM

In *Work Redesign*, Hackman and Oldham (1980) contend that a major factor in organizational improvement is the "person-job relationship," (p. 4). They claim that many problems in the workplace can be traced to the design of work rather than the will of employees to engage it. By focusing on "the work itself" (p. 42), they argue, employers can increase internal work motivation, which eventually leads to higher employee productivity and effectiveness. Their theory is outlined in the JCM displayed in Figure 8.1.

Central to their model (both figuratively and literally) are the "critical psychological states" which the redesign of work is meant to create. Hackman and Oldham (1980) believe that employees should experience greater meaningfulness in their work if they are required to use a variety of skills, if they accomplish a unique and identifiable task from start to finish, and if their work is significant. Employees should feel more responsible for their work when they are given autonomy. Finally, as long as employees are provided with adequate feedback, they will know the results of their work. In sum, if work entails the five core job characteristics on the left, employees will start to experience their work in ways that will motivate them to better outcomes which are shown on the right.

Hackman and Oldham (1980) recognize that a few conditions would moderate the process of redesigned work leading to motivated and productive employees. They hypothesize that individual employees' knowledge and skill and their desire to achieve in the face of challenges and grow professionally (i.e. growth need) would impact whether redesigned work would have the desired effect. They believe that an employee's satisfaction with the workplace would also affect internal motivation and workplace efficiency as well.

Strengths and Weaknesses of the Job Characteristics Model

Researchers have employed the JCM for over a quarter century. Meta-analyses and rigorous empirical research in a variety of settings demonstrate that the model is robust enough to provide an excellent starting point for examining the creation and consequences of a work redesign like distributed leadership (Fried & Ferris, 1987; Johns et al., 1992). Both the multi-dimensionality

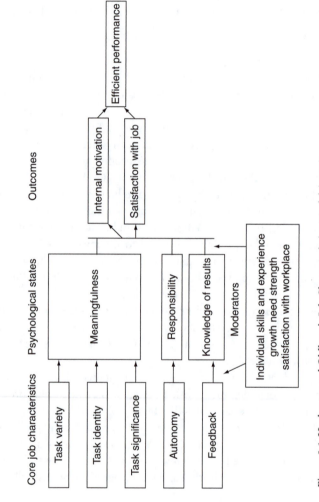

Core job characteristics   Psychological states   Outcomes

Task variety

Task identity

Task significance

Meaningfulness

Autonomy

Responsibility

Feedback

Knowledge of results

Internal motivation

Satisfaction with job

Efficient performance

Moderators

Individual skills and experience
growth need strength
satisfaction with workplace

Figure 8.1 Hackman and Oldham's Job Characteristics Model (1980)

of work redesign, and the correlation of core job characteristics to affective and behavioral outcomes are well-established (Fried & Ferris, 1987).

However, these studies also demonstrate four weaknesses in the original JCM that pose problems to its applicability for studying distributed leadership. First, the research suggests some uncertainty about the role of psychological states as intervening variables. A meta-analysis found that the model worked fine without them (Fried & Ferris, 1987), while another study believed they were important mediators between the core characteristics and the affective and behavioral outcomes (Johns et al., 1992). Most recently, Renn and Vanderberg (1995) concluded that the critical psychological states were only partial mediators.

Second, one of the key findings of the empirical tests of the JCM is that the "relationship between job characteristics and psychological outcomes is more consistent and stronger than the relationship between job characteristics and behavioral outcomes" (Fried & Ferris, 1987, p. 313). That is, the JCM predicts employee motivation and job satisfaction better than it predicts job performance.

Third, researchers are not quite sure how moderators relate to the rest of the model. While Fried and Ferris (1987) find some of their effects to be "largely artifactual" (p. 314), others conclude that individual and contextual variables did have significant relationships to the model (Johns et al., 1992; Loher et al., 1985). Interestingly though, sometimes the moderators from the original JCM operate in the direction opposite to what was expected. In recent years, there have been claims that the JCM is too "context-insensitive" and that it suffers from "important missing components … [including] limited consideration of the contingencies likely to moderate these links [between job characteristics and outcomes]" (Parker et al., 2001, p. 417).

Finally, the JCM is more readily applicable to the study of work redesign for individual employees than for groups. While Hackman and Oldham (1980) devote a section of their book to group work redesign, they largely focus on how the internal workings of the group (e.g. norms and composition) can predict effectiveness. They pay scant attention to organizational factors.

Work Redesign in Schools

An examination of research in schools that is framed by theories of work redesign also provides guidance for how to improve upon the JCM and customize it for a school reform. In the main, research using work redesign theory in schools has been fruitful and its results reinforce the assessments of strengths and weaknesses of the model noted above. Studies demonstrate the power of "enriched work" (i.e. work that shares the core job characteristics of the JCM). For example, teachers who assume non-teaching duties, and therefore have higher skill variety, tend to have better attitudes about their jobs (Rosenblatt, 2001).

With work redesign efforts in schools though (e.g. career ladders, the creation of formal mentor positions, teaming, and participative decision making) there is little spillover from positive emotions to improved performance. For example, teachers in formal mentors roles frequently gain professional satisfaction from working with protégés (Hart, 1985) and most studies show positive affective outcomes from mentoring for veteran and new teachers (Smylie, 1997). However, the results of teacher mentoring program on student achievement are mixed. Similarly, lead teacher programs have had "few benefits at the classroom level" (Smylie, 1997, p. 548) or for other teachers within the building (Smylie, 1994). Participative decision making (PDM) can increase teachers' sense of organizational responsibility (Smylie, 1997) and self-efficacy (Lee et al., 1991), but does little to change instructional behaviors or improve student achievement (Conway, 1984). In fact, too much or too little participation can be counterproductive and lead to dissatisfaction (Conway, 1976). Teacher teaming can lead to professional satisfaction (Crow & Pounder, 2000) and student satisfaction with their teachers (Pounder, 1999), and even teacher self-reports of improved effectiveness (Conley et al., 2004) but generally speaking, the impact of teacher teams rarely leads to student achievement or the overall improvement of the school (Smylie et al., 2002). The general conclusion that we draw from these studies is that the redesign of work in schools does lead to beneficial affective outcomes for the employees whose job is changed but that these effects only reach others rarely. Moreover, we are left to wonder whether the JCM or possibly the redesign efforts themselves are missing elements by which researchers can find wider, behavioral impacts.

Furthermore, in school settings, moderating variables at both the individual and organizational levels were very important in most studies of job redesign efforts. An individual characteristic like years of experience, proved important when studying a career ladder program in Utah. Novice teachers were attracted by the program but it did not make them more likely to stay in their district or in the teaching profession (Hart, 1994; Murphy et al., 1989). However, mid-career teachers said they were more likely to remain in their districts because of it (Ebmeier & Hart, 1992). Organizational components like the trust in a principal can also be crucial. When educators perceive a PDM initiative as a principal's technique for manipulating them, they view that work redesign with skepticism (Firestone, 1977).

Finally, we note that in schools there are both collective and individual work redesigns. Teacher career ladders and mentor programs redesign an individual's work. Teacher teams and the participative decision making policies popular in the 1990s have a collective orientation. These collective work redesigns seem to share a common goal, to foster collaboration and reverse the tradition of teacher isolation in schools.

Our interpretation of these meta-analyses and the empirical studies of work redesign in schools is that the contours of the JCM are sturdy enough and well-suited for understanding distributed leadership projects in schools. However, the original incarnation of the JCM has some important deficiencies generally, and in relation to schools as workplaces specifically. The first problematic area is the strong focus on individual level redesign at the expense of group redesign. Second, the role of motivation as the sole transition mechanism from redesigned work to effectiveness outcomes is questionable. The intervening effect of the three psychological states in the JCM are in doubt and there is a tendency of work redesign research to be more useful for describing affective outcomes like employee satisfaction. In schools, the research usually indicates positive outcomes only for those whose work is redesigned. To study distributed leadership, a reform that is supposed to lead to overall school improvement, we need a better understanding of how redesigned work can lead to behavioral outcomes school wide.

The final underdeveloped area is the insufficient recognition of the importance of context-specific moderating variables. Since we are going to look at a reform that has such broad goals in a complex organization, our model needs to account for more than individual level moderators. We will need to include organizational moderators that impact the process of implementing distributed leadership. In fact, these organizational characteristics can even shape the original design of the reform and serve as antecedents to this model.

An Elaborated Model for the Study of Distributed Leadership

With all of the accumulated wisdom about the JCM and empirical evidence from redesign efforts in schools, we propose a model that elaborates the JCM to understand distributed leadership projects in schools (see Figure 8.2). This model contains our best understanding of how and why efforts to develop distributed leadership in schools would operate and serves as a starting point for predicting the success (or failure) of these reforms. Our conceptual model outlines additional mechanisms by which changes in work would lead to psychological and behavioral outcomes. Recognizing the importance of context, we add multiple moderating/antecedent variables at the organizational level to the individual moderators suggested by the original model.

We note that this model is also based in part, on our early impressions of distributed leadership reforms in six schools. Through some initial rounds of explanation building (Yin, 2004) at regular meetings and the first author's review of completed case study protocols designed to tap our initial theorizing about our schools (Yin, 2004), we determined that all of these additional transition mechanisms and antecedent/moderators were important to distributed leadership development and implementation.

We emphasize that the goal of this manuscript is to provide the field with new insights into how to predict whether distributed leadership projects will take hold and work in schools. Whether distributed leadership can actually

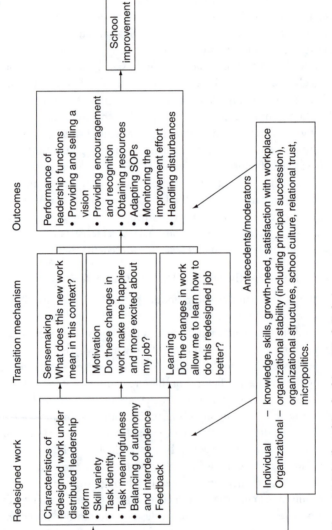

Figure 8.2 Distributed Leadership as Work Redesign

lead to school improvement, and if so, under what conditions, are important empirical questions beyond the scope of what we are trying to achieve here, as we discuss at the end of this chapter.

First, we explicate our model in greater detail. To do this, we start with a description of how these "distributed leadership" projects, at their core, work redesign for both teachers and administrators. In doing so, we provide details of how the five original core job characteristics are important aspects in distributed leadership reform and how they might impact its success or failure. After defining what we mean by the implementation of distributed leadership, we describe how motivation, learning, and sensemaking are transition mechanisms for turning jobs with the characteristics into distributed leadership practice. Then, we look at five contextual antecedent/moderators in greater detail and demonstrate their importance throughout the process of developing distributed leadership, from how they shape the formulation of redesigned work for teachers and administrators, to the way they affect the transition mechanisms, to how they could influence the performance of leadership functions.

Distributed Leadership and the Core Job Characteristics

Based on experiences in our six case study schools, we believe that the original five core job characteristics encompass much of the important aspects of educators' work in the context of a distributed leadership reform. We discuss each job characteristic briefly here and how distributed leadership reforms would influence these elements.

Skill Variety

One of the more recognizable ways in which these distributed leadership reforms redesign work is that they require teachers and administrators to use a variety of skills. Of course, both traditional classroom teaching and school administration are complex and multi-dimensional activities that call upon educators to utilize several technical and interpersonal skills. But when teachers and administrators agree to work together, through distributed leadership, to address the panoply of issues facing schools, many of these skills and more, must be utilized. There can be little doubt that implementing distributed leadership expands the scope of educators' jobs.

State officials overseeing the distributed leadership projects in three of our schools recognized that educators needed to learn or re-learn communication techniques and interpersonal skills to facilitate the uptake of these distributed leadership programs, especially in struggling schools. They hired a consultant to work with successive cohorts of educators from these schools to build such skills.

We hypothesize that as distributed leadership reforms increase skill variety, many educators will become more motivated, as the original JCM predicts.

Simultaneously though, implementers will need to attend to the learning mechanisms (i.e. educators need to learn how to use more skills well) so that the motivation inspired by the greater skill variety can be sustained and lead to denser and more effective leadership practice.

Task Significance

Teachers and administrators already are likely to conceive of their work as significant. However, if educators have their jobs redesigned, there is a danger that they might see their new work, which takes time from their traditional responsibilities, as less meaningful. Specifically, a teacher might feel that any time not spent directly focused on her students is time wasted. On the other hand, one could argue that if teachers engage in new work affecting the whole school, they could perceive that work as highly significant (Willower, 1991). Similarly, administrators need to understand that developing the desire and capacity of teachers to engage in leadership practice is worthwhile and does not threaten their power and authority. Thus, we propose that initiators of distributed leadership in schools will need to "sell" the significance of distributed leadership more than might be expected of work redesigns in other environments to activate the motivational and educational potential of the new work.

Task Identity

Unlike these first two core job characteristics, teachers generally do not experience a great deal of task identity in their traditional work. Like workers on an assembly line, teachers who are "egg-cartoned" in their classrooms might understand their job as taking students from one point to the next (i.e. teaching third grade in preparation for fourth grade). Participating in a distributed leadership reform could enable teachers to climb out of their discipline- and classroom-based mentalities and develop a more system-level understanding of the school and how to improve outcomes for students. Distributed leadership could become an antidote to "a fragmented and incoherent instructional program stem[ming] from weak instructional leadership and … maintained through dysfunctional intraschool communication and norms of noninterference" (Maxcy & Nguyen, 2006, p. 169). Teachers' redesigned work can have task identity if it begins with the creation of a vision and continues through monitoring (see section on leadership functions below). In sum, we predict that through these distributed leadership reforms, educators (especially teachers) can have more task identity that can motivate them and enable them to understand how the school operates.

Autonomy

When viewing distributed leadership as a reform effort, a repeated refrain about its novelty is the push for collective responsibility. One of the earliest calls for distributed leadership urged:

everyone associated with schools – principals, teachers, school staff members, district personnel, parents, community members, and students – to take responsibility for student achievement and to assume leadership roles in areas in which they are competent and skilled ... collective responsibility breeds ownership.

(Neuman & Simmons, 2000, p. 10)

On the other hand, we must recognize that individual autonomy and independence are hallmarks of teachers' work in classrooms (Little, 1990). While several important decisions regarding curricula and content standards are made without their direct input, many teachers believe they can close their classroom door and isolate themselves from interference. So ironically, being a part of a team of teachers and administrators and working on a new initiative within a distributed leadership framework might actually decrease the individual autonomy that a teacher experiences. Indeed, as distributed leadership requires joint work the result can easily be interdependence rather than individual autonomy.

Simultaneously, distributed leadership allows for some measure of collective autonomy for an entire team of educators. That is, a team of teachers may be autonomous in determining the focus and nature of its work. Still, the tension exists between allowing a group to have autonomy and providing specific direction from administrators who are frequently seen as accountable by external actors and as formal organizational leaders by internal ones. We are reminded that "it is important to achieve a balance point between the team's desire for decision making authority and the organization's need for coordination and control" (Conley et al., 2004, p. 693).

Therefore, we believe that distributed leadership reforms will likely decrease individual autonomy of teachers in their traditional work, but may enhance their collective autonomy in their new work. Administrator autonomy will likely decrease within a distributed leadership reform as their traditional work arenas may be open to scrutiny not only from their superiors but also from their faculties. This general shift toward collective autonomy should lead to successful distributed leadership practice given proper organizational conditions like a deep reservoir of trust, healthy micropolitics, and organizational stability (see below).

Feedback

Hackman and Oldham (1980) argue that the best form of feedback comes from the work itself. In a complex endeavor like education, accurate feedback from work is difficult to obtain, but it is possible through techniques like action research and collective inquiry. Since these types of activities often require forethought and planning, we argue that distributed leadership initiatives that neglect some purposeful collection of data about implementation may fail to activate the motivational and educational potential of new work. With or without systematic data collection, the manner in which educators make sense of the initiative and learn from it will be crucial for the success of a distributed leadership reform.

Distributed Leadership Practice

Over the past several decades, the definition of leadership in our field has evolved from individual traits, to an organizational quality (Ogawa & Bossert, 1995), to the descriptive version of distributed leadership – an idea so conceptually vast that it is difficult to separate what does and does not constitute leadership (Lakomski, 2005). For purposes of our model, which focuses on distributed leadership as a tangible reform that could lead to school improvement. Because the original conception of distributed leadership is for description, not for action, there are not many powerful definitions of what a successful distributed leadership reform might look like.

For our model, we select a formulation of leadership that minimizes the importance of role and foregrounds functions. Heller and Firestone's six leadership functions:

- providing and selling a vision;
- providing encouragement and recognition;
- obtaining resources;
- adapting standard operating procedures (SOPs);
- monitoring the improvement effort; and
- handling disturbances

provide a straightforward and concise framework for understanding what leadership might look like in a school with a successful distributed leadership program. They have been empirically tested in the implementation of a social problem solving reform (Heller & Firestone, 1995) and the inclusion of students with special needs in general education classrooms (Mayrowetz & Weinstein, 1999). Spillane et al. (2004) recognized similar "macrofunctions" as crucial for understanding the practice of leadership in schools and others have borrowed this specific framework to study distributed leadership (Maxcy & Nguyen, 2006).

We discuss two important elements of the practice of distributed leadership to demonstrate how these six macro-functions capture some of the work of teachers and administrators as they implement it.

One crucial task in a distributed leadership endeavor is boundary management. Traditionally, the two boundaries that are most important for administrators to attend to are the one between the technical core of teachers and administrators and the one between the school and the community in which it sits. In a school engaged in distributed leadership reform, there are likely to be multiple boundaries to manage, including ones between internal groups of educators that include teachers and administrators, all working on separate but interdependent projects. As organizational theorists have pointed out, for groups to maintain their identities but not be too isolated from the whole organization, group boundaries need "continual management to ensure that it becomes neither too sharply delineated nor too permeable" (Sundstrom et al., 1990, p. 130). In terms of the leadership functions, this type of boundary management is essentially monitoring the innovation of distributed leadership and we imagine that without its adequate performance, eventual school improvement is unlikely.

A related activity in distributed leadership reform is "crafting coherence" (Honig & Hatch, 2004), which is necessary at the school level as well as the district level. If distributed leadership initiatives are to facilitate more open and democratic decision-making processes (Neuman & Simmons, 2000), teachers or other members of the school community will bring their agendas together with those of administrators and external forces whose influence is always present (e.g. school districts, local business groups). With all of these agendas converging, there is a danger that confusion and compromise will lead to incoherence in the school. All educators, but especially administrators who still maintain the formal authority and accountability in schools, must ensure that a coherent vision is established and maintained. These kinds of actions are captured under the first function, providing and selling a vision, and again, without performance of it, schools are unlikely to improve.

Transition Mechanisms

With both the changes in the design characteristics of the work and the practice of distributed leadership explicated, we now focus on transition mechanisms. How do these job characteristics translate into educators engaging in leadership, as defined by multiple individuals performing the six functions?

Motivation

In the original JCM, Hackman and Oldham (1980) believed that a more stimulating work experience would motivate employees to become more satisfied and productive. They proposed:

> When a job is high in motivating potential, people who work on the job tend to experience positive affect when they perform *well*. And performing well, for most people, means producing high quality work of which one can be proud.
>
> (p. 91, emphasis in original)

The potency of work redesign to motivate employees, including teachers, is substantial. For example, teacher teaming has a strong motivational impact and can lead to significantly more teacher satisfaction, professional commitment, and even knowledge of students (Pounder, 1999).

However, as we suggested above, the JCM's sole focus on motivation has clearly kept researchers from looking to other processes that might promote or inhibit the translation of redesigned work into changes in workplace performance. In the shorthand of policy implementation, the JCM has been able to demonstrate how redesigned work is able to spur increased will but it has not shown much in terms of changes in capacity.

In this elaborated model for understanding distributed leadership reforms, we argue that researchers need to consider more than the motivational impact of work redesign. We need to think of other mechanisms by which redesigned work will lead to the widespread leadership practice. We posit that distributed leadership as job redesign will succeed when educators learn how to perform these leadership tasks. Moreover, educators' perceptions of this distributed leadership initiative, and of their school community, will impact their willingness to engage leadership work. We start with the importance of sensemaking.

Sensemaking

Since Karl Weick introduced the notion of sensemaking into the organizational literature in the late 1970s, it has proven to be an important bridge between psychological (i.e. individual-focus) and sociological (i.e. collective-focus) perspectives on organizations. On the one hand, individuals can be said to "make sense" of their individual experiences in organizations (Harris, 1994), largely operating through "schemas" or "mental models" that individuals bring to the setting (Harris, 1994; Louis, 1980). On the other hand, most scholars argue that the organization itself is a social construct within which people test their individual schemas in organized and informal settings, and create a collective understanding that is greater than (or at least different from) the sum of the individual parts.

In particular, it is argued that the concept of organizational culture is a collective phenomenon (it is not possible to reduce the concept of culture to individual attitudes and behaviors) that is based in a collective sensemaking process (Harris, 1994; Louis et al., 2005; Ouchi & Wilkins, 1985). Furthermore, the relationship between individual and organization is dynamic. Under conditions of organizational change, like a distributed leadership project, individual responses help to shape the emerging culture or group shifts. Simultaneously, how individuals respond is also affected by the collective "sense" that members have about "how things should be around here" (Gioia et al., 1994).

What does it mean to "make sense" of a change as radical as a redesigned workplace or job? In general, most popular and scholarly authors assume that changes in a job (e.g. increases in skill variety, task significance and/or autonomy) produce significant stress – stress that in the original JCM, is handled individually. When approached from a collective sensemaking perspective, successful job redesign involves drawing on the organizational culture and creating a new collective set of beliefs that permit the change to take hold among most members, despite stress. Some of the characteristics of the existing organizational culture that support more effective transitions (both of individuals and the group) are unsurprising and consistent with research in schools – trust, and the collective empowerment of the group (Mishra & Spreitzer, 1998).

Studies of other organizational disruptions, like downsizing – which has no apparent positive benefit for individuals, indicate that it is the ability of the "survivors" to make sense of their changed jobs, social context, and functions that allow them to move forward (McKinley et al., 2000). Trice and Beyer (1984) argue that transitions in jobs are often accompanied by participation in rites and rituals that permit people to move forward. In schools, a rite of passage might be an election of teachers to leadership roles. A rite of renewal would be a professional development activity in which a school adopts a new model of teacher leadership, even if everyone acknowledges it to be limited in scope and potential impact.

Learning

The other transition mechanism we add is learning. If teachers are being asked to perform new "enriched work" in this distributed leadership initiative, they will likely need to learn how. Consider, for example, that the skills required to perform the first leadership function, providing and selling a vision, may extend beyond a teacher's traditional repertoire. However, there is a knowledge base about how to exercise influence in this way – how to become a change agent – that might be applicable. Learning from administrators and others within the school community would be a first logical place to acquire these skills. As teachers process information in groups, they will likely generate creative solutions that for some kinds of problems are better than those that could have been found alone. This process of organizational learning is extremely important:

> We identify renewal of the overall enterprise as the underlying phenomenon of interest and organizational learning as a principal means to this end.... [We are] presenting organizational learning as four processes – intuiting, interpreting, integrating, and institutionalizing – linking the individual, group, and organizational levels.
>
> (Crossan et al., 1999, p. 522)

But Brown and Duguid (2001) argue that when we emphasize the importance of "communities of practice," we often overemphasize community and underemphasize practice. In schools, where a lot of knowledge is practice-based, this means that too little attention is given to who knows what, how more knowledge can be attained, and how it can be spread.

To complicate the concept of learning though, we have in mind not only technical learning, but also non-traditional types of learning that are seemingly invisible, both to people in and outside the organization (Weick, 1991). Specifically, adaptations made by high school teachers to long-standing state policies often involve change, but even the teachers themselves have difficulty articulating what is happening in their classrooms as a result of conversations with their colleagues (Louis et al., 2005). Learning may also appear discontinuous, as when there is a major "comprehensive change program" introduced and many practices are disrupted at once, or when a new policy (like data-based decision making) unexpectedly alters the expectations of teachers (Louis et al., 2005). In addition, in schools (as in other organizations), learning about how to do professional work does not require the formal process of unlearning, formally confronting new ideas, testing them out in practice, and the like. Instead, it is gradual, involves trial-and-error, and learning from small errors (Kuwada, 1998).

Moderator/Antecedents

The second major elaboration that we make to the JCM is the addition of organizational level moderators. As we did when briefly describing motivation as a transition mechanism, we stipulate to the importance of an existing element in the model, in this case, the individual level moderators like growth need (i.e. the desire of an employee to develop professionally and achieve). Further, consistent with Harris' (2004) warning: "It would be naïve to ignore major structural, cultural, and micropolitical barriers operating in schools that make distributed forms of leadership difficult to implement" (p. 19), we include those three variables and two others, trust and organizational stability, to our elaborated model. Further, we argue that these crucial contextual elements not only impact the way distributed leadership is implemented (i.e. they are moderators), but they also shape how distributed leadership is formulated at schools (i.e. they are antecedents). We conclude with organizational history and stability because it is a super ordinate consideration that impacts the other four variables.

Organizational Structure

We begin our elaboration of antecedent/moderators with a discussion of organizational structure. Perhaps it is now axiomatic that organizational theorists have overemphasized the importance of workplace structures like rules and policies, organizational charts, and time-on-task, for the accomplishment of desired work outcomes. Nonetheless organizational structures, particularly those that dictate the division of labor and the organization of time, have direct consequences for organizational processes and outcomes.

Organizational structures are important to consider for a number of reasons. First, they not only reflect an organization's unique history including the decisions of its founders (Bobbitt & Ford, 1980) but also its relationship to its environment, especially in the public sector (Lawrence & Lorsch, 1967/86). Thus, public organizational structures can cue cultural, ideological, or power struggles that exist in the larger society. Moreover, other factors like size, available technology, and the regularities of its institutional sector (Meyer & Rowan, 1977) play influential roles in the development of organizational structures. So, structures can also provide insights about the state of a particular sector and deeply embedded cultural norms.

Second, structures enable and constrain the execution of work. How labor, time, and expertise are divided within an organization influence quality and quantity of work production. For example, while early twentieth-century theorists emphasized efficiency through division and specialization of work, by the middle of the last century some scholars realized that organizing workers in semi-autonomous groups and re-complicating jobs was not only more humane but also more productive (Kelly, 1982).

When a school endeavors a work redesign initiative like distributed leadership, these organizational structures can have a powerful effect on both its design and implementation. First, consider a signature division of labor in high schools – the departmental structure based on discipline specialization. Siskin and Little (1995) relay the strength of the department as they: "form the primary organizational unit of the high school, defining in crucial ways who teachers are, what they do, where and with whom they work, and how that work is perceived by others" (p. 1).

Departments have the potential to balkanize a faculty creating relatively isolated social and professional networks based on subject specific identities (Hargreaves & Macmillan, 1995). Even when departments are intentionally weakened through new groupings of teachers, departmental loyalty can remain extremely powerful (Siskin, 1997). So, integrating a group of teachers and administrators from different grade levels or departments to create a distributed leadership work team may be difficult. Furthermore, when educators attempt to perform leadership functions like creating a shared vision, we can expect difficulties as new groupings of teachers and administrators engage in collective sensemaking of their redesigned work and attempt to practice leadership with an eye toward achieving schoolwide objectives.

Second, consider how the division of time in a day might affect the design and implementation distributed leadership. It is now conventional wisdom that time is a scarce commodity in schools. But if a group of educators is to learn new skills, allow trust levels to increase, and simply accomplish leadership work, there must be a concerted effort to carve out the necessary time in a day, a week, a month, a semester, to let these essential elements of distributed leadership happen. There must be time set aside to seek and consider feedback of any work that occurs by a distributed leadership team. Two important factors that likely influence the availability of time for distributed leadership to take hold and operate effectively are teacher releases from classroom duties, and the presence and use of non-instructional time built into teachers' workdays as agreed upon through collective bargaining.

Perhaps the most important structure when considering the design and implementation of distributed leadership reform is hierarchy – one of the ingrained regularities of the institution of schooling that would be difficult to change. Hierarchies serve many purposes within organizations like motivating subordinates, providing expertise, and setting goals. Work redesign, especially in the form of distributed leadership, can potentially substitute for hierarchy and achieve many of these goals (Lawler, 1988). However, it would seem unlikely that educators would completely abandon or ignore their formal hierarchical roles, especially those who derive power and responsibility from them. Even when a school implements a distributed leadership program well, the hierarchical structure can easily impact the sense that educators make of the reform because formal titles still grant few individuals the ability to perform certain leadership tasks and simultaneously signal power differentials. Though distributed leadership is meant to flatten the hierarchy, existing organizational structures will not disappear completely and some of the unique job responsibilities and status afforded by hierarchy will still impact the implementation of this reform.

As the discussion of departmental structures influencing identity demonstrates, structure and culture are closely intertwined in the way we think about and experience the school context. Next, we attend to school culture.

Organizational and Professional Culture

Historically, organizational culture in schools has been defined as a pattern of artefacts, values, and assumptions that bind a school into a coherent whole (Firestone & Louis, 1999). It is the accumulated product of people working, learning and making sense of their world collectively over time. Since the interpretive turn, this relatively narrow view of culture has been altered to the "tool kit" approach for understanding the relationship between culture and action (Swidler, 1986). Specifically, a cultural tool kit contains an assortment of codes that are used eclectically to guide or rationalize action. This view of culture helps to explain contradictory impulses within a school culture, including the development and maintenance of subcultures. The tool kit metaphor also provides room for an individual agency to exist alongside a fairly consistent schoolwide culture.

Organizational culture is important to understanding the development of distributed leadership because scholars view it as both the key to school reform and a major impediment to it. Deal and Peterson (1999) believe that a good school culture rallies stakeholders around a vision, builds a sense of community, and motivates teachers, administrators, and parents to be more productive and effective in educating children. On the other hand, Sarason (1996) points out that certain regularities in the culture of schooling are harmful and resist efforts to change. In either view, if a distributed leadership reform can disrupt the school culture, as we would expect, norms will likely become more explicit.

One aspect of the school culture that is relevant to the design and implementation of distributed leadership initiatives is the professional culture among educators. In schools where a strong professional culture exists there is likely to be (a) a common language and understanding of how to interact and (b) an understanding of teachers' talents, abilities, and shortcomings. In such a cultural setting, educators should be able to coalesce into effective workgroups and administrators should be more willing to grant autonomy to others performing leadership functions. With a strong professional culture, these workgroups may be more open to learning how to perform these functions well, especially if feedback mechanisms are built into their work. Simultaneously, intense and frequent joint work among educators would likely strengthen the professional culture in that work group and school-wide (Louis et al., 1995).

Professional culture is not necessarily a static condition. There is evidence from many studies that administrators have a tremendous influence on professional culture over time (Leithwood et al., 2004). Cultural turnarounds may take several years, but they are possible where administrators and teachers move beyond simplistic perspectives on school improvement (Louis, 1994). One way to do this is to promote teacher leadership and champion collective learning, (Louis et al., 1996; Marks & Louis, 1999) – strategies that sound a lot like distributed leadership.

In the other extreme, we have seen hints in Louis and Miles' (1990) study of urban high schools that a professional culture can reinforce a sense of dispirited fragmentation in schools where teachers experience eroding working conditions and failure over a long period of time. When educators perceive declining resources and demographic change, it can undermine a strong and cohesive sense of professionalism (Hargreaves, 1994). Additionally, unresolved differences among teachers and between teachers and communities take their toll. Brouilette's (1996) case of "Cottonwood District," documents how enduring divisions among well-intentioned leaders, teachers, and parents created conditions that led to an acrimonious fight over the opening of a new high school, which, in turn, reinforced divisions among teachers about fundamental issues, impeding further effective change. Overall, the evidence of how schools overcome the cultural residue of periods of decline and ineffectiveness is slim.

Relational Trust

Tschannen-Moran and Hoy (2000) deduce that trust involves the willingness of individuals to rely upon others and to make oneself vulnerable to others in that reliance. In their words, trust is "one party's willingness to be vulnerable to another party based on the confidence that the latter party is benevolent, reliable, competent, honest, and open" (p. 556; see also Tschennan-Moran, 2004). In the social science literature, trust is generally considered to be a multi-level concept operating in interactive, systemic ways at the individual and at the group or organizational levels (Tschennan-Moran, 2004; Tschannen-Moran & Hoy, 2000). It is developed initially and perhaps provisionally in a social setting, and then can be strengthened, weakened, breached, lost, and restored. Trust can apply to certain aspects of a personal or organizational relationship and not to other aspects of the same relationship. Trust and distrust may exist simultaneously in the same relationship.

Trust can be influenced by individual predispositions to trust or distrust, histories of trust-related interactions, and disclosures of third parties (Kramer, 1999). It can be derived from social categories or organizational roles persons occupy (e.g. minister, doctor) particularly those that are hierarchical. It can also be derived from the norms, formal rules of conduct, and moral authority of the context in which persons interact (e.g. people in hospitals and churches are likely to be trustworthy) or from explicit transactions (e.g. contracts) that define relationships and expectations for those relationships (Bryk & Schneider, 2002; Kramer, 1999).

According to Coleman (1988), trust is important because it lays the foundation for collective activity, mutual assistance, and joint accountability. In Tschannen-Moran's (2004) view, "Trust allows a person to rest assured in a situation where something that person cares about depends, at least in part, on another person" (p. 33). She continues, that trust is important because it serves, paradoxically, as both a "glue" and a "lubricant" in organizational life. As glue, "trust binds organizational participants to one another" (p. 16). As lubricant, "trust greases the machinery of an organization.... [It] contributes to great efficiency when people can have confidence in other people's words and deeds" (p. 16).

Viewing trust as an antecedent to the model, one can imagine that if levels of trust are high, the local developers of distributed leadership probably would:

- develop distributed leadership work that extends to a wider range of tasks on a wider range of topics than if levels of trust are low (skill variety);
- design work that is more challenging and risky but that may also be more meaningful rather than mundane (task significance);

- limit bureaucratic controls, relying more on the trust relationships as a source of control, and extend greater discretion to those who are to perform distributed leadership work (autonomy);
- incorporate into the design of distributed leadership expectations and processes of collaboration and open, bi-directional communication to promote joint problem identification and problem solving, full and accurate exchange of information, and honest and open assessment and feedback not only of work but of performance, like the BASRC cycle of inquiry (Copland, 2003a) (feedback).

With regard to motivation as a transition mechanism, high levels of trust are likely to promote experiences with distributed leadership work and amplify the motivational potential of the work characteristics. Low levels of trust or distrust are likely to impede, suppress, or negatively affect them. Moreover, if collectively, faculty perceives that trust rather than regulation is "lubricating" distributed leadership, they should be more open to the reform.

Finally, the model suggests that how the transition mechanisms of motivation, sensemaking, and learning to operate to promote the performance of distributed leadership may be moderated by the context in which those leadership functions are to be performed. For example, in the performance of distributed leadership functions, trust relationships among teachers and between principals and teachers are important. In a school where faculty felt they were falling out of a "trustzone," a steering committee of influential teachers lost its ability to sustain a unified vision for school improvement (Maxcy & Nguyen, 2006).

Micropolitics

Explicitly describing the ways in which distributed leadership has a political perspective is crucial to understanding its development and operation (Johnson, 2004). The micropolitical perspective offers an insightful alternative to the rational/structural perspective, as it removes the assumption that administrator control is legitimate (Ball, 1987). With a micropolitical lens schools are viewed as "arenas of struggle" (Ball, 1987, p. 19) where self-interest, power, conflict, alliance, and ideology are all in play.

Like others (Hoyle, 1986), we believe that separating the power structures, policies and rules on the one hand, from the interactions among people on the other, is a helpful way to conceptualize micropolitics. For purposes of elaborating our distributed leadership model, we note that both of these elements, power structures and political interactions – particularly in the form of conflicts – can influence the redesign of work and its transition into leadership performance.

For example, autonomy is one of the job characteristics that our model suggests will motivate educators to perform leadership functions. When teachers are asked to encroach into the administrative sphere, as they are expected to do with distributed leadership reforms, the lines between the instructional and administrative spheres will blur. "Conflict ... seems sure to accompany efforts at redefinition" of these deeply ingrained spheres (Willower, 1991, p. 450). Administrators may struggle to surrender the power that existing hierarchical structures grant them and may not allow workgroups that include teachers to make decisions, take risks, and perform leadership functions for change.

Similarly, micropolitics are certain to appear when administrators manage boundaries within and between various internal groups in a school. For example, as educators iron out the power dynamics within each group, there will likely be conflict. Will the group members tolerate or silence dissent? Will they embrace or avoid the conflict? On the one hand, conflict has the potential to spur learning (Achinstein, 2002). On the other, conflict could produce stress that, in turn, could decrease the motivational potential of the redesigned work. So, micropolitics can also impact the transition mechanisms in our model.

Finally, existing sources of power will influence how the educators make sense of the redesigned work and whether they engage in leadership activities. Storey (2004) recounts one school's experience in which a principal and science department chair differed when considering what distributed leadership meant as a strategy for school improvement. The principal wanted to show immediate student achievement results and hoped that distributed leadership would expose poor teachers and force them out of the building. The science department chair wanted distributed leadership to build the capacity of struggling teachers. "When the conflicting stances became evident, the leaders sought support from their different power bases" (Storey, 2004, p. 262) and "buil[t] coalitions as they engaged in support-building behavior" (p. 263). Presumably, the principal had stronger alliances because the science department chairperson decided the conflict was un-winnable and resigned.

Organizational Stability

The stability of the school organization is our final antecedent/moderator and we include it last because it is a super ordinate consideration that influences the model directly and impacts each of the four organizational characteristics above (i.e. structures, culture, trust and micropolitics). The inclusion of this variable in our model demonstrates one of the enduring paradoxes in the school reform literature – change requires stability.

Employing broad sociological and political lenses along with more applied frames, educational scholars have explored the dynamics and the importance of organizational and leadership stability in schools. For example, it is nearly an article of faith in the practitioner literature that the short tenure of many district CEOs, especially large city superintendents, contributes to the educational problems in the nation in general and to the extended periods of decline in many urban school systems. In a related vein, it is often suggested that because of the complex dynamics of school organizations (e.g. their vulnerability to environmental forces, the absence of tight internal linkages) regularities at the schoolhouse and stability of formal leaders in the principal's office are desirable.

Empirical evidence on the stability in school is: (1) generally derivative; that is, it is not the prime element of interest in most studies, it surfaces in the narrative of other variables (e.g. organizational effectiveness); (2) not especially robust; and (3) consistent with theory and research available more generally.

Regarding staff, Rutter and his colleagues (1979) conclude that stability among a school's teachers is associated with more effective education for urban youngsters. In a recent review of educational effectiveness, Murphy and Datnow (2003) found that "promoting staff stability" (p. 267) was a key element in the principal's toolbox to promote organizational coherence, a condition that is in turn, tightly connected to school improvement.

At the school level, principal stability is also linked to more effective schools. Obviously, instability in formal leadership, especially in the principalship, often signals the demise of improvement efforts (Kilgore & Jones, 2003). Or, as Copland and his colleagues discovered in their study of the Bay Area School Reform Collaborative, "of all the challenges involved in reform work, schools point to leadership turnover as the most disturbing factor in the support and encouragement of reform" (Copland, 2003b, p. 176).

More specifically, concerning distributed leadership, principal stability is critical because "it is the principal who occupies the position to bring teacher leadership to life" (Murphy & Datnow, 2003, p. 266), and "the robustness and viability of distributed leadership is dependent on the support and direction of the principal" (Kilgore & Jones, 2003, p. 43). It is the principal, who in many ways, "must set the stage for teacher leadership and allow teachers to seize the opportunity when they recognize the need" (Kahrs, 1996, p. 27). The principal is in a key position to "set the climate that encourages or stifles teachers' attempts to enter the circle of leadership" (Blegen & Kennedy, 2000, p. 4). It is the principal who must step to the forefront to address the "issues that cause a reluctance among teachers to be leaders" (Bishop et al., 1997, p. 77). The principal also "plays a key role in how effectively the teacher leader functions" (Feiler et al., 2000, p. 68). As Katzenmeyer and Moller (2001) conclude from their extensive analysis, teacher leadership is not a chance organizational event. Where teacher leadership thrives, administrators "make teacher leadership a priority and take risks to provide teacher leaders what they need to succeed" (p. 85). The message in the literature is unambiguous; "principals need to know how to develop, support, and manage these new forms of leadership" (Smylie et al., 2002, p. 182). All of these conclusions from the literature demonstrate how the stability in the principal's office can influence the development and implementation of distributed leadership, primarily through building supportive structures and climate, increasing trust and engaging in productive micropolitics.

Finally, an assortment of researchers has concluded that "stability in district leadership [is] linked to successful school reform" (Murphy & Datnow, 2003, p. 270; see Berends et al., 2003; Datnow & Castellano, 2003). These researchers also find that "where school leadership stability is not on the district radar screen, district leaders are as likely to hinder school improvement efforts as they are to enhance them" (Murphy & Datnow, 2003, p. 271).

In short, our model suggests another paradox when it comes to distributed leadership. Despite the explicit goal that distributed leadership initiatives are meant to flatten hierarchies and empower teachers by having them engage high impact and enriched work, by virtue of their positional and symbolic authority, principals still matter a great deal to these reforms. Without stable, consistent leadership in school and district administration, we hypothesize that a reform with as much work redesign as distributed leadership will be incredibly fragile.

Conclusion

By reviving work redesign theory and retrofitting the JCM, we have accomplished two noteworthy results. First, with the proliferation of distributed leadership initiatives spurred by State Action for Education Leadership Projects (SAELPs) and school reformers, we provide scholars with a familiar and relatively manageable theoretical framework that can explain its processes and outcomes. This achievement is especially important at a time when confusion about the definition of distributed leadership abounds and many practitioners do not conceive it to mean what our colleagues in this volume do. Furthermore, embedded within our model is an element of change over time – researchers can use it to study the development and implementation of distributed leadership reforms. Second, we expand the original JCM to overcome its well-documented deficits and to customize it to the study of a decidedly collective reform, distributed leadership.

But despite taking a major step forward in the research of distributed leadership as work redesign, we believe there are a number of tasks necessary to gain a deeper and more thorough understanding of the phenomenon. First, the varied ways with which the new elements (i.e. organizational antecedent/moderators and transition mechanisms) work within the model and interact with each other must be examined more thoroughly. We have started to do this by interrogating our empirical data and exploring the importance of trust for distributed leadership (Smylie et al., in press), and we expect to continue to refine this model as we analyze the data from our field research using elements of the model and the theoretical lenses they imply.

Most important for both research and practice of distributed leadership, the connection between the multiple performance of leadership and school improvement needs to be established clearly. While scholars who have defined distributed leadership descriptively have been very careful in noting that its presence does not necessarily suggest positive or negative outcomes for schools (Spillane, 2006), many authors who use the term in a more prescriptive sense see distributed leadership as a path to school improvement. We tentatively include school improvement as the ultimate result of multiple performance of leadership functions because we believe that redefined and redesigned work in schools can lead to motivated and better-equipped educators with a broader view of their schools and that these educators, in turn, will perform leadership functions which will both deepen and lengthen reform efforts. Simultaneously though, we recognize that not all people in schools can or should be leaders or will wield their leadership for the common good (Kellerman, 2004). Currently, there is very little evidence that demonstrates a causal connection between multiple leadership function performance and school improvement. We urge researchers to investigate that proposed linkage and provide further explanation as to why distributed leadership can end in positive results for schools and students.

Acknowledgments

This manuscript is largely based upon an article published in *Leadership and Policy in Schools*, 6(1).

The research was supported by a grant from the Laboratory for Student Success at Temple University to Vanderbilt University and a separate grant from Vanderbilt University. Responsibility for the conclusions offered here rests entirely with the authors.

References

Achinstein, B. (2002). Conflict amid community: The micropolitics of teacher collaboration. *Teachers College Record, 104*(3), 421–455.

Ball, S.J. (1987). *The micro-politics of the school*. New York, NY: Methuen.

Berends, M., Bodilly, S., & Kirby, S.N. (2003). New American schools: District and school leadership for whole school reform. In J. Murphy & A. Datnow (eds) *Leadership lessons from comprehensive school reforms* (pp. 109–131). Thousand Oaks, CA: Corwin.

Bishop, H.L., Tinley, A., & Borman, B.T. (1997). A contemporary leadership model to promote teacher leadership. *Action in Teacher Education, 19*(3), 77–81.

Blegen, M.B. & Kennedy, C. (2000). Principals and teachers: Leading together. *NASSP Bulletin, 84*(6), 1–6.

Bobbitt Jr, H.R. & Ford, J.D. (1980). Decision-maker choice as a determinant of organizational structure. *The Academy of Management Review, 5*(1), p. 13–23.

Brouillette, L. (1996). *A geology of school reform: The successive restructurings of a school district*. Albany, NY: SUNY.

Brown, J.S. & Duguid, P. (2001). Knowledge and organization: A social-practice perspective. *Organization Science, 12*(2), 198–213.

Bryk, A.S. & Schneider, B. (2002). *Trust in schools: A core resource for improvement*. New York, NY: Russell Sage Foundation.

Coleman, J.S. (1988). Social capital in the creation of human capital. *American Journal of Sociology, 94* (Supplement), S95–S120.

Conley, S., Fauske, J., & Pounder, D.P. (2004). Teacher work group effectiveness. *Educational Administration Quarterly, 40*(4), 663–703.

Conway, J.A. (1976). Test of linearity between teachers' participation in decision making and their perceptions of their schools as organizations. *Administrative Science Quarterly, 21*(1), 130–139.

Conway, J.A. (1984). The myth, mystery, and mastery of participative decision making in education. *Educational Administration Quarterly, 20*(3), 11–40.

Copland, M.A. (2003a). Leadership of inquiry: Building and sustaining capacity through school improvement. *Educational Evaluation and Policy Analysis, 25*(4), 375–396.

Copland, M.A. (2003b). The Bay Area School Reform Collaborative: Building capacity to lead. In J. Murphy & A. Datnow (eds) *Leadership lessons from comprehensive school reforms* (pp. 159–183). Thousand Oaks, CA: Corwin.

Crow, G.M. & Pounder, D.G. (2000). Interdisciplinary teacher teams: Context, design, and process. *Educational Administration Quarterly, 36*(2), 216–254.

Crossan, M.M., Lane, H.W., & White, R.E. (1999). An organizational learning framework: From institution to institution. *The Academy of Management Review, 24*(3), 522–537.

Datnow, A. & Castellano, M. (2003). Success for all: District and school leadership. In J. Murphy & A. Datnow (eds) *Leadership lessons from comprehensive school reforms* (pp. 187–208). Thousand Oaks, CA: Corwin.

Deal, T.E. & Peterson, K.D. (1999). *Shaping school culture: The heart of leadership.* San Francisco, CA: Jossey-Bass.

Ebmeier, H. & Hart, A.W. (1992). The effects of a career ladder program on school organizational processes. *Educational Evaluation and Policy Analysis, 14*(3), 261–281.

Feiler, R., Heritage, M., & Gallimore, R. (2000). Teachers leading teachers. *Educational leadership, 57*(7), 66–69.

Firestone, W.A. (1977). Participation and influence in the planning of educational change. *The Journal of Applied Behavioral Science, 13,* 167–183.

Firestone, W.A. & Louis, K.S. (1999). Schools as cultures. In J. Murphy and K.S. Louis (eds) *Handbook of research on educational administration* (2nd edn) (pp. 297–322). San Francisco, CA: Jossey-Bass.

Fried, Y. & Ferris, G.R. (1987). The validity of the job characteristics model: A review and meta-analysis. *Personnel Psychology, 40,* 287–322.

Gioia, D.A., Thomas, J.B., Clark, S.M., & Chittipeddi, K. (1994). Symbolism and strategic change in academia: The dynamics of sensemaking and influence. *Organization Science, 5*(3), 363–383.

Gronn, P. (2000). Distributed properties: a new architecture for leadership. *Educational Management and Administration, 28*(3), 317–338.

Hackman, J.R. & Oldham, G.R. (1980). *Work redesign.* Reading, MA: Addison-Wesley.

Hargreaves, A. (1994). *Changing teachers, changing times: Teachers' work and culture in the postmodern age.* New York, NY: Teachers College Press.

Hargreaves, A. & Macmillan, R. (1995). The balkanization of secondary school teachers. In L.S. Siskin & J.W. Little (eds) *The subjects in question: Departmental organization and the high school* (pp. 141–171). New York, NY: Teachers College Press.

Harris, A. (2004). Distributed leadership for school improvement: Leading or misleading. *Educational Management Administration and Leadership, 32*(1), 11–24.

Harris, S.G. (1994). Organizational culture and individual sensemaking: A schema-based perspective. *Organization Science, 5*(3), 309–321.

Hart, A.W. (1985, April). *Formal teacher supervision by teachers in a career ladder.* Paper presented at the annual meeting of the American Educational Research Association, Chicago, IL.

Hart, A.W. (1994). Work feature values of today's and tomorrow's teachers: Work redesign as an incentive and school improvement policy. *Educational Evaluation and Policy Analysis, 16*(4), 458–473.

Heller, M.F. & Firestone, W.A. (1995). Who's in charge here? Sources of leadership for change in eight schools. *The Elementary School Journal, 96*(1), 65–86.

Honig, M. & Hatch, T.C. (2004). Crafting coherence: How schools strategically manage multiple, external demands. *Educational Researcher, 33*(8), 16–30.

Hoyle, E. (1986). *The politics of school management.* London, UK: Hodder & Stoughton.

Johns, G., Xie, J.L., & Fang, Y. (1992). Mediating and moderating effects in job design. *Journal of Management, 18*(4), 657–676.

Johnson, B. (2004). Local school micropolitical agency: An antidote to new managerialism. *School Leadership and Management, 24*(3), 267–286.

Kahrs, J.R. (1996). Prinicpals who support teacher leadership. In G. Moller & M. Katzenmeyer (eds) *Every teacher leader: Redefining the potential of teacher leadership* (pp. 19–40). San Francicso, CA: Jossey-Bass.

Katzenmeyer, M. & Moller, G. (2001). *Awakening the sleeping giant: Helping teachers develop as leaders.* Thousand Oaks, CA: Corwin.

Kellerman, B. (2004). *Bad leadership: What it is, how it happens, why it matters (Leadership for the common good).* Boston, MA: Harvard Business School Publishing.

Kelly, J.E. (1982). *Scientific management, job redesign, and work performance.* New York, NY: Academic Press.

Kilgore, S.B. & Jones, J.D. (2003). The modern red schoolhouse: Leadership in comprehensive school reform initiatives. In J. Murphy & A. Datnow (eds) *Leadership lessons from comprehensive school reforms* (pp. 37–56). Thousand Oaks, CA: Corwin.

Kramer, R.M. (1999). Trust and distrust in organizations: Emerging perspectives, enduring questions. *Annual Review of Psychology, 50,* 569–598.

Kuwada, K. (1998). Strategic learning: The continuous side of discontinuous strategic change. *Organization Science, 9*(6), 719–736.

Lakomski, G. (2005). *Managing without leadership: Towards a theory of organizational leadership.* San Diego, CA: Elsevier.

Lawler, E.E. (1988). Substitutes for hierarchy. *Organizational Dynamics, 17*(1) 5–15.

Lawrence, P.R. & Lorsch, J.W. (1967/1986). *Organization and environment.* Cambridge, MA: Harvard Business School Press.

Lee, V.E., Dedrick, R.F., & Smith, J.B. (1991). The effect of the social organization of schools on teachers' efficacy and satisfaction. *Sociology of Education, 64*(3), 190–208.

Leithwood, K., Louis, K.S., Anderson, S., & Wahlstrom, K. (2004). *How leadership influences student learning: A review of research* (Report to the Wallace Foundation). Minneapolis, MN: University of Minnesota.

Little, J.W. (1990). The persistence of privacy: Autonomy and initiative in teachers' professional relations. *Teachers College Record, 91*(4), 509–536.

Loher, B.T., Noe, R.A., Moeller, N.M., & Fitzgerald, M.P. (1985). A meta-analysis of the relation of job characteristics to job satisfaction. *Journal of Applied Psychology, 70*(2), 280–289.

Louis, K.S. (1994). Beyond "managed change": Rethinking how schools improve. *School Effectiveness and School Improvement, 5*(1), 1–22.

Louis, K.S. & Miles, M.B. (1990). *Improving the urban high school. What works and why.* New York, NY: Teachers College Press.

Louis, K.S., Febey, K., & Schroeder, R. (2005). State-mandated accountability in high schools: Teachers' interpretations of a new era. *Educational Evaluation and Policy Analysis, 27*(2), 177–204.

Louis, K.S., Kruse, S.D., & Marks, H.M. (1995). Schoolwide professional community. In F. Newmann (ed.), *School restructuring and student achievement.* San Francisco, CA: Jossey-Bass.

Louis, K.S., Marks, H.M., & Kruse, S. (1996). Teachers' professional community in restructuring schools. *American Educational Research Journal, 33*(4), 757–798.

Louis, M.R. (1980). Surprise and sensemaking: What newcomers experience entering unfamiliar organizational settings. *Administrative Science Quarterly, 25*(2), 226–25.

McKinley, W., Zhao, J., & Rust, K.G. (2000). A sociocognitive interpretation of organizational downsizing. *Academy of Management Review, 25*(1), 227–243.

Marks, H.M. & Louis, K.S. (1999). Teacher empowerment and the capacity for organizational learning. *Educational Administration Quarterly, 35,* 707–750.

Maxcy, B.D. & Nguyen, T.S.T. (2006). The politics of distributing leadership: Reconsidering leadership distribution in two Texas elementary schools. *Educational Policy*, *20*(1), 163–196.

Mayrowetz, D. (in press). Making sense of "distributed leadership": Exploring the multiple usages of the concept in the field. *Educational Administration Quarterly*.

Mayrowetz, D. & Smylie, M.A. (2004). Work redesign that works for teachers. In M.A. Smylie & D. Miretzy (eds) *Teacher Workforce development. The one hundred and third yearbook of the National Society for the Study of Education (Part I)*, (pp. 274–302). Chicago, IL: National Society for the Study of Education.

Mayrowetz, D. & Weinstein, C.S. (1999). Sources of leadership for inclusive education: Creating schools for all children. *Educational Administration Quarterly*, *35*(3), 423–449.

Meyer, J. & Rowan, B. (1977). Institutionalized organizations: Formal structure as myth and ceremony. *American Journal of Sociology*, *83*(2), 340–363.

Mishra, A.K. & Spreitzer, G.M. (1998). Explaining how survivors respond to downsizing: The roles of trust, empowerment, justice, and work redesign. *Academy of Management Review*, *23*(3), 567–588.

Murphy, J. & Datnow, A. (2003). Leadership lessons from comprehensive school reform designs. In J. Murphy & A. Datnow (eds) *Leadership lessons from comprehensive school reforms* (pp. 263–278). Thousand Oaks, CA: Corwin.

Murphy, M.J., Hart, A.W., & Walters, L.C. (1989, April). *Satisfaction and intent to leave of new teachers in target populations under redesigned work*. Paper presented at the annual meeting of the American Educational Research Association, San Francisco, CA.

Neuman, M. & Simmons, W. (2000). Leadership for student learning. *Phi Delta Kappan*, *82*(1), 9–12.

Ogawa, R.T. & Bossert, S.T. (1995). Leadership as an organizational quality. *Educational Administration Quarterly*, *31*(2), 224–243.

Ouchi, W.G. & Wilkins, A.L. (1985). Organizational culture. *Annual Review of Sociology*, *11*, 457–483.

Parker, S., Wall, T.D., & Cordery, J.L. (2001). Future work design research and practice: Towards an elaborated model of work redesign. *Journal of Occupational and Organizational Psychology*, *74*, 413–440.

Pounder, D.G. (1999). Teacher teams: Exploring job characteristics and work-related outcomes of work group enhancement. *Educational Administration Quarterly*, *35*(3), 317–348.

Renn, R.W. & Vanderberg, R.J. (1995). The critical psychological states: An underrepresented component in job characteristics model research. *Journal of Management*, *21*(2) 279–303.

Rosenblatt, Z. (2001). Teachers' multiple roles and skill flexibility: Effects on work attitudes. *Educational Administration Quarterly*, *37*(5), 684–708.

Rutter, M., Maughan, B., Moritimore, P., Ouston, J., & Smith, A. (1979). *Fifteen thousand hours: Secondary schools and their effects on children*. Cambridge, MA: Harvard University Press.

Sarason, S.B. (1996). *Revisiting "The culture of the school and the problem of change."* New York, NY: Teachers College Press.

Siskin, L.S. (1997). The challenge of leadership in comprehensive high schools: School vision and departmental divisions. *Educational Administration Quarterly*, *33*(5), 604–623.

Siskin, L.S. & Little, J.W. (1995). The subject department: Continuities and critiques. In L.S. Siskin & J.W. Little (eds) *The subjects in question: Departmental organization and the high school* (pp. 1–22). New York, NY: Teachers College Press.

Smylie, M.A. (1994). Redesigning teachers' work: Connections to the classroom. In L. Darling-Hammond (ed.), *Review of research in education*, *20*, 129–177.

Smylie, M.A. (1997). Research on teacher leadership: Assessing the state of the art. In B.J. Biddle, T.L. Godd, & I.F. Goodson, (eds) *International Handbook of Teachers and Teaching* (pp. 521–592). Dordrecht, The Netherlands: Kluwer Academic Publishers.

Smylie, M.A., Conley, S., & Marks, H.M. (2002). Exploring new approaches to teacher leadership for school improvement. In J. Murphy (ed.), *The educational leadership challenge: Redefining leadership for the 21st century. The one hundred and first yearbook of the National Society for the Study of Education (Part I)*, (pp. 162–188). Chicago, IL: University of Chicago Press.

Smylie, M.A., Mayrowetz, D., Murphy, J., & Louis, K.S. (in press). Trust and the development of distributed leadership. *Journal of School Leadership*.

Spillane, J.P. (2006). *Distributed leadership*. San Francisco, CA: Jossey-Bass.

Spillane, J.P., Halverson, R., & Diamond, J.B. (2001). Investigating school leadership practice: A distributed perspective. *Educational Researcher, 30*(3), 23–28.

Spillane, J.P., Halverson, R., & Diamond, J.B. (2004). Towards a theory of leadership practice: A distributed perspective. *Journal of Curriculum Studies, 36*(1), 3–34.

Storey, A. (2004). The problem of distributed leadership in schools. *School Leadership and Management, 24*(3), 249–265.

Sundstrom, E., De Meuse, K.P., & Futrell, D. (1990). Work teams: Applications and effectiveness. *American Psychologist, 45*(2), 120–133.

Swidler, A. (1986). Cultures in action: Symbols and strategies. *American Sociological Review, 51*(2), 273–286.

Trice, H.M., & Beyer, J.M. (1984). Studying organizational cultures through rites and ceremonials. *Academy of Management Review, 9*(4), 653–669.

Tschannen-Moran, M. (2004). *Trust matters: Leadership for successful schools*. San Francisco, CA: Jossey-Bass.

Tschannen-Moran, M. & Hoy, W.K. (2000). A multidisciplinary analysis of the nature, meaning, and measurement of trust. *Review of Educational Research, 70*, 547–593.

Weick, K.E. (1991). The nontraditional quality of organizational learning. *Organization Science, 2*(1), 116–124.

Willower, D.J. (1991). Micropolitics and the sociology of school organizations. *Education and the Urban Society, 23*(4), 442–454.

Yin, R.K. (2004). *Case study research: Design and Methods* (3rd edn). Thousand Oaks, CA: Sage.

9
Distributing Leadership to Improve Outcomes for Students

HELEN S. TIMPERLEY

Empirical work on how leadership is distributed more and less successfully in schools is rare. This chapter presents a case for distributing leadership in particular ways that can have positive outcomes for students in a school improvement context in which varying success was evident. Grounding the theory in this practice context led to the identification of some risks and benefits of distributing leadership and to the challenge of some key concepts presented in earlier theorizing about leadership and its distribution. Concepts related to distributed leadership discussed in the chapter include embedding vision in activities and the social distribution of task enactment. Issues addressed within the latter concept include boundary spanning, relationships between leaders and followers and the use of artefacts.

An assumption on which this chapter[1] is based is that leadership in schools is typically distributed and is exercised through the dynamic interactions between multiple leaders and followers (Spillane et al., 2004). The issue I wish to pursue is that the ways in which leadership is distributed may be more or less effective. To this end, I will discuss key concepts related to distributed leadership and illustrate them with an empirical study in a schooling improvement context in which the exercise of distributed leadership was differentially effective in terms of promoting student outcomes. The particular qualities discussed in relation to this differential effectiveness include leadership activities and how they were distributed, the social distribution of task enactment, and the place of artefacts in those interactions. First, however, I will outline some key premises on which the analysis is based because, as with most educational concepts, there is no unified position about the specifics of what constitutes distributed leadership.

Some Issues of Definition

One concept about which most authors appear to agree is that distributed leadership is not the same as dividing task responsibilities among individuals who perform defined and separate organizational roles, but rather it comprises dynamic interactions between multiple leaders and followers. Task responsibilities are distributed across traditionally defined organizational roles. "Decisions about who leads and who follows are dictated by the task or problem situation, not necessarily by where one sits in the hierarchy" (Copland, 2003, p. 378). Spillane et al. (2004) refer to this distribution as being "stretched over" people in different roles.

A second point of agreement is that distributed leadership is particularly important in relation to the instructional aspects of leadership because it is the development of instructional leadership, rather than other organizational functions that has been shown to have the greatest leverage in effecting programmatic changes and instructional improvement (Eraut, 1994; Hargreaves, 1994; Leithwood et al., 1999; Southworth, 1990).

Greater divergence is evident in terms of whether the focus is essentially descriptive or normative. Partly due to the relative infancy of research into distributed leadership, much of the writing is essentially descriptive (e.g. Gronn, 2003; Spillane et al., 2004) with the key task being to develop frameworks and analytical tools to identify how leadership is distributed. An important contribution of this descriptive work is that it has served to focus the unit of analysis on "actors in situations working with artefacts, rather than actors abstracted from situations or artefacts" (Spillane et al., 2004, p. 9). Leadership is no longer seen as separate from the activities in which leaders engage.

The main difference between this essentially descriptive work and that of others, such as Camburn et al. (2003) and Day and Harris (2003) is the normative orientation of these latter writers. An implicit assumption underpinning their work is the perceived desirability of distributing leadership across an increased number of people in an organization because such distribution has the potential to build capacity within a school through the development of the intellectual and professional capital of the teachers. Leadership becomes a collaborative endeavour involving all teachers (Lambert, 1998). Associated empirical work (see, for example, Camburn et al., 2003; Copland, 2003) shows how a variety of comprehensive school reforms, particularly when focused on inquiry-based approaches, create new leadership positions through the appointment of coaches and/or facilitators whose responsibility is typically to provide instructional support and ensure adequate implementation. These authors are less concerned about developing taxonomies, than identifying whether more leadership positions have been created, and if so, how different leadership functions are distributed across them. Surveys of school personnel indicate that greater distribution is typically associated with comprehensive school reform, although this does not happen without some associated challenges.

Despite the differences between those taking a descriptive or a normative stance, there is general agreement that further empirical work is needed, particularly work that provides rich cases of day to day instructional leadership activities using a distributed framework (Camburn et al., 2003; Copland, 2003; Spillane et al., 2004) rather than relying on the more usual self-report surveys. Given that leadership activity – together with the artefacts and relationships that form an integral part – forms the essence of a distributed leadership analysis, such on-the-ground observations are essential to developing these important concepts further.

In this chapter, the data presented are primarily observational, together with interviews related to those observations. The analysis is based mainly on the framework developed by Spillane et al. (2004) because their descriptive focus provides a framework for further development of the constructs. However, if the goal of improving leadership is to be realized so that it has greater influence on instructional practices in the interests of improving schools, I argue that more than a descriptive analysis is needed. The normative position I take, however, is different from the implicit position adopted by others (Camburn et al., 2003; Copland 2003; Leithwood et al., 1999) that greater distribution of leadership is necessarily better. Rather, I suggest that better understanding is needed of how leadership is enacted when it is distributed and of the conditions under which such distribution is differentially effective if it is to make a difference to instructional practices in schools. This perspective, of necessity, judges effectiveness primarily on the quality of task performance (Timperley & Robinson, 2003). The ultimate goal of such instructional task performance, I argue, is to enhance student learning, rather than to change leaders' or teachers' practices per se. Effectiveness judgments, therefore, should be made in relation to this goal of benefit to students. In this study, changes in student achievement (or lack of them) served as such a reference.

The Research Context

This research studied the leadership processes in elementary schools involved in a schooling improvement initiative. In order to understand the context, some background information is needed. Since 1989 schools in New Zealand have experienced a high level of self-management. At this time, all district-level administration was abolished and replaced by Boards of Trustees at each school who were responsible for most operational decisions. There was no mandated national testing in elementary schools, although the Boards of Trustees were required, through the principal and staff, to monitor the progress of students against the achievement objectives outlined in broad curriculum statements (New Zealand Ministry of Education, 1993). A variety of nationally-normed assessments in reading and mathematics are available for schools to use should they wish. Monitoring of results is intended primarily for internal purposes with no expectation that the results will be reported to an external agent for accountability purposes.

An external audit and review agency inspects schools on a regular basis against a set of quality indicators. In 1996, a report (New Zealand Education Review Office, 1996) was published outlining the inadequacy of education offered in approximately half of the schools in two of the poorest communities in the country. Their populations were predominantly Maori (New

Zealand's indigenous people), or first/second generation immigrants from one of the small Pacific Islands nations of Samoa, Tonga, Fiji, Nuie, or the Cook Islands. As part of the intervention in these schools, the Ministry of Education sponsored professional development for literacy leaders and Grade 1 teachers in early literacy acquisition if they wished to take part. The seven schools in this study chose to participate.

Method

The research took place over four consecutive years and involved observations, interviews and the analysis of student achievement data for each year. In any research on leadership, capturing the interactions and activities of leaders is difficult and it was decided that team meetings were likely to provide rich information about the kinds of leadership activities of interest. They had the additional advantage that all schools held such meetings so comparisons could be made across the schools. The participating leaders were asked, therefore, to nominate a meeting in which they discussed either student achievement in literacy or the literacy program that was the focus of the recently completed professional development. A minimum of three such meetings were observed in each school. Observations, however, do not necessarily reveal the inevitable task complexity and ambiguity that form constraints on activities within a meeting, or the impact of what occurred on actions subsequent to the meeting, so interviews were conducted with those in attendance after (and sometimes before) each of the meetings. The participants and data collection procedures are described in more detail below with a summary timeline provided in Table 9.1.

Participants Within Each School

In each of the seven schools, the principal, literacy leader and three teachers of Grade 1 students who represented a range of skills and views were interviewed in each school each year. Meeting observations included all teachers of the Grade 1 students and their literacy leader. The 21 teachers involved in the interviews had completed teacher registration requirements and ranged in experience from one year to more than 20 years. All of the literacy leaders and teachers had participated in professional development in early literacy acquisition during the first year of the study. Principals were interviewed each year in order to understand how their macro-organizational responsibilities cohered (or not) with the more micro-activities occurring in the team meetings.

Data Collection Methods

The observational and interview data were collected each year for three years beginning with the year of the professional development. Student achievement data were collected the year prior to the professional development as baseline, in addition to the following three years. Individual school

Table 9.1 Research-Related Activities

Year and Professional Development Undertaken	Research Data Collection
Baseline Professional development n/a	Achievement data as students completed first year of schooling in all schools. No other research data collected
Year 1 First six months – literacy leader and teachers participated in professional development Second six months – no external professional development	Achievement data Observation of one team meeting in each school Interviews of principal, literacy leader and three teachers in each school Written feedback to individual schools followed by discussion
Year 2 No external professional development	Achievement data (as for Year 1) Observation of one team meeting in each school Interviews of principal, literacy leader and three teachers in each school Written feedback to individual schools Combined schools discussion and critique of research report
Year 3 Training session for literacy leaders on the analysis of data (Group 1 Schools)	Achievement data (as for Year 1) Observation of one team meeting in each school Interviews of principal, literacy leader and three teachers in each school Combined schools discussion and critique of research report

reports compiled by the researcher were discussed with participants each year and comments were taken into account in the more comprehensive reports written at the end of Years 2 and 3. These latter reports were critiqued by the schools involved in a public forum.

Interviews and Meeting Observations

The interviews were designed primarily to probe the reasons underpinning particular activities that were observed during the meetings. Some interview questions were asked of all participants and are indicated in the data descriptions. The three observed meetings in each school were analyzed in terms of the frequency with which they occurred and the material artefacts such as student achievement data, that were part of the meeting activity. In addition, a dialogue analysis of the tape recorded transcripts was coded by the first author and independently checked by a registered teacher who had no other involvement with the research.

Reliability between the two coders of greater than 85 percent was obtained for all transcripts. Disagreements in coding were discussed and resolved to the satisfaction of both coders. The coding categories were designed to be mutually exclusive and a single code assigned to whatever length of text was relevant to that code. The coding schedule was developed to distinguish among the following types of meeting discussions: (a) external or organizational issues that did not relate directly to the instructional program, (b) descriptions of programs and teaching approaches without reference to any achievement information, (c) understanding the meaning of data without reference to any teaching implications, (d) problems identified from the achievement data that were specific to individual students with the teaching implications discussed, and (e) other (e.g. social discourse). The percentage of time spent for any one code was calculated by using the number of lines per topic as a proportion of the total lines. Quotes were extracted from the transcripts to illustrate the meaning of particular codes and how they reflected the differences in meeting activities.

The meeting analyses showed differences in activities and material artefacts between two groups of schools. The Group 1 schools had either no achievement information available for the meeting (Pine[2], Kauri, and Olive) or had achievement data that were aggregated for all students across the year level, so the achievement of individual students, or the teachers who taught them, could not be identified (Mangrove, Beech). These data were not discussed in terms of their teaching implications, rather these schools spent most of their time describing programs and teaching approaches or examining data without examining the teaching implications. The Group Two schools (Avonside and Allendale), in contrast, had nationally benchmarked student achievement information on the table in front of them. Each student's reading level was identified with an X on a scatter plot, colour coded by class with a clear indication of whether the student was above, at, or below national benchmarks and the teaching implications arising from these data formed the basis of most of the meeting discussion. An analysis of the percentage of time spent in the meetings in the seven schools in Year 3 is presented in Table 9.2.

After receiving feedback on the research findings at the end of Year 2, the observed differences in meeting activities between the two groups of schools was reduced. The profile of activities in the Group One schools more closely resembled those of Group Two. More time was spent in the Group One schools identifying targeted students and discussing relevant program adjustments. Table 9.3 identifies the changes in the amount of time spent in the same activities in Year 3 as those identified in Table 9.2.

Student Achievement

Two sets of student achievement information were used. The first related to literacy skills at school entry and the second to their achievement after one year at school. Details of all achievement measures and the analysis used are

Table 9.2 Percentage of Meeting Time Spent in Different Activities During Years 1 and 2 Combined

School	External or Organizational	Program Descriptions and Teaching Approaches	Meaning of Data (No Teaching Implications)	Data-Identified Achievement Problems Specific to Individuals[a]	Other
Group 1					
Pine	3.1	96.5	0	0	0.4
Mangrove	32.2	42.0	2.5	0	
Kauri	0	99.0	0	0	1.0
Beech	11.1	7.0	26.8	3.0	
Olive	9.6	67.2	5.5	1.7	
Group 2					
Avonside	3.7	0	6.5	72.6	
Allendale	6.9	30.3	9.5	46.4	

Note
a Includes suggested solutions.

Table 9.3 Average Percent of Time Spent in Different Activities in the Group 1 and Group 2 Schools in Year 3

School	External or Organizational	Program Descriptions and Teaching Approaches	Meaning of Data (No Teaching Implications)	Data-Identified Problems Specific to Individuals[a]	Other
Group 1 Schools	7.8	63.2	6.7	1.7	20.6
Group 2 Schools	3.5	29.5	16.6	29.2	21.2

Note
a Includes suggested solutions.

described in detail in a technical report (Timperley & Wiseman, 2003) so a general outline only is provided here.

School Entry

Although it can be assumed that the children's scores at school entry were unlikely to be significantly different because all the children were attending schools located in communities categorized as the poorest 10 percent in the country, this assumption was checked by assessing a random sample of 10 percent of children whose data are included in the research in each school. Statistical analyses were not possible because the small sample and variable performance within schools led to very high standard deviations. The raw scores did not show a discernible pattern among the schools in achievement at school entry.

End of First Year of Formal Instruction

In each school all students were regularly assessed, after one year at school, on six different literacy measures by a trained assessor. The assessor recorded the results with a summary given to the classroom teacher. If a child performed poorly, the results were sometimes accompanied by teaching recommendations. In no school were these recommendations followed up to ensure their implementation. The assessment had very "low stakes" for either the literacy leader or the teachers. Only two schools (Beech and Avonside) aggregated the results in any form. These data were ideal for research purposes because the records for all schools were complete for all years of the study. They were not the data discussed at the observed meetings.

The two measures used in this study were selected because they required relatively sophisticated reading knowledge and were at greatest risk of not being achieved by students from these low-income communities (Phillips et al., 2001). These were text reading accuracy (Clay, 1993) and generalized word recognition using the BURT word list (Gilmore et al., 1981).

In order to determine a particular school's reading profile so that the students' achievement in the schools could be compared using multivariate statistics, a combined reading z score from the Text level and BURT scores was created with a mean of 10 and a standard deviation of 2. These z scores are those reported for each school with mean reading scores for all children after one year of instruction in each school for each of the four years presented in Table 9.4.

Analysis of Student Achievement Data

A one-way analysis of variance in Year 2 showed a significant difference between the schools' reading scores [$F(6406) = 8.736$, $p < 0.01$]. A Sheffé test of multiple comparisons established that in Year 2 (18 months after the completion of the professional development) the schools fell into three groups that were significantly different from one another ($\alpha.05$). The reading scores in Pine and Mangrove were significantly different from those in Kauri, Beech,

Table 9.4 Number of Children (n), Mean Reading Scores (M) and Standard Deviations (SD) for Each School for Baseline and Years 1 to 3

School	Baseline		Year 1		Year 2		Year 3	
	n	M (SD)	n	M (SD)	n	M (SD)	n	M (SD)
Group 1								
Pine	69	9.19 (1.51)	64	8.72 (1.2)	81	9.23 (1.5)	48	9.74 (2.15)
Mangrove	70	8.17 (0.90)	59	8.86 (1.65)	65	9.45 (2.00)	57	*10.58 (1.91)
Kauri	53	9.20 (1.51)	50	9.94 (1.95)	45	10.09 (2.00)	73	*10.71 (2.40)
Beech	27		53	9.88 (1.51)	44	10.13 (1.56)	62	10.43 (2.12)
Olive	66	9.27 (1.24)	50	9.02 (1.30)	42	10.20 (1.73)	21	*10.99 (2.27)
Group 2								
Avonside	63	10.42 (1.85)	90	10.53 (2.20)	70	10.96 (2.24)	114	11.29 (2.12)
Allendale	119	10.12 (1.97)	105	10.63 (2.03)	64	11.21 (2.18)	59	*10.48 (1.72)

Notes

In Year 2, the achievement in the Group 1 schools was significantly lower than that in the Group 2 schools (Sheffé test of multiple comparisons).

* indicates that the difference in mean scores for Years 2 and 3 are significant ($p < 0.05$).

and Olive, which were, in turn, significantly different from those in Avonside and Allendale. In Year 3, when the five lower achieving schools adopted the same data analysis and meeting activities as the two higher achieving schools, the scores in all these schools had improved. There was no statistical difference in the students' achievement scores for six of the seven schools. The scores for Pine, however, remained significantly different from the scores for Avonside. The only school with a decline in scores was Allendale, although the scores at this school were not significantly different from the other schools.

Analysis of Leadership Activities

The remainder of this chapter focuses on the leadership activities in the different schools using a distributed leadership framework. The schools were divided into two groups for comparative analysis. Pine, Mangrove, Kauri, Beech, and Olive are referred to as Group 1 because the leadership activities were similar in Years 1 and 2 of the research and achievement was significantly lower than in the other two schools. Avonside and Allendale are referred to as Group 2 because while similar to each other, their meeting activities were very different from those in Group 1 during Years 1 and 2 of the research and achievement was significantly higher than in the other five schools. All schools' meeting activities became more alike in Year 3, as did the students' achievement.

For the sake of clarity, detailed descriptions and quotes are given for two schools only. Mangrove is used to illustrate the activities in Group 1 and Allendale the activities in Group 2. When the activities in these two schools differ from others in their group, these differences are noted.

How Leadership Was Distributed

Isolating key constructs in an analysis of distributed leadership is inevitably difficult because the concept itself involves a web of task, situation, and people. The two constructs on which I have chosen to focus in this chapter include embedding visions in activities and the social distribution of task enactment.

Embedding Vision in Activities

Under the self-managing school legislation in New Zealand, schools are required to have charters that began with vision statements with accompanying goals. Neither the charters nor the vision statements within them were observed to form the basis of leadership activities in practice. On the other hand, the leadership visions in action in the Group 1 schools had embedded within them very different visions of what it meant to be effective from their Group 2 counterparts and it is these that are the subject of the following analysis.

Achievement in literacy was the major focus of the schooling improvement initiative, and of course, the professional development. In Years 1 and 2, the two Group 2 schools communicated their vision that all students were capable of reaching national benchmarks in reading through the meeting activities. Also communicated was their responsibility to develop teaching strategies to accomplish this outcome. They did this by analyzing student achievement against national benchmarks of expected achievement, identifying slow progress students who had not reached the benchmarks together with the teachers who taught them, and then working together as a team to diagnose each individual student's reading difficulties and helping the teachers concerned to develop strategies to accelerate progress. The meeting discussion focused on how to move these students from below the benchmark to reaching or exceeding it. The possibility that some students were not capable of doing so never entered into the discussions.

At no time were explicit vision type statements articulated, such as, "We believe all our students can achieve," rather, the assumption that they could if they were taught effectively was embedded in the activity. Through analyzing the reading difficulties experienced by the low achieving students and examining what they, as teachers, could do to assist them, the vision was clear. For example, in Allendale, two students whose achievement sat below the benchmark had not made progress over the last ten weeks. After identifying their reading level, the following conversation took place:

TEACHER: I've had to keep them at this level because they were not coping when I tried them on harder books. They just didn't know the words.
LITERACY LEADER: What does the running record [assessment] say?
TEACHER: They both got all the little words mixed up. R said "we" for "when." M said "were" for "is."
LITERACY LEADER: These sound like different problems to me. Let's have a look at R's running record first. I wonder if he is not making any sense of what he is reading or just not looking carefully enough at the words.
TEACHER: He has no idea what he is reading.

The discussion continued with a more detailed analysis and some agreed-on teaching strategies. One teacher explained how it impacted her teaching in a follow-up interview.

[The literacy leader] graphs them for us and we can see who is falling behind which is good. With my lowest group I see them four times a week and try to push them up. You can see who is struggling and where you have to close the gap. So it's good and we talk about that. You don't want any of them to be below.

In four of the five Group 1 schools in Year 2, on the other hand, the vision embedded in the meeting activity gave a different message to the teachers –

their responsibility was to implement the program that was presented during the professional development, as well as they were able. In none of the schools was the adequacy of student achievement discussed, nor was program implementation linked in any way to the students' achievement. Exactly how this message was communicated through the meeting activities was different in the individual schools. Pine, Kauri, and Olive did not use any material artefacts at the meeting. The teachers in Pine spent their time taking turns to describe their writing programs with the aim of promoting quality writing. Defining quality of teaching process or student outcomes was left to individual teacher judgment because all programs described were treated as equally effective. Kauri focused on expected lesson sequences and Olive talked about classroom organizational problems when implementing the literacy program. Beech was different in that they had achievement data present at their meetings but they spent most of the meeting time discussing how to interpret the data. Although it was benchmarked, the teachers had difficulty understanding the meaning of the benchmarks. Neither the adequacy of the students' progress nor the implications for teaching were mentioned during the meeting.

In Mangrove, the Group 1 school from which illustrative examples are selected, the focus of the meeting was to improve program implementation by developing greater consistency across the classes. The specifics of how the program was implemented were essentially the group's choice provided they all taught the same way. Nothing was imposed.

> I've been talking to L [a teacher] and we think that some of us are using the little white boards and some of us are using paper for word work. There are some other little differences too. We thought it's probably best if we all do the same thing. I want to spend some time just talking about it to see what you want to do.

This emphasis on consistency was embedded in the meeting analysis in Year 2 when nearly a third of the time was spent organizing classroom observations to determine how the program was being implemented in each class.

The literacy leader did present achievement data at the meetings but the way they were presented and the associated meeting activities were very different from those in Group 2. The students' scores from all Grade 1 classes were aggregated to indicate the percentage of students reading above, at, or below grade level expectations. The benchmarks used were the same as those in the Group 2 schools, but the absence of individual student or class-specific data meant that the teachers could not identify whose students were below grade level. The data showed that more students were below the benchmark near the end of the year than at the beginning of the year and the literacy leader had disclosed to the author prior to the meeting that she believed the reason for the decline in scores was a drift in the quality of program implementation. She had called the meeting to discuss the issue. When presenting the information to the teachers, however, she did not identify her concerns immediately:

> What we're going to do today is I just wanted to just very quickly go through the latest bit of data – I've given you a copy but I know it's a paper war and just have a look at it today and if you don't want it just give it back to me. You don't have to file it or anything like that at this stage … it's just hand-written.

The embedded message for her teachers appeared to be that the data were not important, despite her private indication prior to the meeting that she believed them to be vitally important because they identified the decline in scores.

Later in the meeting she disclosed to the teachers her concern that reading levels had declined in relation to the expected levels for that time in the year. She had prepared some notes identifying possible reasons that she paraphrased for her teachers in the following quote. In this statement only two of the seven reasons given for the decline in scores reflected her concern about non-implementation of the program as taught in the professional development.

> I've put some of the reasons why [the achievement was declining] – and I'm really, at this stage just looking at why are there still such a large percentage of children under average. The most obvious one is the large classes in the second half of the year, that we finished the professional development in July and weren't given that intensive fortnightly burst of keeping us on track all the time. I wasn't monitoring as closely in the second half of the year as I was in the first half of the year. We had all those timetable things and a million others. Teachers moving away from the programme because it was sort of an experimental time and we wanted to just try other things and get new ideas from different courses and things and putting those into the literacy sessions. I added parents in there. I don't know whether you agree with that or not. But maybe parents being unsure of how to support what we were doing at school back at home still. Absences is another good one. Can anybody think of any other reasons why it might be happening?

Not surprisingly, her invitation to the teachers to identify further reasons did not elicit her hoped-for response of a classroom focus. For example, one teacher responded in the following way:

Well, I still would come back to the same barriers that we know exist. Are they having breakfast? Are they sleeping? Are they coming with the right clothes? I mean those all are factors especially for these kids that are disadvantaged to begin with. If that hasn't changed, then maybe it isn't just their reading but their education in general could still be down here so I still feel that those – those physical aspects of it as still a barrier to those kids moving up. I'd also just be interested to know if those kids that we have seen as a success – did they go to pre-school or were they non pre-schoolers?

The literacy leader did not challenge these types of statements. Rather she replied, "I haven't done that analysis yet."

From a distributed leadership perspective, the different kinds of visions in the two groups of schools were conveyed through a complex interactive web of leaders, followers and artefacts that did not operate independently of one another. In the case of Mangrove, the form of the artefact, aggregated student achievement data, the leader's anticipation of the followers' responses, and the followers' diversion from the leader's agenda all came together to create a situation that failed to develop a coherent vision of what they wanted to achieve or how they might achieve it.

When the meeting activities changed in Year 3 in the Group 1 schools, to more closely resemble those of the two high achieving Group 2 schools through a close analysis of individual student achievement against national benchmarks (see Table 9.3), the same literacy leader presented the data this way:

This is a valuable time – collecting all that data in and just looking at it. Although it is a pain getting it ready, it is the only way we are going to make a difference. I will give it out to you in a minute and you can have a look to see in your class who is below and who is above [the national benchmark] and look especially at the ones just below and think: "What am I going to do to make sure they are not below next time?"

Each teacher then identified the students of concern with a follow-up discussion of how they might best be assisted. When the author asked about how she had managed to overcome the focus of discussions about barriers external to the teacher and school, the literacy leader replied: "They just disappeared, they never come up. Once we started looking at the data in this way, nobody mentions it any more." A different form of the artefact combined with different leadership behavior created a situation that elicited very different responses from the followers.

Interviews with the teachers following the meeting indicated how differently they now perceived the situation and how these perceptions, in turn, impacted on their activities.

Well I keep saying the word focus. If you don't have that focus, well then another few weeks go by and things can crop up, like you can do some folk dancing and a marvellous unit on something else. Now we know that every five weeks we are going to look at the data, and so you don't let reading go, you let other things go, but you don't let that go. We used to think about getting through the day, keeping the room tidy, having a quiet class. At the end of the day, we would go home with a warm fuzzy feeling. "Oh, that was a good day. Maybe I will do some more of that tomorrow." I think the focus has come right back to "What have I done today in reading today, who is moving and who isn't moving and why aren't they moving?" That is what you are taking home in your head.

By situating leadership activities in an interactive web of actors and artefacts, rather than focusing on the attributes of a particular leader, a rich picture of the connections between leadership activities and the visions teachers held for students and their responsibilities is conveyed. These visions were rarely stated explicitly, but rather embedded within the activity. The meeting analysis in Mangrove over the different years showed how it was possible to change the activities and the collective vision of the team. A focus on articulated visions or decontextualized tasks would fail to capture the essence of this change.

Social Distribution of Task Enactment

The focus of distributed leadership on interactions among tasks, relationships and artefacts makes analysis of these separate attributes rather arbitrary. While the section above made some reference to the social interactions within the enactment of a task, I wish to expand this particular aspect further in this section by describing additional aspects of the social relationships between the participants, paying particular attention to Spillane and Sherer's (2004) concept of stretching activities over people. The activity of analyzing data and understanding the instructional implications in the Group 2 schools were stretched over the principal, literacy leader, and teachers. The literacy leader effectively acted as a "boundary spanner" between the other two parties. These boundary-spanning activities will be presented in the first part of this section. The second part discusses issues related to developing teacher leadership. A central concern of distributed leadership is how it is exercised by those without formally designated roles (for example, see Barth, 2001; Day & Harris, 2003; Wenger, 1998). Expertise, rather than formal position should form the basis of leadership authority and this type of leadership often resides within the larger professional community of teachers (Copland, 2003; Day & Harris, 2003; Wenger, 1998). This examination, therefore, focuses on how teacher leadership was developed in the schools by following through on some of the illustrative examples from Mangrove and Allendale. The final part of this section will examine the relationship between leaders and followers. Earlier formulations of leadership that focused on the individual leader were based on an implicit assumption that it was the role of the leader to influence followers. As more studies of micro-politics of leadership situations were undertaken, it became apparent that followers also influence leaders (Smylie & Hart, 1999). A distributed leadership perspective assumes more permeable boundaries between leaders and followers and positions followers as an essential constituting element of leadership activity (Gronn, 2003; Spillane & Sherer, 2004).

Boundary Spanning

An obvious potential problem with distributing leadership is the possibility of developing incoherence within an organization. Those to whom leadership is distributed may have different agendas from the official leaders and ensuring coherence within schools can be a defining issue in the success of schooling improvement initiatives (Bryk, 1999). What was of particular interest in this study was how the literacy leaders acted as boundary spanners between the principal and the teachers and the ways in which these activities impacted on the coherence of beliefs and activities within the school.

Although when asked directly, all principals expressed the belief that improving student achievement was an important focus of their efforts, the main differentiating quality in the two groups of schools related to implicit beliefs about professionalism in pursuit of that goal as evident in their activities. The theory-in-use analysis was more telling than an espoused theory analysis. In the Group 1 schools, professionalism was defined through the meeting activities essentially as trusting teachers to make sound judgments to implement programs well and giving them sufficient support to be successful. In the Group 2 schools, professionalism was defined in terms of having a positive impact on student achievement. Programs were the vehicles for achieving this outcome. These differences in beliefs were evident in the principals' activities in relation to supporting the program and how they judged its success. In Years 1 and 2 a remarkable consistency existed between the principals' beliefs and activities and those evident in the meetings analyzed above even though the principals were not physically present. This consistency, once again, will be illustrated using data from Mangrove and Allendale as representative of others in their group.

Guided by the recommendations of the literacy leader, the Mangrove principal approved the substantial classroom release time from teaching activities for the teachers to undertake the professional development. He trusted the literacy leader's professional judgment because he knew little about junior school reading. He received reports from the literacy leader on student achievement, but said that he did not feel qualified to interpret them. When asked by the author how he would judge the success of the program, he replied: "I guess that you can judge a program by the attitude of staff, and they do feel comfortable." Consistent with these views was his belief that his role was to "support the teachers and celebrate their successes" which he did by providing the necessary resources and making statements at staff meetings about how much he appreciated the teachers' efforts and commitment. The principals from the other Group 1 schools described similar actions focusing on staff satisfaction and support.

It is not surprising that the meetings referred to above focused on supporting teachers to implement the program well and that the literacy leader in Mangrove was so tentative about her requests for change. Other literacy leaders in Group 2 schools were similarly tentative. They spent many hours discussing program implementation, but no rules were ever laid down about how the teachers should teach in any of the Group 1 schools. No check of effectiveness was made against student outcomes.

The literacy leaders in the Group 2 schools also acted as effective boundary spanners between their principals and teachers in Years 1 and 2, but the message about what was involved in being professional was different. Both Group 1 principals received and analyzed student achievement information and were very aware of trends in the data. The principal in Allendale had taken part in the professional development herself in order to develop a good understanding of the program. She had previously taught junior reading and felt confident in this leadership role. She occasionally attended the team meetings when student achievement was discussed so she could "understand how things were going and the difficulties the teachers were experiencing" and would be in a better position to support the teachers. She had more limited views on teacher judgment than her counterpart at Mangrove. She first wanted the teachers to understand how to implement the program because it had proven success in her view. Then, if they wanted to make changes they could experiment, but effectiveness would be assessed against student reading progress. The teachers reported a similar belief but had not wanted to change anything "because it worked."

In both groups of schools in Years 1 and 2, therefore, all literacy leaders were effective in their boundary spanning activities in the sense that they achieved coherence between the principals' beliefs and activities and those of the teachers. This coherence, however, was differentially effective in terms of gains in student achievement.

Effective boundary spanning and coherence, however, can be very fragile. Any changes in the social structure can impact on the coherence and effectiveness of the leadership activity. In Year 3, the Allendale principal left and a new principal was appointed. The literacy leader was no longer able to act as an effective boundary spanner because the new principal held very different beliefs about professionalism and appropriate associated activities. She expressed a belief to the author that the literacy leader was ineffective in her role, and explained it like this:

> An effective teacher doesn't slavishly follow one program, like ... [the literacy leader] is doing. She should go to lots of different courses, then develop a program to meet the needs of the children she is teaching. It should be a combination of many programs. I have tried to get her to think about other ways of teaching, but she won't listen. She keeps saying she wants to do just this program.

Reading scores declined significantly in Allendale in Year 3. The principal was unaware of the decline, but the literacy leader was acutely aware. For her, the blame was placed squarely at the door of the new principal. "She keeps taking away our literacy [instructional] time. This term we've lost a third of our literacy time because she has organized other things [school events]. She doesn't respect it like ... [the previous principal] did." The principal denied the accusation and it was impossible to verify it independently. The similarity of her beliefs about professionalism to those of the Group 1 principals, however, was obvious. Being professional was about preferred program implementation, not the impact of that program on student achievement.

The changes in Allendale highlighted the fragility of the effectiveness of distributed leadership and boundary spanning activities. Under one principal the literacy leader was highly effective. Coherence was maintained and student achievement was high. Under another principal, her authority and effectiveness were undermined dramatically and conflict came to dominate the social interactions and relationships.

Teacher Leadership

Teacher leadership has been promoted as a way of developing organizational capacity (Lambert, 1998; Sergiovanni, 1988). While distributed leadership among teachers may be desirable, some caution needs to be sounded about the potential difficulties involved. Although formally appointed leaders do not automatically command respect and authority, teacher leaders may be particularly vulnerable to being openly disrespected and disregarded because they do not carry formal authority. On the other hand, nomination of teacher leaders by colleagues may not realize potential expertise within the group because colleagues may select their leaders using other criteria. Each of these issues will be discussed in turn through two vignettes of activities in Allendale and Mangrove.

In Years 1 and 2, Allendale actively distributed leadership for successful program implementation over teachers as well as designated leaders. During the meetings, the literacy leader frequently invited other teachers to offer ideas and assistance. Many times these activities resembled Spillane et al.'s (2004, pp.

18–19) description of "the collective cognitive properties of a group of leaders working together to enact a particular task" as different teachers took leadership roles in assisting their colleagues to reach the common objective of raising the achievement of the slow progress students. This collective leadership and responsibility is illustrated by the response of the literacy leader when one teacher indicated that she needed assistance with the slow progress students: "Be thinking team about the kind of help that we may be able to offer."

Leadership in this school was also more formally assigned to particular individuals. The achievement data showed that one teacher was particularly successful in raising the achievement of students in her class and her advice was often sought. One strategy involved other teachers observing in her class and receiving coaching from her. The Grade 1 teachers expressed how much they valued such opportunities.

The success of such a strategy, however, is dependent on the social context, not just the qualities of the leader in relation to the task. The impact the Grade 1 teachers were having in raising student achievement led the principal to send the Grade 2 teachers to the same professional development in the first half of Year 2. Many experienced implementation problems, so the principal decided to release the proficient Grade 1 teacher from teaching duties each morning to assist the Grade 2 teachers. These teachers, however, were not receptive to her expertise. She explained the reception she received:

> I go in there [Grade 2 classrooms] and they say, "Well this child can't read and because you are so good you can teach him." I want to help them with their teaching, but they don't want to know. They just want me to take the kids out [of class] and fix them.

The tension between the Grade 1 and 2 teachers was no doubt caused partly by the attention and praise given by the principal for the success of the Grade 1 students the previous year and the implied criticism of the poor results achieved in Grade 2. When asked by the researcher, the Grade 2 teachers explained that they believed the Grade 1 teachers exaggerated the reading scores and that the new program had little merit. Needless to say, the Grade 2 teachers welcomed the difficulties that arose between the new principal and the Grade 1 literacy leader in Year 3.

An alternative approach that could overcome the kinds of difficulties experienced by the designated teacher leader in Allendale might be to allow teachers to seek their own assistance from respected colleagues or create forums for this to happen which occurred in Mangrove. The teachers were encouraged by the principal and literacy leader to seek assistance from their peers. When they were asked in the interviews whom they believed to be the most effective Grade 1 teacher, two nominated one person and two others different people. They also all indicated that they believed their nominated person had leadership qualities and that they regularly discussed programs and sought advice from them. The informal leadership networks appeared to be working well to the extent that no teacher indicated that they felt alone or unsupported. Each teacher blamed others for the declining achievement patterns because they believed that they themselves, and the nominated person with whom they discussed their programs, were teaching effectively.

The problem identified with this informal system based on existing respect was that advice was sought most frequently from ineffective teacher leaders. The most frequently nominated person was quoted above as believing that the main achievement problems were caused by the students' home and educational backgrounds: "Are they having breakfast? Did they go to pre-school?" This teacher had a particularly strong influence on, and provided a great deal of support to, a newly qualified teacher who was experiencing both management and instructional difficulties in her classroom. Causes external to her teaching competence were an attractive option to consider. These vignettes from Allendale and Mangrove indicate that one of the challenges in developing teacher leadership is to integrate leadership qualities of acceptance by followers, with expertise in the particular area because followers construct leadership activity as much as the other way around. Neither acceptance nor expertise guaranteed the other quality, and their integration was not satisfactorily achieved in any of the schools. In the next section, I examine the issue of the reciprocal relationship between leaders and followers more closely.

Relationships Between Leaders and Followers

When leadership is viewed from a distributed perspective, the analysis of power relationships inevitably changes (West et al., 2000) and distinctions between leaders and followers blur (Gronn, 2003). This section examines this reciprocal influence between leaders and followers in Mangrove.

In the section above describing embedding of visions in activities, a quote from the literacy leader in Mangrove in Year 2 illustrated how she disguised her beliefs that poor program implementation was responsible for the decline in test scores by listing factors outside of the classroom. During an interview after the meeting, she expressed her frustration to the researcher that the discussion was dominated by these external causes. The reason she gave for not challenging the teachers follows:

LITERACY LEADER: That discussion – it coming in about no lunches and all that sort of thing and I do remember trying to cut that off because I think we're past that. We've been through all that blame sort of thing.

RESEARCHER: What stopped you from saying something like that?

LITERACY LEADER: Probably because I sympathize with how they feel because it shows things that are a reality for some children and I want to kind of say "Yes," and acknowledge that we've got to move on from there. There are a group of teachers that are like that and it's almost like, "Well that's where they're at at the moment." I'm hoping that people will come to a natural conclusion of getting past that.

When she changed her meeting activities in Year 3 to focusing the meeting on identifying and targeting failing students, she no longer allowed herself to be so influenced by the teachers. She explained it like this:

> While I still try to sympathize with the problems the teachers are having, I know that if we want to raise achievement we have to get past all that. Since we changed focus, it never comes up about blaming kids and homes. The teachers are now focused on what they can do. I don't know how it happened, it just happened.

In Year 2, the leadership activity in the meeting was focused on the teachers, their beliefs and their preferences. Trying to shift them toward a different set of beliefs, together with the hope of "getting past all that," that left the leader in a position of being led by the followers. How she acted was determined largely by the teachers' responses, and she felt powerless to change their thinking or actions until they were ready. In Year 3, when the activity was more explicitly focused on raising student achievement, followers influenced the leader only to the extent of providing the support needed to reach agreed goals. By using student achievement (rather than teachers) as the reference point and structuring the meeting activities around the data, divergence from teaching and learning issues was constrained, and the relationships between leaders and followers changed. This example illustrates how different forms of artefacts can exert a powerful influence on other attributes of the situation, and it is a more focused analysis to which I turn next.

The Use of Artefacts

From a distributed leadership perspective, artefacts and how they are used are a constitutive part of leadership activities. Spillane et al. (2004) refer to artefacts as "externalized representations of ideas and intentions" (p. 23). These authors include a range of artefacts in their definition, including: materials such as memos, structures such as timetables, and symbols such as language. The use of language as an artefact to represent central ideas has been illustrated in the previous sections.

In this section, I focus on achievement data as a material artefact and how it shaped and was shaped by the leaders. Rather than reiterate how these data were stretched over leadership activities, I am taking a slightly different perspective on the role of this artefact. First, I examine how the form of the achievement data and the conversations around it served to either integrate it with or decouple it from instruction. Second, I discuss briefly how artefacts that are stretched over functions and roles might need to change in form if they are to be effective in spanning boundaries between principals, literacy leaders, and teachers.

Forms of Artefacts, Instruction and Spanning Boundaries

Artefacts can both enable and constrain practice (Spillane et al., 2004). The presence in the meetings of benchmarked individual student achievement information that could be compared across classes did both these things in the Group 2 schools in Years 1 and 2 and all schools in Year 3. As noted in the section above, the artefacts constrained the meeting activities in the sense that they focused on students, their achievement, and the teachers' actions associated with that achievement. However, the achievement data also enabled practice, in that they served as the basis of the discussion on how to teach the students more effectively. One of the reasons that the meeting and related activities could reasonably be associated with improvements in student achievement, is that the activities and artefacts were closely integrated with instruction. The following quote from a teacher at Mangrove in Year 3 illustrates how the *X* on the scatter plot representing children's progress triggered a complex web of cognitions about children, their progress, how that progress fitted with others in the group and what actions she could take next:

TEACHER: I find that it has been quite beneficial because the graph is marked for each child. I can actually see where they're at, whether they are above the line or below the line [national benchmark]. So it's really looking at each individual in my classroom, so I can see what I need to do. Like we spoke now [in the meeting], I look at which ones I should be moving above the line and work with those particular children in the group

AUTHOR: They're only marks on a graph. Those little crosses – they don't tell you how to teach.

TEACHER: But you the teacher know the children, so you're basically linking the graph and what you know about your children. Do you know what I mean? It is different for you because you're looking at it just as X's. But for me as a teacher and my class, I'm linking the X's to children. Although L is at red level I know he's going to be moving faster than the other two in the group. And I think about the [teaching] prompts I'm using, because each level has its own prompts. So you see if I'm going to be working at Level 1, I know that these are the prompts that I must be using at this particular level. And if I can see that one child in that particular group is able to move a bit faster than the rest of the group. I can say, "OK, I've got another group at Level 3 and this child is at the end of Level 3 so I can move her up to that group."

In contrast, the form of the achievement data in Year 2, in those Group 1 schools that used them, were irrelevant to the teachers in terms of their practice when the data were combined for all students. In Mangrove, for example, the data were presented as a summary table of the percentages of students performing below, at, and above expectations. They had little meaning for the teachers because the collated data across all students did not cater to the teachers' primary interest in "my students in my class." No relationship to teaching, therefore, was made.

Forms of material artefacts need to be different for those with different task responsibilities if they are to be useful. In this study, the achievement data needed to be analyzed one way for teachers and another way for principals if they were to be useful in their different roles. Given the boundary-spanning function of the literacy leader, it would be her responsibility to make the necessary adjustments.

In Avonside and Allendale in Year 2 and all schools in Year 3, the teachers had available to them detailed scatter plots that identified individual students' reading levels from which they could make various comparisons. This level of detail, however, was inappropriate for a principal whose function was to understand the picture of the whole school at each grade level. A key boundary-spanning task for the literacy leader was to modify the artefact to enable the principal to perform more macro-level tasks by summarizing the data appropriately.

Modification of artefacts to meet the task requirements for people performing different organizational roles may appear an obvious requirement but it was not apparent in any of the Group 1 schools in Years 1 and 2. When achievement data were analyzed, they were presented in the same form to people having different functions. By changing the form of the data in Mangrove, and the other Group 1 schools in Year 3, they became more meaningful for the teachers who were then able to use them to integrate them into their practice.

Conclusions

The value of analyzing activities, artefacts, and situations in determining differential effectiveness in leadership activities is well-illustrated in this study. By changing the artefacts and the situation, the same leaders who in one year had failed to accomplish the task of accelerated student outcomes, were able to become much more effective in the following year. This "transformation" could not be understood if leadership traits, behaviors, tasks, or artefacts had been analyzed separately. The change involved a complex interplay among all these aspects, resulting in different leadership activities situated in these contexts. This activity proved to be the useful unit of analysis.

Spillane et al.'s (2004) descriptive framework provided an important set of constructs on which to base the analysis in this paper. Particularly useful is their emphasis on activity and how it is stretched over people. The conceptual robustness of the framework has accommodated the shift from their descriptive work to the more normative position I have taken to examine the differential effectiveness of leadership. The dimensions of interest to most researchers who adopt a normative position, that greater distribution is more desirable than containing leadership within formally specified roles (Camburn et al., 2003; Day & Harris, 2003), however, is different from the one I have adopted. Distributing leadership over more people is a risky business and may result in the greater distribution of incompetence. I suggest that increasing the distribution of leadership is only desirable if the quality of the leadership activities contributes to assisting teachers to provide more effective instruction to their students and it is on these qualities that we should focus.

These qualities cannot be understood in isolation from the situation in which leadership is exercised. Leadership by its very nature involves others who are situated in a cultural, historical and institutional setting (Spillane et al., 2004). The way followers interpret the situation and respond to the leader influences how leaders think and act. These reciprocal responses can have very different outcomes. The way in which artefacts are constructed and presented to followers also serves to shape different social interactions and outcomes yet artefacts are rarely identified as a constitutive and influential component of leadership activity.

The power of leadership activities in shaping teachers' visions for and expectations of student achievement was apparent in the different schools and phases of this study. Changed activities developed different visions about what was possible in tackling the problems of student underachievement. By externalizing the reference point for the meetings from teachers' beliefs and preferences about a generalized problem of underachievement to concerns about the achievement of individual students in their classes, solutions to the problems became manageable. The solutions made sense to the teachers within their existing knowledge and experience (Spillane et al., 2002). They knew about teaching individual students and, with assistance, improving achievement became possible. When the meeting activities were structured in this way for the teachers, looking for solutions outside of the classroom disappeared. The vision in action, as evidenced in the meetings, became far more powerful than any written statements of goals and strategies.

Boundary spanning by the middle managers provided some interesting challenges. In many ways it was up to these key people to transform, through the use of language and material artefacts, the macro-functions undertaken by principals into a meaningful form so teachers were able to translate them into the more micro-functions of teaching students. One of the challenges they faced was to change the form of the artefacts, in this case student achievement data, to meet task requirements. When principals and teachers received the same form of student achievement information, for example, neither made use of it in many of the schools. For the teachers, in particular, the achievement data needed to be in a form that allowed them to integrate the information into their instructional practice. This form was too detailed to be useful for the principals' macro-functions.

Another challenge was to achieve coherence across the organization in ways that promoted student achievement. While coherence was successfully accomplished in all schools in the early stages of this study, through the boundary spanning activities of the literacy leaders, it was not always the kind of coherence that promoted student achievement. Accomplishing coherence and instructional improvement proved difficult and fragile.

Developing teacher leadership in ways that promoted student achievement, a goal for many advocates of distributed leadership (Leithwood et al., 1999; Southworth, 1990), also presented difficulties. Teacher leaders with high acceptability among their colleagues were not necessarily those with expertise. Conversely, the micro-politics within a school can reduce the acceptability of those with expertise. More research is needed into issues and dilemmas related to teacher leadership and how they might be resolved, rather than assuming that distributing leadership among teachers develops instructional capacity.

Distributed leadership is a relatively new theoretical concept. Individual leaders, their personal characteristics and behavior, the standards they should meet (Gronn, 2003) and the influences they exert on followers (Camburn et al., 2003) have dominated the leadership literature. Yet leadership has always been distributed within organizations so it is a little surprising that we have taken so long to recognize it and develop the associated conceptual frameworks. Having begun to do so, it is important that enthusiasm for the possibilities it may unfold does not mean we become blinkered to the limitations of the concept itself, and our ability to think about it and outside of it.

Acknowledgments

The author wishes to acknowledge the openness of the leaders in the schools involved in this research to having their practice scrutinized, and their willingness to make changes in response to feedback. The funding support provided by the New Zealand Ministry of Education is also acknowledged. The helpful comments on an earlier draft of this manuscript by Associate Professor James Spillane and Professor Viviane Robinson were greatly appreciated.

Notes

1 This chapter is based on a previously published article (see Timperley, 2005).
2 Pseudonyms have been used for all schools. In the interests of clarity, Group 1 schools have the names of trees and Group 2 schools have a geographical association.

References

Barth, R.S. (2001). *Learning by heart.* San Francisco, CA: Jossey-Bass.
Bryk, A. (1999). Policy lessons from Chicago's experience with decentralization. In D. Ravitch

(ed.), *Brookings Papers on Education Policy* (pp. 67–128). Washington, DC: Brookings Institution Press.

Camburn, E., Rowan, B., & Taylor, J.E. (2003). Distributed leadership in schools: The case of elementary schools adopting comprehensive school reform models. *Educational Evaluation and Policy Analysis*, 25(4), 347–373.

Clay, M.M. (1993). *Reading recovery: A guidebook for teachers in training.* Auckland, NZ: Heinemann.

Copland, M.A. (2003). Leadership of inquiry: Building and sustaining capacity for school improvement. *Educational Evaluation and Policy Analysis*, 25(4), 375–395.

Day, C. & Harris, A. (2003). Teacher leadership, reflective practice, and school improvement. In K. Leithwood & P. Hallinger (eds) *Second international handbook of educational leadership and administration* (Chapter 27). Dordrecht, The Netherlands: Kluwer.

Eraut, M. (1994). *Developing professional knowledge and competence.* London, UK: Falmer Press.

Gilmore, A., Croft, C., & Reid, N. (1981). *BURT Word Reading Test: New Zealand revision.* Wellington, NZ: New Zealand Council for Educational Research.

Gronn, P. (2003). Leadership: Who needs it? *School Leadership and Management*, 23(3), 267–290.

Hargreaves, A. (1994). *Changing teachers, changing times: Teachers' work and culture in the postmodern age.* New York, NY: Teachers College Press.

Lambert, L. (1998). How to build leadership capacity. *Educational Leadership*, 55(7), 17–19.

Leithwood, K., Jantzi, D., & Steinbach, R. (1999). *Changing leadership for changing times.* Buckingham, UK: Open University Press.

New Zealand Education Review Office. (1996). *Improving schooling in Mangere and Otara.* Wellington, NZ: Education Review Office.

New Zealand Ministry of Education. (1993). School charters and the revised national education guidelines. *The Education Gazette* (p. 3). Wellington, NZ: Ministry of Education.

Phillips, G.E., McNaughton, S., & MacDonald, S. (2001). *Picking up the pace: Effective literacy interventions for accelerated progress over the transition into Decile One schools* (Final report). Wellington, NZ: Ministry of Education, available at: http://www.minedu. govt.nz/web/document/document_page.cfm?id=6444.

Sergiovanni, T.J. (1988). Leadership as pedagogy, capital development and school effectiveness. *International Journal of Leadership in Education*, 1(1), 37–47.

Smylie, M.A. & Hart, A.W. (1999). School leadership for teacher learning and change: A human and social capital development perspective. In J. Murphy & K.S. Louis (eds) *Handbook of educational administration: A project of the American Educational Research Association* (pp. 421–442). San Francisco, CA: Jossey-Bass.

Southworth, G. (1990). Leadership, headship and effective primary schools. *School Organization*, 10(1), 3–16.

Spillane, J.P. & Sherer, J.Z. (2004, April). *A distributed perspective on school leadership: Leadership practice as stretched over people and place.* Paper presented at the Annual Meeting of the American Educational Research Association. San Diego, CA.

Spillane, J.P., Halverson, R., & Diamond, J. (2004). Towards a theory of leadership practice: A distributed perspective. *Journal of Curriculum Studies*, 36(1), 3–34.

Spillane, J.P., Reiser, B.J., & Reimer, T. (2002). Policy implementation and cognition: Reframing and refocusing implementation research. *Review of Educational Research*, 72(3), 387–431.

Timperley, H. (2005). Distributed leadership: Developing theory from practice. *Journal of Curriculum Studies*, 37(4), 395–420, also available at http://www.informaworld.com.

Timperley, H.S. & Robinson, V.M.J. (2003). Partnership as intervention strategy in self-managing schools. *School Effectiveness and School Improvement*, 14(3), 249–274.

Timperley, H.S. & Wiseman, J. (2003). *The sustainability of professional development in literacy: Part 2. School-based factors associated with high student achievement.* Wellington, NZ: Ministry of Education, available at: http://www.minedu.govt.nz/index.cfm?layout=document&documentid=8638&data=l.

Wenger, E. (1998). *Communities of practice: Learning, meaning, and identity.* New York, NY: Cambridge University Press.

West, M., Jackson, D., Harris, A., & Hopkins, D. (2000). Leadership for school improvement. In K. Riley & K.S. Louis (eds) *Leadership for change* (pp. 35–47). London, UK: Routledge.

10
Distributing Leadership to Make Schools Smarter
Taking the Ego Out of the System

KENNETH LEITHWOOD, BLAIR MASCALL, TIIU STRAUSS,
ROBIN SACKS, NADEEM MEMON, AND ANNA YASHKINA

In this study, we inquired about patterns of leadership distribution, as well as which leadership functions were performed by whom, the characteristics of non-administrative leaders, and the factors promoting and inhibiting the distribution of leadership functions. We consider our account of distributed leadership in this district to be a probable example of "best practice" at the present time – not perfect, but likely more mature than average by a significant degree. The most noteworthy detail to emerge from our study was the critical part played by formal school and district leaders in helping to foster apparently productive forms of distributed leadership.

The study of leadership practices or functions has traditionally located them in individuals, usually people in roles or positions with formal authority and not infrequently people to whom "heroic" capabilities and charismatic qualities are attributed. This is "focused leadership." Most organizations have always relied heavily on the leadership provided by many other members of the organization to actually get work done. The current flurry of interest in distributed leadership could be interpreted as an effort to shift these sources of leadership from the informal to the formal side of the organizational chart – to explicitly acknowledge the presence of such leadership so as to better understand its contribution to organizational functioning.

With the exception of leadership distributed through formally established committees and teams, we have almost no systematic evidence about the relative contribution to the achievement of organizational goals of different patterns of distributed leadership; limited to school organizations, such evidence is virtually non-existent.

This chapter reports evidence from the first phase of a two-staged, multi-methods study. The first phase entails the collection of qualitative evidence in a small number of schools followed by a second phase entirely based on quantitative data. Including both phases of the research, our study aims to provide systematic evidence in response to questions about:

- differences in patterns of leadership distribution (touched on in this phase but addressed more fully in Phase Two);
- who performs which leadership functions;
- characteristics of those in non-administrative roles performing leadership functions;
- factors which assist or inhibit the development of distributed leadership; and
- the outcomes of distributed leadership including both organizational effects and effects on student learning (Phase Two).

Unlike most distributed leadership studies to date, our perspective on these questions spans both schools and their district. Our end goal, furthermore, is to help move research on distributed leadership beyond its current, largely descriptive state, to a state which offers more insights about the improvement of leadership practice.

Review of Literature

This section of the chapter reviews evidence relevant to four of the five issues pursued in our two-phase study. The fifth issue, outcomes of distributed leadership, will be addressed when we report results of the second phase of the research. In addition to summarizing conceptual orientations and empirical evidence about each of the four issues, we also formulate a series of hypotheses warranted by those orientations and evidence which is to be tested during the course of our project as a whole. Not all of these hypotheses have been tested in this first phase, however.

Patterns of Distributed Leadership

Both Gronn (2003) and Spillane (2006) have conceptualized two distinct forms of distributed leadership. Gronn labels these forms *additive* and *holistic*. The additive label describes an uncoordinated pattern of leadership in which many different people may engage in leadership functions but without much, or any, effort to take account of the leadership activities of others in their organization. This would seem to be the most common meaning of the term assumed by those advocating that "everyone is a leader" (e.g. Manz & Sims, 1980).

Holistic or, in Spillane's (2006) terms, *person-plus* labels refer to consciously-managed and synergistic relationships among some, many, or all sources of leadership in the organization. These forms of distributed leadership assume: the sum of leaders' work adds up to more than the parts; there are high levels of interdependence among those providing leadership; and the influence attributed to their activities emerges from dynamic, multidirectional, social processes which, at their best, lead to learning for the individuals involved, as well as for their organizations (Pearce & Conger, 2003).

Based on his review of a small corpus of research conducted in an array of different organizational contexts, Gronn (2002) has suggested that holistic forms of distributed leadership may take three forms. The first of these is spontaneous collaboration. "From time to time," Gronn explains, "groupings of individuals with differing skills and knowledge capacities, and from across different organizational levels, coalesce to pool their expertise and regularize their conduct for duration of the task, and then disband" (p. 657). A second form of concertive distribution is referred to by Gronn as *intuitive working relations.* This form of concertive distributed leadership emerges over time "as two or more organizational members come to rely on one another and develop close working relations" and, as Gronn argues, "leadership is manifest in the shared role space encompassed by their relationship" (p. 657). Finally, citing committees and teams as their most obvious embodiment, Gronn's institutionalized practice includes such formalized structures as arising from design or through less systematic adaptation.

The extent and nature of coordination in the exercise of influence across members of the organization is a critical challenge from a holistic perspective. Interdependence between two or more organizational members may be based on role overlap or complementarity of skills and knowledge. When role overlap occurs in a coordinated fashion there can be mutual reinforcement of influence and less likelihood of making errors in decisions. When performance of complementary functions is the form of interdependence, those providing leadership have opportunities to do what they know best, as well as increase their own capacities by observing their colleagues doing the same, a "huddle effect" according to Gronn (2002, p. 671).

Our conception of distributed leadership patterns builds on and extends Gronn's three holistic forms. We focus on the extent to which the performance of leadership functions is consciously aligned across the sources of leadership. In addition, we speculate about the beliefs and values which would support each of these different forms of alignment.

PLANFUL ALIGNMENT

In this configuration, comparable to the holistic form which Gronn labels *institutionalized practice,* the tasks or functions of those providing leadership have been given prior, planful thought by organizational members. Agreements have been worked out among the sources of leadership about which leadership practices or functions are best carried out by which source.

Although we assumed that alignment was a good thing for the organization, positive contributions of this configuration to productivity cannot be assumed for several reasons. Patterns of task distribution determined through planning may turn out to be sub-optimal in some manner. And even if the distribution is optimal, one or more leaders may enact their agreed-on functions in an unskilled manner. But we assumed that the "pre-thinking," reflective, or planful processes associated with this configuration would increase the chances of a productive pattern of leadership distribution.

Shared values and beliefs that seem likely to be associated with planful alignment include:

- reflection and dialogue as the basis for good decision making;
- trust in the motives of one's leadership colleagues (see Gabarro, 1978 cited in Gronn, 2002);
- well-grounded beliefs about the capacities of one's leadership colleagues;
- commitment to shared whole-organization goals; and
- cooperation rather than competition as the best way to promote productivity within the organization.

SPONTANEOUS ALIGNMENT

In this configuration, essentially Gronn's *spontaneous collaboration* form of concertive distribution, leadership tasks and functions are distributed with little or no planning. Nevertheless, tacit and intuitive decisions about who should perform which leadership functions results in a fortuitous alignment of functions across leadership sources. There is no significant difference in the contribution to short-term organizational productivity of this method of alignment, as compared with planful alignment. However, the tacit nature of decisions this method entails seems likely to reduce the flexibility and adaptability of the organization's responses to future leadership challenges. Spontaneity offers few guarantees of fortuitous alignment.

Shared values and beliefs which seem likely to be associated with spontaneous alignment include:

- "gut feelings" as the basis for good decision making;
- trust in the motives of one's leadership colleagues;
- idealistic beliefs about the capacities of one's leadership colleagues;
- commitment to shared organizational goals; and
- cooperation rather than competition as the best way to promote productivity within the organization.

SPONTANEOUS MISALIGNMENT

This configuration mirrors spontaneous alignment in the manner of leadership distribution, as well as its underlying values, beliefs and norms. Only the outcome is different or less fortuitous – misalignment (which may vary from marginal to extensive). Both short- and long-term organizational productivity suffer from this form of (mis)alignment. However, organizational members are not opposed, in principle, to either planful or spontaneous alignment thus leaving open reasonable prospects for future productive alignment of one sort or another.

ANARCHIC MISALIGNMENT

This configuration is characterized by active rejection, on the part of some or many organizational leaders, of influence from others about what they should be doing in their own sphere of influence. As a result, those leaders' units behave highly independently, competing with other units on such matters as organizational goals and access to resources. Active rejection of influence by others, however, stimulates considerable reflection about one's own position on most matters of concern.

Shared values and beliefs likely to be associated with anarchic misalignment include:

- reflection and dialogue as the basis for good decision making about one's own work and sphere of influence;
- mistrust in the motives and capacities of one's leadership colleagues;
- commitment to individual or unit, but not whole organization goals; and
- competition rather than cooperation as the best way to promote productivity across units within the organization.

HYPOTHESES

Based on this conceptualization of leadership distribution patterns, we expect evidence accumulated across the two phases of our study to demonstrate that:

1. Planful and spontaneous patterns of alignment contribute equally to short-term organizational productivity and more than either spontaneous misalignment or anarchic misalignment.
2. Planful alignment contributes significantly more than other patterns of alignment to long-term organizational productivity.
3. Both spontaneous misalignment and anarchic misalignment have negative effects on short- and long-term organizational productivity.
4. Organizational members associated with both spontaneous alignment and misalignment will be more attracted to planful alignment than will organizational members associated with anarchic misalignment.

Leadership Functions

Fundamental to the study of distributed leadership are questions about just what it is that is being spread around. Our general answer is leadership functions, actions or "practices"; the term practices, as we use it, conforms to most dictionary definitions of the term and is more or less synonymous with leadership behaviors. It is not, we should stress, the conception of practices created by Spillane (2006) in his distributed leadership study – interactions that occur among leaders, followers and the situations in which they work. While such interactions are obviously critical to an understanding of how leadership influence is enacted, we limit our conception of practices to the behaviors or functions of leaders during such interactions.

From our perspective, both leaders and followers engage in practices that need to be understood and the context or situation in which they interact has important influences on what both leaders and followers do in response to one another. One of the most important missions for leadership research (and one of the most practical) is to uncover those leadership behaviors or practices that have predictable and desirable influences on followers, especially influences that can be predicted across a significant range of contexts or situations.

Evidence from leadership studies in both school and non-school contexts points to several broad categories of leadership functions with such predictable effects; they served as our initial conception of what is being distributed in this study and we have described them, as well as the evidence giving rise to them, quite extensively elsewhere (e.g. Leithwood et al., 2004; Leithwood & Riehl, 2005). These categories of leadership practices reflect a transformational approach to leadership which Bass (1997) claims, has proven to be useful in many different cultural and organizational contexts. This claim is demonstrably the case for educational organizations, generally (e.g. Geijsel et al., 2003; Southworth, 1998; Yu et al., 2002) and, specifically, for the success of some large-scale reform efforts in schools (e.g. Day et al. 2000). We consider these categories and the specific practices they encompass to be the "basics" of good leadership in most organizational contexts.

SETTING DIRECTION

A critical aspect of leadership is helping a group to develop shared understandings about the organization and its activities and goals that can undergird a sense of purpose or vision (e.g. Hallinger & Heck, 2002). The most fundamental theoretical explanations for the importance of direction-setting practices on the part of leaders are goal-based theories of human motivation (e.g. Bandura, 1986; Ford, 1992; Locke et al., 1988). According to such theory, people are motivated by goals which they find personally compelling, as well as challenging, but achievable. Having such goals helps people make sense of their work (e.g. Thayer, 1988; Weick, 1995) and enables them to find a sense of identity for themselves within their work context (Pittman, 1998).

Often cited as helping set direction are such specific practices as:

- identifying and articulating a vision;
- fostering the acceptance of group goals;
- creating high performance expectations; and
- promoting effective communication.

(Bennis, 1984)

DEVELOPING PEOPLE

While clear and compelling organizational directions contribute significantly to members' work-related motivations, they are not the only conditions to do so. Nor do such directions contribute to the capacities members often need in order to productively move in those directions. Such capacities and motivations are influenced by the direct experiences organizational members have with those in leadership roles (Lord & Maher, 1993), as well as the organizational conditions within which people work (Rowan, 1996), as we discuss below.

The ability to engage in such practices depends, in part, on leaders' knowledge of the "technical core" of schooling – what is required to improve the quality of teaching and learning – often invoked by the term "instructional leadership" (Hallinger & Murphy, 1985; Sheppard, 1996). But this ability also is part of what is now being referred to as leaders' emotional intelligence (Goleman et al., 2002). Recent evidence suggests that such intelligence displayed, for example, through the personal attention devoted by a leader to an employee and the use of the employee's capacities increases levels of enthusiasm and optimism, reduces frustration, transmits a sense of mission and indirectly increases performance (McColl-Kennedy & Anderson, 2002).

More specific sets of leadership practices significantly and positively influencing these direct experiences include, for example:

- offering intellectual stimulation;
- providing individualized support (e.g. Louis et al., 1999); and
- modeling appropriate values and practices. (e.g. Ross, 1995; Ross et al., 1996).

REDESIGNING THE ORGANIZATION

Successful educational leaders develop their schools as effective organizations that support and sustain the performance of teachers as well as students. This category of leadership practices has emerged from recent evidence about the nature of learning organizations and professional learning communities (Leithwood et al., 1998) and their contribution to staff work (e.g. Louis & Kruse, 1995; Louis et al., 1996) and student learning (Marks et al., 2000; Silins et al., 2000). Such practices assume that the purpose behind organizational cultures and structures is to facilitate the work of organizational members and that the malleability of structures should match the changing nature of the school's improvement agenda. Specific practices typically associated with this category include strengthening school cultures (e.g. Leithwood & Jantzi, 1990), modifying organizational structures (Louis & Kruse, 1995; Roberts, 1985), and building collaborative processes (e.g. Sleegers et al., 2002).

MANAGING THE INSTRUCTIONAL PROGRAM

This category acknowledges the special nature of schools and the core technology of schooling, in particular; it also recognizes the crucial contribution that reliable standard operation procedures make to the effectiveness of almost any organization. Evidence about the nature of instructional leadership (e.g. Alig-Mielcarek & Hoy, 2005) and effective school improvement processes (Leithwood et al., 2006) narrow our focus to four subsets of tasks in this category:

- staffing the instructional program;
- monitoring the progress of students and the school's improvement strategies;
- buffering staff from unproductive external demands for attention; and
- allocating resources to foster the school's improvement efforts.

HYPOTHESES

The leadership functions which have been described are typically portrayed as "core" or "basic" functions that successful leaders need to exercise in most circumstances; evidence also suggests that they are relatively comprehensive of what leaders do (Day & Leithwood, 2007). So we hypothesized that:

5. Leadership functions distributed in schools and across the district will be encompassed by the four categories of functions described above.

Sources and Extent of Leadership Distribution

Who and how many people engage in which leadership functions appears to depend at least on which functions are to be performed, their level of complexity and the organizational context in which they are to be carried out.

WHO EXERCISES WHICH LEADERSHIP FUNCTIONS?

Locke's (2003) *integrated model* of leadership includes the potential for considerable coordination in a distributed leadership environment. This model acknowledges both the reality and the virtues, in most organizations, of distributed leadership based on multiple forms of lateral influence. Also acknowledged by the model, however, is what Jaques (1989) claims to be "inevitable" sources of vertical or hierarchical leadership in virtually any successful organization. As Locke comments, "No successful, profit-making company that I know of has ever been run by a team" (2003, p. 273). Relationships involved in vertical leadership entail a two-way flow of influence that assists with the coordination problem left unresolved in conceptions of distributed leadership, which usually imply only the lateral forms of leadership in Locke's model.

Locke (2003) argues that, among the range of functions and tasks associated with leadership, several should not be distributed or shared while the remainder should be – at least in part. From the perspective of our core leadership functions, Locke would assign "top leaders" (his term) the job of deciding on the organization's vision (including its core values), determining an overall strategy for realizing the vision, and making sure the organizational structure supports its strategy. While top leaders are likely to engage many people in processes leading up to such decisions, top leaders have the final responsibility for them. At least partly shareable leadership tasks, according to Locke, are goalsetting in relation to the vision, intellectual stimulation, individualized support and building a collaborative culture. These are tasks which need to be carried out at all levels if the organization is to succeed in moving toward its vision.

TASK COMPLEXITY

Organizational theorists have long argued that task complexity is a key variable shaping productive leadership responses. This body of evidence argues that more directive forms of leadership (akin to what most people think of as "supervision") are productive when the tasks to be performed are relatively simple. More participatory, shared or distributed forms of leadership work best in response to relatively complex tasks (Rowan, 1996). This is the case because the collective capacities of the organization theoretically far exceed the capacities of any one organizational member. Distributing leadership is a strategy with some potential for accessing and bringing to bear the organization's collective cognitions on the achievement of complex tasks and organizational goals.

Conceptions of distributed cognition, furthermore, support "unconstrained" forms of distributed leadership. Whereas constrained forms of distributed leadership entail leadership functions carried out by one formal leader or shared among formal leaders only, unconstrained forms include the distribution of leadership to whomever has the expertise required for the job, rather than only those in formal leadership roles. Leadership functions may be: shared among formal leaders and one, or a few, exceptional "others" because of their unique personal expertise; widely shared among formal and informal leaders depending on their existing expertise; or widely shared among formal and informal leaders based on their existing expertise, as well as the opportunities provided by such distribution for developing additional expertise. This last form of unconstrained distribution seems the most sophisticated or preferred because it conceives of leadership distribution not only as a means of using the shared expertise in the organization but also as a means of further building that expertise.

HYPOTHESES

Based on this perspective about leadership distribution, we expected to find that the most effective forms of distribution:

6. Demonstrate differentiation in the performance of functions depending on role.
7. Vary the numbers of people providing leadership in response to the complexity of the tasks to be performed – more in the case of complex tasks and fewer in response to simple tasks.
8. Reflect unconstrained forms of distribution especially in the performance of complex leadership tasks.

Characteristics of Non-Administrator Leaders

Our attraction to unconstrained forms of distributed leadership is based on its potential to leverage organizational expertise. But in addition to expertise, people may be viewed as leaders by their colleagues because they are perceived to be "prototype" organizational members and/or because of their personal traits.

PROTOTYPICALITY

Leadership research guided by *social identity theory* suggests that one's self identity can be located along a continuum from personal to social identity (Reicher et al., 2005). Personal identity includes idiosyncratic attributes such as abilities and interests, whereas a social identity encompasses salient group classifications such as gender, nationality and organizational affiliation (e.g. I am a teacher at Carleton High School).

Organizational identity is a specific form of social identification. As people begin to identify with their organizations, they usually assume the prototypical characteristics of the organization as part of their own self concept. They are motivated to form such identities because of a need for "self-categorization" (the need to make sense of their own place in society), and the need for "self-enhancement" (feelings of self-worth from membership in an organization). In sum, then, identification with the organization helps define self-concept and contributes to feelings of self-worth. Applied to leadership, social identity theory suggests that when people identify strongly with their group or organization, they are most likely to identify, as leaders within their group or organization, those with the most prototypical characteristics, not necessarily those with the greatest expertise (Lumby, 2006; Pierro et al., 2005). An ideal or prototypical person is one who is most like other members of the group and most different from those outside the group. There seems to be good evidence to suggest that groups often ascribe leadership to those with the most prototypical features of the group (Lipponen et al., 2005).

When informal leadership is ascribed to prototypical persons, those persons may or may not have the capacity or motivation to move their organization forward. Indeed, their motivation might be just the opposite – to preserve strongly-held group norms that, nevertheless, stand in the way of the group becoming more effective. Prototypical leadership nomination, therefore, has the potential to exercise a highly conservative influence on the organization unless the existing group or organizational norms are highly supportive of change. Potentially the most effective informal leaders would seem likely to be those with high levels of relevant expertise, as well as high levels of acceptance based on their prototypicality. These leaders begin with the trust of their colleagues and are likely to be more successful in convincing their colleagues of the need for change should that be required.

TRAITS

Several recent reviews of evidence (Day & Leithwood, 2007; Zaccaro et al., 2004) associate a bundle of cognitive and "affective traits" with successful leadership. Among the cognitive characteristics or traits identified in these reviews are intelligence, problem solving capacities and knowledge relevant to the content of the challenges facing the organization; successful leaders, the evidence suggests in brief, have higher than average amounts of these things. Among affective traits associated with successful leadership are aspects of personality, motivation, and social appraisal skills.

Substantial evidence associates successful leadership with a bundle of personality traits including: maintenance of emotional stability; extraversion or proactivity (sociable, gregarious, assertive, talkative, active); agreeableness (e.g. courteous, flexible, trusting, good natured, cooperative); and, conscientiousness (e.g. hardworking, achievement oriented, persevering). Successful leaders also are open to experience (e.g. imaginative, curious, original, broad minded), are optimistic, and have a good deal of confidence in themselves or high levels of self-efficacy as leaders.

Evidence from non-school contexts indicates that successful leaders have motivational profiles characterized by the need for dominance or power, achievement, affiliation, and responsibility. Within schools, recent evidence paints successful school leaders as passionate about their work, highly committed emotionally and highly motivated. Many of them have high energy levels likely to be motivational to others, as well as being determined, persistent, and industrious.

The final category of affective leadership traits or characteristics associated with successful leadership is social appraisal skills, the ability to understand the feelings, thoughts, and behaviors of oneself and others and to act appropriately upon that understanding. Capacities included in this broad category of traits refer to leaders' abilities to appreciate the emotional states of colleagues, to discern those states in complex social circumstances, to respond in ways that are considered helpful, and to understand and manage one's own emotions. Social appraisal skills of successful leaders identified in a broad array of evidence include self-monitoring skills, as well as both social and emotional intelligence. These social intelligence or social appraisal skills of leaders have been the object of considerable research. It seems reasonable, in addition, to assume that emotional intelligence, a concept popularized by Goleman (e.g. 1998), is part of this broad category of traits. Research specifically about the emotional intelligence of leaders is relatively new, however. Overall, this evidence indicates that social appraisal skills have strongly related to leadership success. This relationship may vary in strength depending on type of job. Wong and Law suggest, for example, "emotional management skills would be more strongly related to performance in a highly emotionally laborious job than in those involving less emotional labor" (quoted in Zaccaro et al., 2004, p. 116). School leadership undoubtedly qualifies as emotionally laborious.

HYPOTHESES

We expected that non-administrative leaders would emerge because of their expertise, their prototypicality, as well as their traits. This evidence led us to expect that:

9. Non-administrative leaders identified because of their prototypicality only will be less effective than those who emerge because of their expertise, or because of both their expertise and prototypicality.
10. Non-administrative leaders identified as prototypical by their colleagues, as well as possessing significant expertise, will be more effective than those with expertise alone.
11. Attribution of leadership to those in non-administrative roles will be significantly shaped by the perceived traits associated with attributions of leadership to those in formal administrative roles.

Influences on the Development of Distributed Leadership

Most of what we know about factors influencing the development of distributed leadership in schools is the product of research on teacher leadership. This body of evidence suggests that the extent to which teachers take up organizational leadership functions depends on features of the school's structure and culture, opportunities for capacity building, the nature of teacher–principal relations, and active encouragement and support for distributed forms of leadership by principals (Day & Harris, 2002; Harris, 2005;

Harris & Lambert, 2003; Lieberman & Miller, 2005; Leithwood, 2003; Leithwood et al., 2003; MacBeath, 2005; Murphy, 2005; Smylie et al., 2002).

Hierarchical school structures diminish the likelihood of the changes in relationships between teachers and administrators that are needed to encourage leadership practices by teachers. Distributed leadership is greatly encouraged, in contrast, by flatter organizational structures at both school and district levels, structures which provide opportunities for collaboration among colleagues – such as common planning times – and norms which sustain collegial relationships among school staff. Talbert and McLaughlin (1993), for example, found that teachers who came together to discuss problems and solutions, to sort out curriculum issues, and to learn from one another, formed professional learning communities that nurtured the exercise of leadership by them (also see Lieberman & Miller, 2005).

The likelihood of teacher leadership is also increased when teachers have access to professional development aimed at developing the skills and knowledge they will require to effectively enact leadership roles (Day & Harris, 2002; Murphy, 2005). Particularly important capacities for teachers to acquire through such professional development are: "finely honed skills in communication, group process facilitation, enquiry, conflict mediation and dialogue" (Harris & Lambert, 2003, p. 46).

Principals (and the rest of the school community, as well) can find it difficult to accept changes in power structures (Harris & Lambert, 2003; Murphy, 2005). In order to participate in distributed leadership, individual teachers and administrators need to recognize and accept new professional roles. As Harris and Lambert point out, "Changing roles grow out of changing self-perceptions; and, in turn, new roles provide 'spaces' in which individuals can redefine what it is to be a teacher, parent, pupil, administrator. New roles are accompanied by new responsibilities" (2003, p. 124).

Principals have a great deal of responsibility for making distributed leadership work in the school (e.g. Harris, 2005; Smylie et al., 2002). Somewhat paradoxically, the success with which leadership is distributed to teachers depends quite crucially on administrative initiative. Principals encourage distributed forms of leadership when they create problem-solving teams to substitute for administrative leadership. Principals often have to select teachers to take on leadership responsibilities and, as some evidence suggests, it is important that principals base their selections on knowing what teachers are capable of doing but may be reluctant to tackle (MacBeath, 2005) and what kinds of professional development would benefit individual teachers (Leithwood, 2003). Principals can observe how teachers deal with leadership tasks and "as people prove their ability to exercise leadership they are given more" (MacBeath, 2005, p. 360).

Leadership distribution is influenced either positively or negatively by teachers' and principals' willingness to view their jobs differently. Good teachers are already busy and may be reluctant to take on new functions. They come to the job focused on working with their students rather than with other adults (MacBeath, 2005) and may easily conclude that additional leadership responsibilities will only erode the time they have for their students. Similarly, some principals view the distribution of leadership as erosion of their own power.

In addition to the importance of organizational structures and training, Murphy (2005) describes several other influences that affect the distribution of leadership to teachers:

- resources (including enough time for all aspects of preparing for and participating in leadership roles);
- incentives and recognition (including monetary and non monetary rewards such as public acknowledgement of teacher-leaders' work); and
- role clarity (including an effort to avoid creating resentment among colleagues).

In the face of traditional understandings of how schools work, the development of distributed leadership among teachers depends on changes being made at all levels of the organization. There is little or no evidence concerning the factors that might encourage members of the school community (e.g. students, support staff, parents), other than teachers, to assume leadership functions.

HYPOTHESES

Evidence about factors influencing the emergence of distributed leadership supports two hypotheses:

12. The likelihood of teachers exercising leadership in their schools and districts will increase as:
    - hierarchical school structures are replaced or supplemented with flatter structures such as teams, committees, and working groups with significant decision-making responsibilities;
    - opportunities are available for teachers to develop the capacities they need to exercise leadership effectively;
    - principals demonstrate their willingness to share leadership with teachers;
    - principals actively encourage selected teachers to assume leadership functions for which they seem especially well suited;
    - principals provide resources and incentives within the school for leadership by teachers.
13. Other members of the school community, in addition to teachers,

will be likely to engage in leadership functions when they experience the same conditions which foster teacher leadership.

Methods

Context for the Study

This study was conducted in a large urban/suburban district in southern Ontario serving more than 100,000 increasingly diverse students in approximately 25 secondary and 140 elementary schools with an annual budget of almost $900 million. The elementary student population had grown almost 20 percent in the five years prior to our study, prompting the building of some four dozen new schools with more to be opened in the next few years. Senior district administration included a director of education (the CEO) who reported to a fully elected board of trustees. Working as part of the senior leadership team was an associate director for business services, four superintendents responsible for different business areas reporting to the director for business services. In addition, the senior leadership team included three coordinating superintendents of education, each with substantial staffs. The district was divided into four geographical regions, each of which had two field superintendents in charge of elementary and secondary education.

An especially significant part of the context for this study was the long tenure of the director of education (14 years) who brought to the job, in addition to a provincial reputation as a curriculum leader, the explicit intention to significantly flatten a district organization noted for its hierarchy and focused leadership. As a consequence, the district had been working for many years prior to our study to establish norms and practices supporting shared and distributed forms of leadership at both district and school levels. The results of our study at the school level should be interpreted as the outcome of a "best case scenario" at the district level; school staffs were strongly urged to follow both the words and deeds of district leaders in so far as approaches to leadership were concerned.

Sample

The eight schools included in Phase One of our study were selected, with help from district staff, to reflect a balance of elementary and secondary schools (four each), a two- or more-year tenure of the school principal (M = four years, but one principal had only one year tenure), demonstrable commitment to a shared or distributed approach to school leadership, and evidence of improvement in student achievement on provincial tests over the previous three years. One school was in a rural location, the rest were suburban.

Based on our conception of leadership as an attribution (Lord & Maher, 1993), all teachers in each of the eight schools (N=515) were sent a preliminary survey requesting them to nominate non-administrative colleagues in their schools whom they believed were providing leadership – however they defined that term. Two hundred and twenty-five teachers responded to this survey[1] (a 43.6 percent return rate). These respondents nominated a total of 296 non-administrative leaders. When we narrowed our focus to the two district initiatives of highest priority to each school, 19 of these nominees qualified as leaders suitable to include in our study.

Included in the study at the district level were nine district administrators: the director (CEO), two coordinating superintendents, the board chair, two superintendents of education, two curriculum coordinators and one consultant. These people were selected because of the central role they played in promoting distributed approaches to leadership in schools and their close knowledge of each of the district's primary initiatives for change.

Instruments and Data Collection Procedures

Our initial contact with principals of the selected schools provided them with an explanation of the purpose of the research and requested basic demographic information about their schools and the district initiatives on which they were focused as priorities.

A total of 31 nominators and 19 nominees were interviewed. Including the principal, in each school we conducted individual interviews with an average of seven educators and one focus group interview with six students (reported separately). This chapter is based on interview data from a total of 67 district staff, school administrators, non-administrative school leaders, and teachers.

Four instruments were used for the collection of interview data in schools, one for district leaders and three for school staffs (one for those nominated as leaders by their peers, one for nominators, and one for principals). In general, the questions asked about district initiatives, leaders' practices with respect to the initiatives, characteristics of non-administrator nominated leaders, influences on the distribution of leadership, the impact of distributed leadership, and relationships between school and district leadership. At each school, interviews were conducted by teams of two or three people over the course of one day.

Analysis

All interviews were audiotaped and extensive notes were taken during the interviews, often by a second researcher not conducting the interview. The interview notes were elaborated on immediately after each set of interviews and checked for accuracy with the audio recordings. Illustrative direct quotations were taken from the audio recordings as well.

The primary coding categories were the five main themes or questions guiding this first phase of the research:

- patterns of leadership distribution;
- sources of leadership functions;

- characteristics of non-administrative leaders;
- influences on the development of distributed leadership; and
- outcomes associated with distributed leadership.

Frequency tables were created (number of times something was mentioned, the number of people who mentioned it, and the number of schools in which it was mentioned). Secondary coding categories were developed from frameworks encountered in the literature review, where such frameworks existed, and in a grounded way where they did not.

Results reported in this chapter are based on a synthesis of results across the eight schools about each of the five themes or questions. Factors, such as school level, that appear to explain some of the differences in responses across the eight schools are identified.

Results and Discussion

Patterns of Distributed Leadership

While we have left to the next phase of our research the systematic exploration of patterns of leadership distribution and their relative effects on schools and students, data from this first phase provide some preliminary information about such patterns. Our framework proposed four distinct forms of alignment, each associated with a cluster of unique values and beliefs. We hypothesized that the most effective pattern would be planful alignment followed, in order of effectiveness, by spontaneous alignment, spontaneous misalignment, and (least effective) anarchic misalignment.

Our results uncovered many instances of planful alignment. This form of alignment was most likely with the school's highest priority initiative. The likelihood of planful alignment dropped off precipitously, however, as the focus shifted to lower priority initiatives. Arguably the most obvious reason for this disparity was the attention and effort of the principal. Our evidence seems to be telling us that planful and aligned forms of distributed leadership are unlikely in the absence of focused leadership on the part of the school's formal leader. Planfully aligned leadership distribution depends on the establishment of facilitating structures and this function seems to be considered by staff as the purview of the school's chief administrator: "The principal has a good sense of vision. She is fair and also makes sure things get done – the right people get things done. There are teacher leaders to get things done" (Secondary Teacher).

Some of our evidence also suggested that distributing leadership to teams of teachers in a planfully aligned structure, if it is to be effective, still depends on the regular monitoring of progress by the principal and sometimes a quite active form of intervention to move the agenda forward if it is stalled. By themselves, for example, a group of teachers working together as a leadership team can find themselves going in circles with little benefit to their colleagues or students; we found several examples of this. "In terms of the Assessment and Evaluation Committee, they have not been influential at all. They just keep arguing. They have never produced anything teachers can use" (Secondary Teacher). So effective forms of distributed leadership may well depend on effective forms of focused leadership – leading the leaders.

Sources of Leadership Functions

Our framework identified four broad categories of core leadership functions – setting direction, developing people, redesigning the organization, and managing the instructional program. Within each of these categories are to be found three or four more specific sets of functions. Our results allow us to identify which of these leadership functions were being performed by each of three groups of leaders – non-administrator and informal leaders, school administrators (mostly principals), and senior district leaders. Table 10.1 summarizes the results and allows for a comparison of the functions performed by each of the three groups of leaders. In our interview with him, the director told us that one of his objectives for distributing leadership was to flatten the school system. Evidence summarized in this table describes a more complex reality at this point in the district's evolution. It may also suggest a more complex ideal for future aspirations. Flattening implies an undifferentiated sharing of all or most leadership functions across those in many different roles (of course, the director may well have had a more nuanced understanding of the term).

The complex reality evident in Table 10.1, suggests some specialization in leadership functions depending on such factors as position, opportunity, expertise, disposition, and widely held expectations:

- With respect to the setting direction category, informal leaders had more involvement with creating high performance expectations and motivating others than formal school leaders, while formal leaders had more to do with identifying and articulating a vision. Eight of the nine district level leaders were also focused on identifying and articulating a vision.
- In relation to developing people, non-administrator leaders were more focused on providing individual support and modeling appropriate values and practices than were formal school leaders. Contributing to professional development was an important function for leaders in all three groups.
- Informal leaders were more involved with redesigning the organization than the formal leaders. Of particular importance were the functions of building collaborative processes/teamwork and building community in the school. Eight district leaders mentioned their commitment to building collaborative processes.

- Non-administrator leaders were devoting more of their attention to managing programs, committees, and meetings and sharing information than were the administrator leaders, while school administrators were more often taking care of delegating. All the district leaders were fulfilling the function of managing programs, committees, and meetings.

This more complex reality includes some functions performed by those in many different official positions – but enacted differently depending on position, context, and the like. It also includes some functions primarily performed only by those in one of several positions. This more complex reality mirrors our findings from an earlier study of leadership distribution across the entire country of England in the context of implementing the government's National Literacy and National Numeracy projects (Leithwood et al., 2004). This reality also is consistent with two claims that are part of Locke's (2003) model of distributed leadership. First, some hierarchy is unavoidable and necessary in any large organization. Second, for greatest impact some leadership functions need to be performed by those in particular positions or with special expertise, not just anyone in the organization.

These results, it should be noted, describe the reality in one school district, just as our results from England described the reality in one country. And as analytic philosophers would remind us, you cannot get directly from an "is" to an "ought" – although our discussion of these results has begun to trend in that direction. What we can do, however, is agree that the distribution of leadership practices observed in our one district and eight schools was the product of working hard to get it right over more than a decade. So, while the distribution of leadership functions we discovered may not be perfect, there is a very good chance that it is significantly more productive than average; it may very well represent the current state of best practice when it comes to distributing leadership functions.

We can further test this claim about being best practice by comparing the results with the three hypotheses we initially formulated from our review of prior evidence about the most effective forms of distribution.

First, we expected that effective distribution of leadership functions would encourage some degree of differentiation in the performance of functions depending on role. This is clearly what we found and what is most evident in Table 10.1. That said, the functions most likely to be performed by informal and non-administrator leaders were more likely to be managerial in nature, and less likely to entail direction setting functions. "My role is to facilitate, organize, set the agenda, make calls, remind people about meetings, get people together, and then we sit and discuss. I make sure people stay on task: 'Here's what we decided. Let's do it. All take responsibility and work as a team'" (Secondary Teacher).

Table 10.1 Leadership Functions of Non-Administrator School Leaders, Formal School Leaders, and District Leaders

Leadership Functions	Types of Leaders		
	Non-Administrator Leaders N = 58/8[a]	Formal School Leaders N = 58/8	District Leaders N = 9
Direction Setting			
Creating High Performance Expectations/Motivating Others	13/8[b]	3/3	7[c]
Identifying and Articulating a Vision	12/7	26/8	8
Fostering the Acceptance of Group Goals	2/2	6/5	6
Promoting Effective Communication	3/2	–	1
Total[d]	25/8	26/8	
Developing People			
Contributing to Professional Development	16/7	13/7	8
Providing Individualized Support	15/7	5/2	5
Modeling Appropriate Values and Practices	12/6	5/3	7
Mentoring	6/3	2/2	n/a
Total	26/8	17/7	
Redesigning the Organization			
Building Collaborative Processes/Teamwork	19/8	10/8	8
Building Community in the School	11/6	2/2	n/a
Getting Involved in Community Outside School	6/4	4/4	n/a
Developing a Professional Learning Community	4/3	3/3	1
Strengthening School Culture	2/2	–	n/a
Modifying Organizational Structures	1/1	3/3	4
Working with the Board	n/a	7/5	n/a
Total	26/8	13/8	

Managing the Instructional Program

Managing Programs, Committees, Meetings	24/8	10/7	9
Sharing Information	13/6	3/3	n/a
Staffing the Instructional Program	n/a	5/5	4
Monitoring Students' Progress and the School's Improvement	9/7	4/4	n/a
Providing Resources	9/6	9/7	5
Knowing What's Happening/Staying up to Date	7/6	3/3	4
Delegating	2/2	14/7	n/a
Total	29/8	22/8	

Notes

a Number of respondents includes nominated informal leaders, nominators, and principals/at all schools.
b Number of respondents who mentioned a particular function/number of schools where a particular function was mentioned.
c Number of respondents who mentioned a particular function.
d Number of respondents who mentioned a function in this category.

Although district leaders understood the value of having those in many different roles shaping the systems direction, these leadership functions largely remained the purview of senior administrator leaders. While this conforms to Locke's (2003) claims about the inevitability of hierarchy in large organizations and the specialization of leadership functions across roles, it begs the question of whether or not such distribution most effectively utilized the full capacities of the school system. This is a complex question but one worthy of further consideration by those in the school system.

Second, our review of prior evidence led us to hypothesize that the most effective distribution of leadership functions would vary the numbers of people providing leadership in response to the complexity of the tasks to be performed – more in the case of complex tasks and fewer in response to simple tasks. There was some evidence of this variation, especially from one of our district interviewees, but it seems likely that the district and schools could refine their practices substantially (and save a good deal of precious time) by being more sensitive to task complexity.

Finally, our review of prior evidence led us to hypothesize that effective leadership distribution would encourage unconstrained forms of distribution, especially in the performance of complex leadership tasks in order to maximize the use of existing expertise. While our data did uncover some instances of people who were perceived to be offering leadership to their colleagues without formal leadership designation, most people nominated as leaders by their colleagues had been designated leaders by the school or district. This result could well be a function of our research methods; specifically our decision to ground our data collection in district reform initiatives. Such initiatives are much more likely than "grass roots" initiatives to have formal leadership roles associated with them. So our data are likely to have underestimated that amount of informal leadership exercised in our case schools.

Characteristics of Non-Administrator Leaders

What is it that prompts others to think of you as a leader, especially if you are not in an administrative position? We hypothesized in our review of literature that such an attribution might reflect something about you that others believe to be prototypical of the organization; it might also reflect your colleagues' positive judgments about your relative expertise. From other lines of research, we also know that the direct experience of your work and its value to the organization might lead to such an attribution, as might your match to people's pre-existing leadership prototypes (Lord & Maher, 1993) and some of your basic personality traits (Zaccaro et al., 2004).

Our interview data asked about qualities, experiences and factors giving rise to the attribution of leadership among those in non-administrative roles. As Table 10.2 indicates, ten categories of characteristics were identified: *interpersonal skills, organizational skills, personal qualities, professional qualities, commitment to an initiative, range of undertakings, respect for others' cultures, source of good ideas, breadth of experience,* and *designation as formal leader.*

The characteristics most frequently associated with non-administrative leaders in our study mirror many of the results of prior research about the characteristics of formal administrative leaders. By far the most frequently identified category (17 people in eight schools) was *personal qualities.* Attributions of openness, care, and extraversion are quite consistent with prior evidence, primarily about those in formal leader roles. And being *quiet but effective* is a characteristic we discovered in our earlier research on teacher leadership, in particular (Leithwood et al., 1999).

The second most frequently mentioned set of characteristics (11 people in all eight schools) was *commitment* to whatever the initiative was. Once again, this finding is very similar to characteristics attributed to successful principals in all eight national contexts included in a recent international leadership study (Day & Leithwood, 2007). In addition, the *interpersonal skills* category mentioned by eight people in seven schools reflects the growing body of evidence about the importance attributed to these skills (e.g. empathy) on the part of formal administrative leaders (Zaccaro et al., 2004).

So the largest proportion of our evidence about characteristics attributed to non-administrator and informal leaders suggests no difference as compared with the attributes of formal administrative leaders. This seems to indicate that people's leadership prototypes do not discriminate among formal or informal roles; it suggests, in addition, that people are influenced

Table 10.2 Characteristics of Nominated Non-Administrator Leaders

Characteristics	Elementary Leaders	Secondary Leaders	Total
Interpersonal Skills	4/4[1]	5/3	9/7
Organizational Skills	2/2	2/2	4/4
Personal Qualities	11/4	6/4	17/8
Easygoing	3/2	0/0	3/2
Open/Approachable	5/3	0/0	5/3
Caring	3/3	5/4	8/7
Vocal	0/0	2/2	2/2
Quiet	3/2	1/1	4/3
Professional Qualities	5/3	2/4	9/5
Committed to Initiative	4/4	7/4	11/8
Involved in a Range of Undertakings	4/3	1/1	5/4
Source of Good Ideas	10/4	1/1	11/5
Breadth of Experience	5/3	1/1	6/4
Shows Respect for Others' Cultures	0/0	1/1	1/1
Designated as a Formal Leader	2/2	7/3	5/9

Note

1 Number of individuals who mentioned a particular characteristic/Number of schools where the characteristic was mentioned.

by approximately the same types of direct experiences in forming their opinions about the leadership potential of their colleagues.

Reinforcement also can be found in these results for the claim made by many leadership theorists that leadership is an attribution and followership is a voluntary state (e.g. Lord & Maher, 1993). Our evidence, in sum, confirms one of our original expectations about leadership characteristics – attributions of leadership to those in non-administrative roles will be significantly shaped by the perceived traits associated with attributions of leadership to those in formal administrative roles. "That's in part too because … [the Principal] is so supportive. He will do whatever he can to support us. He learns right along with us…. And when he models it like that people are motivated to do it" (Elementary Teacher).

Our framework suggested two additional expectations about the characteristics of non-administrator leaders. One of these was that informal leaders who emerge because of their prototypicality only, will be less effective than those who emerge because of their expertise, or because of both their expertise and prototypicality. The second expectation was that informal leaders identified as prototypical by their colleagues, as well as possessing significant expertise, will be more effective than those with expertise alone. We do not have sufficient evidence to directly test either of these expectations. But the importance attached by our interviewees to *breadth of experience, being a source of good ideas* and having *organizational skills* does suggest that expertise figures strongly in teachers attributions of leadership among their colleagues.

Influences on the Development of Distributed Leadership

Distributing leadership to non-administrators in a way that actually benefits the district or school presents some obvious challenges. For example, those to whom leadership is being distributed already have full time jobs; how will they apportion their time to take on these additional functions? We cannot assume much opportunity for non-administrative leaders to become skillful in the exercise of those leadership functions which they assume or are expected to take on; how will they develop the new capacities they need? Some administrators may value the power they have over decisions in their organizations and be reluctant to share that power with others; how can these concerns be addressed?

Interviewees identified significant numbers of positive and negative influences on the development of distributed patterns of leadership. School-based staffs spoke about some five positive and four negative influences, while district interviewees identified eight positive and five negative influences. There was considerable overlap among the influences identified by both groups. These results, as a whole, indicate that distributed patterns of leadership are nurtured when collaborative structures are established, when the numbers of people collaborating on an initiative are kept manageable, and when influence is exercised through expert rather than positional power. "[When leadership is shared] peer involvement is more influential than when there is administrative leadership only" (Secondary Teacher). Distributed patterns of leadership are nurtured, as well, by an organizational culture which is open, encourages strong staff commitment to students and is free of favoritism and internal dissent. ("Not just one person goes to workshops. Administration sends a wide range of people depending on people's interests" [Teacher Leader].) Staff will be motivated to participate more fully in distributed approaches to leadership with visible support and tone-setting from their formal leaders, when those leaders provide full explanations (exemplifying an open culture) for their decisions and when they go out of their way to ensure staff are aware of new directions and activities. Finally, distributed leadership is more likely to develop when there are opportunities for staff to acquire the capacities they need to participate effectively, along with the autonomy and time to act in accord with their professional beliefs and values. ("The board provided a lot of professional development last year because it was the first year for the Literacy Teacher [Teacher Leader]"; "The principal asked me, and then left it to me what I thought was best to do [Teacher Leader]".)

These results are entirely consistent with our initial hypothesis about conditions giving rise to increased teacher leadership. We have no evidence from this phase of the study to test our hypothesis that these same conditions will foster leadership on the part of others in the school community (e.g. students, parents).

Conclusion

This first phase of our two-phase study inquired about patterns of leadership distribution, which leadership functions were performed by whom, characteristics of non-administrative leaders, and factors promoting and inhibiting the distribution of leadership functions. We inquired about these issues in eight elementary and secondary schools located in one large school district which had been encouraging distributed forms of leadership for well over a decade. As the district's CEO (director of education) told us, his purpose for such encouragement had been to "take the ego out of the system" – to create forms of collaborative work that would make the most of staff members' collective capacities, encourage the development of new capacities, and reduce unproductive knowledge hoarding and competition practices that had been common across the district.

We consider our account of distributed leadership in this district to be a probable example of best practice at the present time – not perfect, but likely more mature than average by a significant degree. So this best practice evidence assists our broader purpose of moving the study of distributed leadership beyond its largely descriptive character. If, as is typically argued, organizational learning (Marquardt, 1996) and systems thinking (Senge, 1990) are paths to organizational effectiveness, some patterns of distributed leadership should be, as well. Each of these three ways of thinking and acting promise to enlist and productively apply organizational members' collective skills and knowledge beyond what is likely in their absence.

The "devil," as usual, is in the details, however. And the most noteworthy detail to emerge from this first phase of our study was the critical part played by formal school and district leaders in helping to foster apparently productive forms of distributed leadership. First, coordinated patterns of distributed leadership were common to initiatives given high priority and attention by principals but quite uncommon among other initiatives. Second, the structures, cultural norms and opportunities for staffs to build their leadership capacities depended heavily on the intentional work of principals. Third, staffs attributed leadership to those of their peers who shared traits and dispositions typically associated with formal administrative leaders such as principals and superintendents. Fourth, reflecting some earlier theorizing on the matter (Locke, 2003), it fell to principals to enact those critical direction-setting leadership functions associated with our multi-dimensional conception of successful leadership. Finally, central office leaders created a district culture which modeled distributed leadership in many different ways, from the requirements they established for how district initiatives were to be implemented in schools through the active forms of engagement of teachers and school administrators in district decision making.

Our evidence as a whole indicates that distributing leadership to others does not seem to result in less demand for leadership from those in formal leadership positions. However, it does produce greater demand: to coordinate who performs which leadership functions, to build leadership capacities in others, and to monitor the leadership work of those others, providing constructive feedback to them about their efforts. These results are remarkably similar to much earlier evidence about the consequences of school-based management for the work of central office administrators (e.g. Murphy, 1994); their work changed but did not diminish. Perhaps we should not be surprised since school-based management represents the most determined, explicit, and widespread effort to date, to planfully distribute leadership functions among districts and their schools as a strategy for school improvement.

Acknowledgment

An earlier version of this chapter was published in *Leadership and Policy in Schools*, 6(1).

Note

1. Questions on the survey included, for example:
   1 Who provides some form of leadership for this initiative?
   2 Why have you nominated X as a leader?
   3 What does each of the people you nominated as a leader do that counts in your mind as leadership?

4   How have they come to do these things? Do you know who decided they would?
5   Can you give some examples of things that have happened as a result of their leadership?

References

Alig-Mielcarek, J. & Hoy, W.K. (2005). Instructional leadership: Its nature, meaning, and influence. In W. Hoy & C. Miskel (eds) *Educational leadership and reform* (pp. 29–51). Greenwich, CT: Information Age Publishing.

Bandura, A. (1986). *Social foundations of thought and action*. Englewood Cliffs, NJ: Prentice Hall.

Bass, B. (1997). Does the transactional-transformational leadership paradigm transcend organizational and national boundaries? *American Psychologist, 52*(2), 130–139.

Bennis, W. (1984). Where have all the leaders gone? In W.E. Rosenbach & R.L. Taylor (eds) *Contemporary issues in leadership* (pp. 5–23). Boulder, CO: Westview.

Day, C. & Harris, A. (2002). Teacher leadership, reflective practice and school improvement. In K. Leithwood & P. Hallinger (eds) *Second international handbook of educational leadership and administration* (pp. 957–978). Dordrecht, The Netherlands: Kluwer.

Day, C. & Leithwood, K. (eds) (2007). *Successful principal leadership: An international perspective*. Dordrecht, The Netherlands: Springer.

Day, C., Harris, A., Hadfield, M., Tolley, H., & Beresford, J. (eds) (2000). *Leading schools in times of change*. Buckingham, UK: Open University Press.

Ford, M. (1992). *Motivating humans: Goals, emotions, and personal agency beliefs*. Newbury Park, CA: Sage.

Geijsel, F., Sleegers, P., Leithwood, K., & Jantzi, D. (2003). Transformational leadership effects on teacher commitment and effort toward school reform. *Journal of Educational Administration, 41*(3), 228–256.

Goleman, D. (1998). *Working with emotional intelligence*. New York, NY: Bantam Books.

Goleman, D., Boyatzis, R., & McKee, A. (2002). *Primal leadership*. Boston, MA: Harvard Business School Press.

Gronn, P. (2002). Distributed leadership. In K. Leithwood & P. Hallinger (eds) *Second international handbook of educational leadership and administration* (pp. 653–696). Dordrecht, The Netherlands: Kluwer.

Gronn, P. (2003). Leadership: Who needs it? *School Leadership and Management, 23*(3), 267–290.

Hallinger, P. & Heck, R. (2002). What do you call people with visions? The role of vision, mission, and goals in school leadership and improvement. In K. Leithwood & P. Hallinger (eds) *Second international handbook of educational leadership and administration* (pp. 9–40). Dordrecht, The Netherlands: Kluwer.

Hallinger, P. & Murphy, J. (1985). Assessing the instructional management behavior of principals. *Elementary School Journal, 86*(2), 217–247.

Harris, A. (2005). Distributed leadership. In B. Davies (ed.), *The essentials of school leadership* (pp. 160–172). London, UK: Paul Chapman.

Harris, A. & Lambert, L. (2003). *Building leadership capacity for school improvement*. Berkshire, UK: Open University Press.

Jaques, E. (1989). *Requisite organization*. Arlington, VA: Cason Hall.

Leithwood, K. (2003). Teacher leadership: Its nature, development and impact on schools and students. In M. Brundrett, N. Burton, & R. Smith (eds) *Leadership in education* (pp. 103–117). London, UK: Sage.

Leithwood, K. & Jantzi, D. (1990). Transformational leadership: How principals can help reform school cultures. *School Effectiveness and School Improvement, 1*(4), 249–280.

Leithwood, K. & Riehl, C. (2005). What we know about successful school leadership. In W. Firestone & C. Riehl (eds) *A new agenda: Directions for research on educational leadership* (pp. 22–47). New York, NY: Teachers College Press.

Leithwood, K., Jantzi, D., & McElheron-Hopkins, C. (2006). The development and testing of a school improvement model. *School Effectiveness and School Improvement, 17*(4), 441–464.

Leithwood, K., Jantzi, D., & Steinbach, R. (1999). *Changing leadership for changing times*. Buckingham, UK: Open University Press.

Leithwood, K., Jantzi, D., & Steinbach, R. (2003). Fostering teacher leadership. In N. Bennett, M.

Crawford, & M. Cartwright (eds) *Effective educational leadership* (pp. 186–200). London, UK: Paul Chapman.

Leithwood, K., Leonard, L., & Sharratt, L. (1998). Conditions fostering organizational learning in schools. *Educational Administration Quarterly*, 34(2), 243–276.

Leithwood, K., Louis, K.S., Anderson, S., & Wahlstrom, K. (2004). *How leadership influences student learning: A review of research for the Learning from Leadership Project.* New York, NY: The Wallace Foundation.

Leithwood, K., Jantzi, D., Earl, L., Watson, N., Levin, B., & Fullan, M. (2004). Strategic leadership for large-scale reform: The case of England's National Literacy and Numeracy Strategies. *Journal of School Leadership and Management*, 24(1), 57–80.

Liebermann, A. & Miller, L. (2005). Teachers as leaders. *Educational Forum*, 69(2), 151–162.

Lipponen, J., Koivisto, S., & Olkkonen, M.-E. (2005). Procedural justice and status judgements: The moderating role of leader ingroup prototypicality. *Leadership Quarterly*, 16(4), 517–528.

Locke, E.A. (2003). Leadership: Starting at the top. In C.J. Pearce & C. Conger (eds) *Shared leadership: Reframing the hows and whys of leadership* (pp. 271–284). Thousand Oaks, CA: Sage.

Locke, E.A., Latham, G.P., & Eraz, M. (1988). The determinants of goal commitment. *Academy of Management Review*, 13, 23–39.

Lord, R.G. & Maher, K.J. (1993). *Leadership and information processing.* London, UK: Routledge.

Louis, K. & Kruse, S. (1995). *Professionalism and community: Perspectives on reforming urban schools.* Newbury Park, CA: Corwin Press.

Louis, K.S., Marks, H.M., & Kruse, S. (1996). Teachers' professional community in restructuring schools. *American Educational Research Journal*, 33(4), 757–798.

Louis, K.S., Toole, J., & Hargreaves, A. (1999). Rethinking school improvement. In J. Murphy & K.S. Louis (eds) *Handbook of research on educational administration* (2nd edn). San Francisco, CA: Jossey-Bass.

Lumby, J. (2006). Conceptualizing diversity and leadership. *Educational Management, Administration and Leadership*, 34(2), 151–165.

MacBeath, J. (2005). Leadership as distributed: A matter of practice. *School Leadership and Management*, 25(4), 349–366.

Manz, C.C. & Sims Jr, H.P. (1980). Self-management as a substitute for leadership: A social learning perspective. *Academy of Management Review*, 5(3), 361–367.

Marks, H.M., Louis, K.S., & Printy, S. (2000). The capacity for organizational learning. In K. Leithwood (ed.), *Understanding schools as intelligent systems* (pp. 239–265). Stamford, CT: JAI.

Marquardt, M.J. (1996). *Building the learning organization.* New York, NY: McGraw-Hill.

McColl-Kennedy, J.R. & Anderson, R.D. (2002). Impact of leadership style and emotions on subordinate performance. *Leadership Quarterly*, 13(5), 545–559.

Murphy, J. (1994). The changing role of the superintendency in restructuring districts in Kentucky. *School Effectiveness and School Improvement*, 5(4), 349–375.

Murphy, J. (2005). *Connecting teacher leadership and school improvement.* Thousand Oaks, CA: Corwin Press.

Pearce, C.J. & Conger, C. (2003). *Shared leadership: Reframing the hows and whys of leadership.* Thousand Oaks, CA: Sage.

Pierro, A., Cicero, L., Bonaiuto, M., van Knippenberg, D., & Kruglanski, A.W. (2005). Leader group prototypicality and leadership effectiveness: The moderating role of need for cognitive closure. *Leadership Quarterly*, 16(4), 503–516.

Pittman, T.S. (1998). Motivation. In D.T. Gilbert, S. Fiske, & G. Lindzey (eds) *The handbook of social psychology* (4th edn, Vol. 1, pp. 549–590). Boston, MA: McGraw-Hill.

Reicher, S., Haslam, S.A., & Hopkins, N. (2005). Social identity and the dynamics of leadership: Leaders and followers as collaborative agents in the transformation of social reality. *Leadership Quarterly*, 16(4), 547–568.

Roberts, N.C. (1985). Transforming leadership: A process of collective action. *Human Relations*, 38, 1023–1046.

Ross, J.A. (1995). Strategies for enhancing teachers' beliefs in their effectiveness: Research on a school improvement hypothesis. *Teachers College Record*, 97(2), 227–251.

Ross, J.A., Cousins, J.B., & Gadalla, T. (1996). Within-teacher predictors of teacher efficacy. *Teaching and Teacher Education, 12*(4), 385–400.

Rowan, B. (1996). Standards as incentives for instructional reform. In S. Fuhrman & J. O'Day (eds) *Rewards and reform: Creating educational incentives that work.* San Francisco, CA: Jossey-Bass.

Senge, P.M. (1990). *The fifth discipline: The art and practice of the learning organization.* New York, NY: Doubleday.

Sheppard, B. (1996). Exploring the transformational nature of instructional leadership. *Alberta Journal of Educational Research, XLII*(4), 325–344.

Silins, H., Mulford, B., Zarins, S., & Bishop, P. (2000). Leadership for organizational learning in Australian secondary schools. In K. Leithwood (ed.), *Understanding schools as intelligent systems.* Stamford, CT: JAI Press Inc.

Sleegers, P., Geijsel, F., & van den Borg, R. (2002). Conditions fostering educational change. In K. Leithwood & P. Hallinger (eds) *Second International handbook of educational leadership and administration.* Dordrecht, The Netherlands: Kluwer.

Smylie, M., Conley, S., & Marks, H. (2002). Exploring new approaches to teacher leadership for school improvement. In J. Murphy (ed.), *The educational leadership challenge: Redefining leadership for the 21st century* (pp. 162–188). Chicago, IL: University of Chicago Press.

Southworth, G. (1998). *Leading improving primary schools.* London, UK: Falmer Press.

Spillane, J.P. (2006). *Distributed leadership.* San Francisco, CA: Jossey-Bass.

Talbert, J.E. & McLaughlin, M.W. (1993). Understanding teaching in context. In D.K. Cohen, M.W. McLaughlin, & J.E. Talbert (eds) *Teaching for understanding: Challenges for policy and practice.* San Francisco, CA: Jossey-Bass.

Thayer, L. (1988). Leadership/communication: A critical review and a modest proposal. In G.M. Goldhaber & G.A. Barnett (eds) *Handbook of organizational communication* (pp. 231–263). Norwood, NJ: Ablex.

Weick, K.E. (1995). *Sensemaking in organizations.* Thousand Oaks, CA: Sage.

Yu, H., Leithwood, K., & Jantzi, D. (2002). The comparative effects of transformational leadership on teachers' commitment to change in Hong Kong and Canada. *Journal of Educational Administration, 40*(4), 368–384.

Zaccaro, S.J., Kemp, C., & Bader, P. (2004). Leader traits and attributes. In J. Antonakis, A.T. Cianciolo, & R.J. Sternberg (eds) *The nature of leadership* (pp. 101–124). Thousand Oaks, CA: Sage.

11
Distributed Leadership and Knowledge Creation

ALMA HARRIS

In a knowledge based economy, the new coin of the realm is learning.

Robert Reich

This chapter focuses on the relationship between distributed forms of leadership in schools and the processes of knowledge creation. The chapter argues that knowledge creation is best supported and nurtured by forming communities of practice based on social processes where individuals collaborate and work together. These "micro-communities of knowledge" provide the shared space that encourages and nurtures participation on many different levels. The chapter provides illustrations from "development and research" (D and R) school networks in England that are actively seeking ways of restructuring and redefining leadership practice. Within these D and R networks, schools are focused upon deep and distributed leadership. It is suggested that distributed leadership provides the "organizational circuitry" that can support knowledge creation within and between schools.

As societies face the challenges brought about by globalization and the new technologies, the critical importance of innovation and knowledge creation has become clear to all. Most leaders would say that their main challenge is one of generating and sustaining innovation. This is particularly true in education where the economic and social costs if the system fails to innovate, will be substantial. As Fullan et al. (2007) note, education needs a system that will support the day to day transformation of instruction for all students – a system that is both practical and powerful.

But how do we generate this system? If knowledge creation is the key to transformation, will major shifts and changes in organizational forms inevitably be needed? In addition, will new forms of leadership be required to create new knowledge and to sustain innovation? Krogh et al. (2006, p. 7) suggest that effective knowledge creation depends on an enabling context, and a shared space that fosters emerging relationships. They suggest that knowledge creation is best supported and nurtured by forming communities based on social processes where individuals collaborate and work together. These "micro-communities of knowledge" provide the shared space that encourages and nurtures participation on many different levels.

It is clear that neither bureaucracies nor hierarchies provide the optimum structures for knowledge creation. Instead organizations that are inter-dependent and collaborative are more likely to be the enabling contexts required for knowledge creation to occur. These "collaborative enterprises" will be networked, virtual ecosystems consisting of actual and potential allies and partners (Heckscher, 2007, p. 25). They will have extended, dynamic and diverse systems of interaction requiring leadership practices that go far beyond the current structural boundaries of teams, partnerships or networks.

The collaborative enterprise will sustain two sets of relationships – the vertical and the horizontal. The dominant organizational infrastructure will depend on strong collaborative teams, both real and virtual. The distinguishing mark of the collaborative enterprise will be its interdependence, its networking and its adaptability, rather than its conformity or authority. It will be an organization where the quality of leadership practice will matter more than leadership roles or positions.

Leadership that is flexible, responsive and able to re-align itself to a changing environment and changing needs will be required in this new organizational form. Distributed leadership will have a major role to play as the hierarchical structures fall away, so too, will hierarchical forms of leadership (Harris, 2006). In their place will emerge forms of leadership practice based on relationships rather than on organizational divisions or boundaries. Relationships are at the heart of knowledge creation (Krogh et al. 2006). Nonaka and Takeuchi (1995) argue that the organization moves from tacit knowledge to explicit knowledge by "sharing, creating concepts, justifying concepts, building an archetype, and cross-levelling knowledge" (p. 84). So the knowledge spiral continues. In organizations where it occurs, knowledge is co-constructed through interactions and between people. As a result learning takes place.

The fragility of knowledge creation means that it needs to be supported by a leadership circuitry or infrastructure that enables it to happen. This infrastructure should allow the sharing of tacit knowledge and effective conversations across various organizational levels. It is suggested that distributed leadership provides an infrastructure for professional interaction, co-construction, and learning to occur at multiple levels.

Distributed Leadership and Knowledge Creation

In their latest work on distributed leadership practice, Spillane and Diamond (2007) illustrate the power of co-construction through conversations and interactions between teachers. Their work focuses on the relationship between leadership and classroom practice and the way leadership is distributed across leader, follower, and the context. Their work makes the relationship between instruction and leadership explicit and shows how one aspect of instruction, the school subject, is a potentially powerful explanatory variable in leadership practice.

From a distributed perspective, Spillane and Diamond (2007) argue that aspects of the situation such as organizational routines and tools are not simply a backdrop or an accessory for school leadership and management practice. Rather by framing interactions among leaders and followers, organizational routines and tools are a core defining element of practice. Their position is that leadership practice takes shape in these interactions and that the routines and tools can transform leadership practice over time.

However it is also clear that the patterns of leadership activity both within and across organizational forms heavily influence the situation, routines, and tools that are used. The structural configuration of leadership roles and responsibilities will ultimately determine and shape the nature and type of interactions within the organization. A hierarchical model of leadership provides a very different organizational architecture for professional interaction than a school with a lateral or horizontal leadership structure.

The basic point here is to agree with Spillane and Diamond (2007) that leadership is a function of the interactions between leaders, followers, and their situation but to argue that these interactions are heavily influenced and framed by organizational structures and settings. In other words that the practice of leadership cannot be seen in isolation from the organizational structure that ultimately determines the types of routines, practices and norms in each context or setting.

Spillane and Diamond (2007) highlight that the important question is not that leadership is distributed but how it is distributed. Taking a normative rather than an analytical stance on distributed leadership means exploring how leadership is distributed. It implies looking at the ways in which different organizational forms detract or add to patterns of leadership distribution. It also means attending to organizational design and focusing on whether knowledge is created or re-cycled.

Currently distributed leadership is theoretically rich and empirically poor. As argued elsewhere, we undoubtedly need more specific empirical studies of distributed leadership (Harris, 2007). However, the empirical evidence we have to date, and the evidence that is emerging, is encouraging, if not definitive. It points toward a positive relationship between distributed leadership and organizational change (Harris, 2007; Leithwood et al. 2007). It also is beginning to show that the patterns of distribution make a difference to organizational outcomes (Day et al. 2007).

Recent research into the relationship between leadership and student outcomes has found that "'substantial leadership distribution was very important to school' success in improving pupil outcomes" (Day et al. 2007, p. 17). The findings showed that distributed leadership cultivated a sense of ownership and agency on the part of staff and that leadership distribution commonly took one of two broad forms or patterns. One pattern, *consultative distribution*, featured considerable participation of key staff in providing information and advice on school wide decisions but final decisions were retained by those in formal leadership positions. The second pattern, *decisional distribution*, awarded full responsibility and a high degree of autonomy to teacher leaders for all decisions in a designated area of responsibility.

The project found that the leadership structures in the most effective school were becoming "fatter" rather than flatter and the relationship between vertical and horizontal leadership was becoming more porous and inter-changeable. It was clear from the research evidence that the principals largely determined the nature and pattern of leadership distribution in their schools. The patterns they chose to orchestrate were determined by three influences:

a their personal view of leadership (e.g. need for control)
b their own stage of development as a leader
c their estimates of the readiness of their staff to take on greater leadership responsibilities (Day et al. 2007, p. 19).

Spillane and Diamond (2007) suggest that a distributed take on leadership is not an effective prescription for effective leadership in and of itself. But if we have sufficient evidence that certain organizational forms are more effective than others, why should we shy away from prediction or prescription? While there are some inherent challenges and methodological difficulties in exploring the way different patterns of leadership practice impinge on organizational outcomes, as Leithwood et al. (2007) have shown, it is possible to explore such patterns.

The remainder of this chapter focuses on how distributed leadership, in a structural and normative sense, contributes to knowledge creation and organizational growth. It looks at how schools are deliberately distributing leadership functions in order to build lateral capacity. The chapter presents some initial findings from an empirical study that is exploring distributed or deep leadership practices.

Distributed Leadership in Practice

In 2005, the Specialist Schools and Academies Trust, in England, established a network of schools committed to the creation of the new professional practices and system wide transformation. The Development and Research (D and R)[1] networks are viewed as integral to system-wide renewal and transformation within England and they are all actively engaged in innovation, dissemination and co-construction. There are currently 55 hub schools that are the catalysts and the focal point for the school to school networks, and over 376 D and R schools across the country.

The establishment of D and R networks is consistent with the idea of knowledge creation developed by Nonaka and Takeuchi (1995). The D and R networks are premised on the notion that new ideas, research breakthroughs and applications arise anywhere in the sector, not just within the boundaries of formal Research and Development (R and D) activities. In D and R networks, users play more of a role in the process of knowledge creation and dissemination.

In school to school D and R networks, practitioners lead and disseminate new ideas, they are central to the "sparking, shaping, validating and spreading of innovation" (Bentley & Gillinson, 2007, p. 4). As Chesbrough (2003) argues, "it's about harnessing the most effective sources of innovation – from wherever they are derived. This is not just about ideas – it is about their realization". In his model of "open innovation" users are involved in shaping the service and are active participants in knowledge creation (p. 23).

The D and R model is premised on the idea of open innovation as the aim of the practitioner networks is to create new knowledge. The networks are guided by the "3 D's Model" – they are de-centralized (in their structure); disciplined (in the way that innovation is organized) and distributed (in the construction of the innovation agenda) (Hargreaves, 1999). While there is no overall blueprint for the networks, schools have been required to lay out clear plans for innovation that had the core purpose of creating new and better practices in learning. The latest group of D and R networks have focused their activities on distributed or deep leadership. Hargreaves (2006) suggests that "deep leadership means re-designing education so that, through a culture of personalization and co-construction with shared leadership, the school secures deep experience, deep support and deep learning for all its students" (p. 2).

During 2007 an empirical study was undertaken to provide summative and formative feedback about the impact of the deep leadership work in schools (Harris, 2007). In particular the research focused upon the nature, type, and forms of leadership required to promote and sustain knowledge creation. It explored how school leaders were creating and sustaining a culture of co-construction and provided evidence of various forms and configurations of distributed leadership practice.

The research utilized data from the D and R network database and also collected in depth case study data[2] from 11 D and R schools. These schools were selected for the project on the basis that they were engaged in innovative leadership practice and were committed to working with other schools in a de-centralized, disciplined, and distributed manner. All the schools demonstrated a commitment to sharing practice and supporting other schools that were aspiring to gain expertise in the area of distributed or deep leadership.

A range of data was collected which included semi-structured interviews with key leaders involved in the work (i.e. head, hub co-ordinator, and other staff members, students) in each school to explore the way in which deep leadership is being implemented and sustained. The data provided insights into the way in which schools were conceptualizing leadership practice and actively re-organizing structures so that alternative forms of leadership practice could emerge. It was also clear that the hub schools were important catalysts for action and played an important role in ensuring that schools continued to push the boundaries of their leadership re-design process.

Models of Distributed Leadership Practice

The data from the study showed that through their various activities schools were involved in vertical or lateral leadership differentiation. They were actively seeking to "stretch leadership" (Spillane, 2006) by creating the opportunities and the spaces for greater participation in leadership within and across schools. In his work, Weick (1976) talks about loosely and tightly coupled systems. In his seminal paper, Weick (1976) argues that the coupling imagery provides organizational researchers with a powerful new way of talking about organizational complexity. Loose coupling conveys an image that separate parts are "somehow attached" and that "each retains some identity and separateness" (p. 678).

This imagery is particularly helpful in representing different forms of distributed leadership practice. Unlike the model of distributed leadership practice provided by Spillane and Diamond (2007), which focuses upon the relationship between leaders, followers and their situation, the model outlined below focuses on the structural alignment, composition and patterns of distributed leadership practice. It is primarily concerned with outlining various ways in which schools are rearranging leadership practice.

The two axes of the model represent tight versus loose organizational coupling and diffuse (uncoordinated) versus deep (coordinated) forms of leadership distribution. This typology provides four different forms of distributed leadership practice:

Ad Hoc Distribution

A more flexible, lateral and loose organizational structure has been created but the distributed leadership practice is uncoordinated and random. As a consequence the benefits to the organization are limited.

Autocratic Distribution

Structures remain relatively unchanged but participation and involvement in development work is encouraged. However, it is restricted by the existing structure, therefore, its impact is limited.

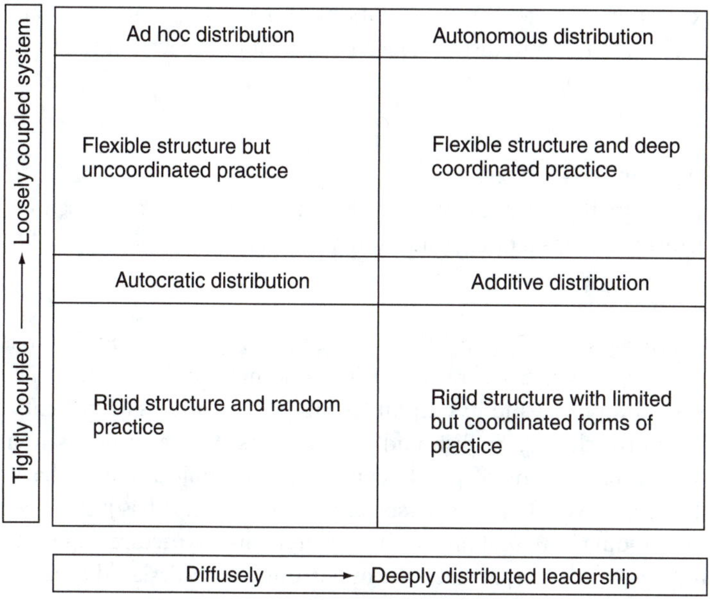

Ad hoc distribution	Autonomous distribution
Flexible structure but uncoordinated practice	Flexible structure and deep coordinated practice
Autocratic distribution	Additive distribution
Rigid structure and random practice	Rigid structure with limited but coordinated forms of practice

Loosely coupled system → Tightly coupled

Diffusely ——→ Deeply distributed leadership

Figure 11.1 A Model of Distributed Leadership Practice

Additive Distribution

Structures remain relatively unchanged but opportunities have been deliberately created for limited forms of developmental and innovative work. This work is coordinated but its impact on the organization is additive rather than transformative.

Autonomous Distribution

A more flexible, lateral and loose organizational structure has been created with the prime purpose of generating innovation and change. The leadership work is coordinated and disseminated in ways that impact positively upon the organization and other organizations. There is clear commitment to co-construction and to transformational processes.

The D and R schools are clear examples of organizations that were loosely but purposefully coupled. As Weick (1976) points out such organizational configuration can be good for swift and substantial localized adaptation – any one element can adjust to, and modify, a local unique contingency without affecting the whole system. The data showed that all of the D and R schools had abandoned certain practices, they had actively restructured to maximize teacher to teacher interaction, and a number were trying to develop more sophisticated forms of student leadership. The teacher to teacher element was an important dimension of their work, as well as the drive to increase collaboration and staff cohesiveness.

The next section provides some illustrations of the type of work the D and R schools had undertaken to distribute leadership more widely and to embed it more deeply.

Distributed Leadership Practice

The following vignettes illustrate some of the ways in which D and R schools are re-structuring and re-defining leadership practice.

School A

School A is an ages 11–19 comprehensive school with 1200+ pupils. It is located in a suburban area where the socio-economic profile is mixed. The school performs very well and its current GCSE[3] performance is 65 percent A to C, 60 percent including English and Mathematics. It is a diverse school with more than 82 percent of pupils coming from ethnic minority backgrounds. There are over 40 languages spoken in the school. It has just moved into a new building (30 million) with a campus-like structure based on faculty buildings which has provided the opportunity to re-design the leadership structures.

DISTRIBUTED LEADERSHIP

The school has deliberately flattened and extended its leadership team. The school has moved from one headteacher and two deputies, to one headteacher, three deputy heads, and eight assistant heads (including one job share). Each assistant head leads a faculty or phase with one non-teacher as a key support. The school has also tried to distribute leadership through subject teams and has tried to inculcate a culture where leadership goes right down to the classroom teacher.

The school also has a Junior Leadership Team where students apply for the post and shadow the senior leadership team members. This opportunity is open to all students through a formal application process. The two leadership teams take responsibility for joint planning and decision making. There is succession planning and training for both leadership teams that is provided at the school and in a residential setting. The school invests heavily in leadership development and training of both staff and students.

IMPACT

The junior leadership team has had a major impact on the extent to which students feel that they are part of decision making in the school. They feel that through this form of distributed leadership that they have a voice and can influence the direction of the school. The school staff are also more involved in decision making and feel that they can take an active role in leading innovation and change.

School B

School B is a large secondary school in a rural area with 1950 pupils.

It has a split site and a wide catchment area. The socio-economic indicators suggest that the school is an area with some deprivation. There is an even spread of ability among pupils with about 10 percent of pupils having English as a second language and 10 percent being eligible for free school meals. Standards of pupil achievement are steadily improving – GCSE results are currently 68 percent in the A to C grade range in 2007.

DISTRIBUTED LEADERSHIP

Leadership has been distributed among the "four deeps" identified by Hargreaves (2006):

Deep Leadership – Principal, vice principal, and business manager;
Deep Experience – Assistant principal + consultant + technology leaders (emphasis on new technologies);
Deep Learning – Assistant principal + consultant;
Deep Support – Three assistant principals + those with Key Stage responsibilities + head of sixth form.

There is a core Leadership Team consisting of a principal, vice principal, and business manager with assistant principals. There is also an extended team that consists of the core plus a range of consultants. Consultants take a leading role in Continuing Professional Development (CPD) including sophisticated approaches to observing teaching, outreach work to other schools, and conferences.

New teachers are introduced to the processes and principles of distributed leadership during their induction. The school has been particularly successful in attracting high quality staff because of their reputation for distributed leadership practice.

IMPACT

There has been a shift within the school toward a professional learning culture. Personalized learning has led to learning to learn formats for teachers to use, techniques for accelerated learning, and the adoption of assessment for learning. The structural re-alignment around the four deeps has had a positive impact on learning and pupil achievement. In addition, assessment-for-learning is now embedded in the school and this would not have been possible without the structural changes that have located leadership practices closer to teaching and learning.

School C

School C has just short of 1600 students on roll. It is a comprehensive school serving the full range of ability in what might seem a leafy suburb, an impression not reflected in the intake of the school. It is a high performing school and seen as "a very good school poised to become outstanding" by Office for Standards in Education (OFSTED).

DISTRIBUTED LEADERSHIP

Leadership has been dramatically reconfigured within the school. The leadership team has been restructured to reflect the discourse of deep leadership. Distributed leadership is a core part of its philosophy and at the core of trying to change things. The school wanted to develop the leadership capacity and potential of all staff and therefore set up their own, year long Emerging Leaders course for support staff using the leadership framework they had developed. The aim was to maximize the leadership potential of those in support roles and to generate leadership capacity through internal, targeted training.

IMPACT

There are closer working relationships between support staff and teaching staff as both groups see themselves as potential leaders. Also accountability has deepened as a result of distributed leadership. In particular, as a result of the leadership training subject leaders have taken greater responsibility for working with other teachers to create new materials, ideas, and knowledge. Both teachers and support staff tend to see themselves as accountable for educational attainment on behalf of the school. This is a new mindset and a more collaborative approach to raising attainment.

School D

School D is a primary school in a suburban setting. It is a school that has grown in terms of student numbers significantly in the last five years. During that time the leadership structure and practices within the school has changed.

DISTRIBUTED LEADERSHIP

The leadership responsibilities have been extended from just the head teacher to a model of a head and several co-deputies. Each deputy takes on the role for one half term. They all have more than five years of experience and when they are not in the deputy head role are full time classroom teachers. As the head is a regional leader of a Leadership Network and is out of school two days per week, a co-head has been appointed from within the staff. This means that the leadership team is structurally flexible and relies on extended membership that is constantly renewing itself as members come into the team and leave the team.

In addition, the school is now leading a network of 30 schools that are interested in system redesign and distributed forms of leadership practice between schools. The aim is to create a network of schools that are actively innovating around leadership practice and trying different models and configurations of leadership activity.

IMPACT

The flexible and extended leadership team has encouraged teachers to engage more with decision-making processes and to take on temporary leadership roles. The links to schools within the network have created the opportunity for trialing alternative innovative practices between schools and to look for ways of connecting leaders at different levels across the network.

The school has become much more outward facing and is generally recognized as a source of innovative practice. Teachers tend to stay in the school and are able to combine leadership experience without relinquishing teaching duties permanently. This has created a vibrant interface between leadership and learning that has had a positive impact on teachers and students at the school.

Bentley and Gillinson (2007) argue that the potential of reorganizing traditional R and D into D and R has the potential to have powerful effects on performance. There are certainly some signs that this is the case, although the evidence base is still emerging. There is emerging evidence that the D and R networks are beginning to have a positive impact at three levels (Harris, 2007). First, at the level of the individual, where there is enhanced professional practice. Second, at the level of the school where there is much greater commitment, willingness, and energy for sharing and implementing new ideas. Third, instructional practices are being influenced by the D and R networks, particularly the processes and practices associated with personalized learning.

There is evidence that the new leadership arrangements prompted by the D and R networks are providing a platform for knowledge creation, application, and dissemination. The new leadership structures are encouraging teachers to share knowledge with other teachers, both within their own school and across the network. In this respect, D and R networks provide a powerful platform for the leverage of knowledge and the acceleration of innovation.

Nonaka and Takeuchi (1995) identify two sets of dynamics that drive the process of knowledge amplification: converting tacit into explicit knowledge; and moving knowledge from the individual level to the group, organizational, and inter-organizational levels. The latter require some form of knowledge leveraging which is very visible within the practices of the D and R networks. This leveragable body of knowledge is all the knowledge available to the community via all participants in the system. The repository for "captured" knowledge, the knowledge base, must provide feedback in support of its own continued development and evolution. It must also support the following types of interactions from each of the participants within the system.

It is clear that effective knowledge creation depends on an enabling context or a "knowledge space" where knowledge is shared and where the tacit becomes the explicit. D and R networks seem to be powerful knowledge spaces (Krogh et al. 2006). They are encouraging collaboration, communication, and dialogue in a supportive context. They are essentially micro-communities of knowledge (Krogh et al. 2006). They are fluid, rather than fixed, continually evolving with accumulated collective experience.

Lave and Wenger (1991) and Wenger (1998) propose that when learning in communities of practice, participants gradually absorb and are absorbed in a culture of practice giving them exemplars leading to shared meanings, and a sense of belonging and increased understanding. D and R networks are distinguished by their emphasis on group or collective learning, their mutual trust and professional respect.

Hargreaves (1999) suggests that "a network increases the pool of ideas on which any member can draw" and that "networks extend and enlarge the communities of practice with enormous potential benefits" (p. 9). There is emerging evidence that the D and R networks provide the spaces for knowledge creation which impacts positively upon instructional processes. Choo (1998) argues that organizational innovations "germinate from the seeds of tacit knowledge" (p. 27) and that implicit knowledge generates new value when it is made explicit. As knowledge moves from an individual to an organization in the form of teams, groups, and networks, it can provide the shared context where knowledge creation takes place. It provides a social context in which the meaning of objects, problems, events, and artefacts are constructed and negotiated.

We need to know much more, however, about the nature, processes, and impact of distributed leadership. We need to know whether the D and R networks can be scaled up, if they are sustainable in the mid to long term, whether and how the networks connect to each other and the effect such "macro-communities of practice" might have on the system. Work is already underway to address some of these questions and to focus on whether and how distributed forms of leadership, in the long term, contribute to knowledge creation and innovation at the school and system level (Harris, 2007).

Comment

Organizational theorists have long emphasized the differentiated and even fragmented nature of organizations (Martin & Frost, 1996). Many writers have explored the issue of organizational complexity and differentiation in some depth (Lima, 2007). According to Jablin (1987) organizational complexity develops through two processes of internal differentiation vertical differentiation (the number of different hierarchical processes in an organization relative to its size) and horizontal differentiation (the number of department divisions within it).

It is clear that many schools, districts and systems are now actively engaged in both vertical and horizontal differentiation. They are deliberately restructuring leadership functions, redefining leadership roles, and rearranging leadership responsibilities. They are seeking to provide the spaces and opportunities for knowledge creation to take place.

While it is clear that extending and enhancing leadership density should not be regarded as the only or even main strategy for transforming school and school systems, it remains a powerful lever. Evidence shows that high performing and complex organizations are highly differentiated and have leadership structures that provide maximum flexibility for organizational growth and change. They are organizations which have optimized vertical and horizontal leadership differentiation.

If we are really serious about system transformation, we need to do things differently. The process of school and system transformation is unlikely to be achieved without some radical, long-term change in leadership structures and practices. The danger is that token, superficial changes will be implemented instead of the deep-rooted changes that are required. If this happens then new "old leadership practices" will simply be recreated that will actively undermine any transformational process. As Fullan et al. (2007) note: what is needed now is proactive leadership in which individuals and groups seek ways of connecting to adjacent layers of the system. In the end, distributed leadership will make it work. Many schools have recognized this need and are already moving towards alternative forms of leadership structures and practices.

The question is whether they are moving fast enough. The pace of technological change is quickening, the demands on schools and school systems are increasing. Our present ways of organizing are fast becoming outmoded yet we seem hypnotized with current structures and ways of leading. It is possible that the new or alternative leadership approaches may not be any better than those currently in operation. We will not know this unless we change the structures and the practice. By deliberately constructing fluid, organic structures premised on widely distributed forms of leadership, we might just be inventing organizational forms more suited to the twenty-first century than a previous age.

Acknowledgments

I am grateful to the Specialist Schools and Academies Trust for allowing me to draw upon their D and R work. However the views expressed in this chapter do not represent the views held by the Specialist Schools and Academies Trust. In particular, I wish to acknowledge the contribution of Professor David Hargreaves and also thank Sue Williamson, Emma Sims, and Kai Valcher at the Specialist Schools and Academies Trust and Gill Ireson and Toby Greany at the National College for School Leadership in England for allowing me to draw upon the research work.

Notes

1 The D and R networks are funded by the Specialist Schools and Academies Trust – http://www.specialistschools.org.uk/.
2 A full account of methodology can be found in Harris, 2007.
3 External examination in England at age 16. Grades A to C are pass grades.

References

Bentley, T. & Gillinson, S. (2007). Innovation: *A D and R system for education*. London, England: DfES Innovation Unit.

Chesbrough, H. (2003). The era of open innovation. *Sloan Management Review, 44*(3), 35–41.

Choo, C. (1998). *The knowing organization: How organizations use information to construct meaning, create knowledge, and make decisions*. New York, NY: Oxford University Press.

Day, C., Sammons, P., Harris, A., Hopkins, D., Leithwood, K., Gu, Q., Penlington, C., Mehta, P., & Kington, A. (2007). *The impact of school leadership on pupil outcomes* (Interim report). London, England: Department for Children, Schools and Families.

Fullan, M., Hill, P., & Crevola, C. (2007). *Breakthrough*. Thousand Oaks, CA: Corwin Press.

Hargreaves, D. (1999). The knowledge-creating school. *British Journal of Educational Studies, 47*(2), 122–144.

Hargreaves, D. (2006). *A new shape for schooling?* London, England: Specialist Schools and Academies Trust.

Harris, A. (2005). *Crossing boundaries and breaking barriers: Distributing leadership in schools*. London, England: Specialist Schools Trust.

Harris, A. (2006). Opening up the black box of leadership practice: Taking a distributed perspective. *International Journal of Educational Administration, 34*(2), 37–46.

Harris, A. (2007). *Deep leadership and knowledge creation* (Interim research report). Nottingham, England: SSAT/NCSL.

Heckscher, C. (2007). *The collaborative enterprise*. New Haven, CT: Yale University Press.

Jablin, F.M. (1987). Formal organization structure. In F.M. Jablin, L.L. Putnam, K.H. Roberts, & L.W. Porter (eds) *Handbook of organizational communication: An interdisciplinary perspective* (pp. 389–419). Newbury Park, CA: Sage.

Krogh, G.V., Ichijo, K., & Nonaka, I. (2006). *Enabling knowledge creation*. Oxford, England: Oxford University Press.

Lave, J., & Wenger, E. (1991). *Situated learning: Legitimate peripheral participation*. Cambridge, England: Cambridge University Press.

Leithwood, K., Mascall, B., Strauss, T., Sacks, R., Memon, N., & Yashkina, A. (2007). Distributing leadership to make schools smarter: Taking the ego out of the system. *Leadership and Policy Studies, 6*(1), 37–67.

Lima, A. (2007). Teachers' professional development in departmentalized, loosely-coupled organizations: Lessons for school improvement from a case study of two curriculum departments. *School Effectiveness and School Improvement, 18*(3), 273–301.

Martin, J. & Frist, P. (1996). The organizational culture war games: A struggle for intellectual dominance. In S.R. Clegg, C. Hard & W.R. Nord (eds) *Handbook of organizational studies* (pp. 599–621). London, UK: Sage.

Nonaka, I. & Takeuchi, H. (1995). *The knowledge-creating company: How Japanese companies create the dynamics of innovation*. Oxford, England: Oxford University Press.

Spillane, J. & Diamond, J.B. (2007). *Distributed leadership in practice*. New York, NY: Teachers College Press.

Spillane, J.P. (2006). *Distributed leadership*. San Francisco, CA: Jossey-Bass.

Weick, K.E. (1976). Educational organizations as loosely coupled systems. *Phi Delta Kappan, 63*(10), 673–676.

Wenger, E. (1998). *Communities of practice: Learning, meaning, and identity*. New York, NY: Cambridge University Press.

Part 4

What We Have Learned and Where We Go From Here

12

What We Have Learned
and Where We Go From Here

KENNETH LEITHWOOD, BLAIR MASCALL, AND TIIU STRAUSS

The chapters in this volume, as a whole, portray an area of study in an adolescent stage of development. It is an area no longer naively confident of its own value; greater distribution of leadership is not likely to be *the* answer to what ails schools, for example (although it seems likely to be a part of that answer). Furthermore, it is a field, struggling with complex identity issues. How can concepts of distributed leadership be distinguished from, say, models of participatory leadership or the behaviors associated with professional learning communities? It is a field striving for some measure of independence while, at the same time (and sometimes reluctantly), acknowledging the important influence of its parentage. After all, it is those long-studied leadership practices that are being distributed, along with the knowledge, skills, and dispositions on which they are based. Hierarchy still seems an essential property of organizations for purposes of coordination (and possibly direction-setting, as well). Influence still lies at the heart of what leadership entails. And the concept of leadership still depends on the concept of followership to have any meaning at all.

Clearly, however, the study of distributed leadership is experiencing a growth spurt that would do any teenager proud, a growth spurt nicely captured between the covers of this book. The maturity accompanying this growth spurt is manifest, for example, in the efforts to grapple with normative and descriptive purposes for engaging with the distributed leadership concept. Maturity is also evident in the prevalence of efforts to build on the ideas and evidence of others working in the same area, and in the increasingly sophisticated empirical inquiry aimed at exploring what until recently has been, to turn an old phrase on its head, "dust bowl" theorizing.[1] Current approaches to inquiry, as the chapters in this text make clear, include efforts to explore distributed leadership concepts with well-established theoretical tools and to examine an increasingly broad array of questions about the nature, causes, and consequences of leadership distribution.

This final chapter offers some closure to the text by summarizing key research results, developing some further clarity about selected concepts, and by offering a fairly substantial list of questions worth careful consideration by those who undertake research related to distributed leadership in the future. Occasionally an implication for practice pops out of this thicket. But we have quite intentionally suppressed our urge to dwell at length on such implications. First, leadership distribution is already a "hot topic" among practicing leaders and policy makers and needs no additional promotion by us. Second, the amount of empirical research on distributed leadership in school and district organizations does not actually extend very far beyond the covers of this book. So we consider it premature to suggest that this corpus of research, as provocative, engaging and diverse as it is, offers the kind of robust direction for practice for which systematic and formal research is valued. For the most part, we encourage readers who are practicing leaders and policy makers to find their own implications in the fairly rich sets of ideas and diverse sets of data the chapters have provided.

Our concluding remarks are organized around three issues with comments about a fourth at the end. These are issues concerning the overall purposes for research on distributed leadership (the descriptive versus normative distinction), the different ways in which patterns of distributed leadership have been conceptualized, which leadership functions are included in this body of research, and what we seem to have learned about the development of distributed leadership when that is the goal. Our final comments are about the effects of leadership distribution on school conditions and student outcomes.

Descriptive Versus Normative Purposes for Distributed Leadership Research

Authors of most chapters in the text have explicitly positioned themselves as pursuing either descriptive/analytical purposes (e.g. describing how leadership is distributed in schools) or normative purpose (e.g. figuring out how leadership ought to be distributed to have its most positive effect on schools) for their research. Normative purposes are explicitly and heavily favored by our authors. For any research community closely aligned to a professional field of practice such as education, a strongly normative emphasis would seem to be the obvious and most defensible choice. The venerable claim by Kurt Lewin – that the best way to understand something is to try to change it – could be invoked to quell any prolonged debate on the matter, in any event.

While the argument favoring normatively-oriented research seems a hands down winner in the abstract, it is far less compelling in the face of specific questions about which more knowledge is needed. Descriptively-oriented research, to begin with, is an eminently appropriate point of departure in a new field of study. We have good examples in this text of research conducted with descriptive orientations in mind serving to inform normative goals in quite powerful ways. A descriptive orientation toward distributed leadership is most explicit in chapters by Gronn (Chapter 2) and by Spillane et al. (Chapter 5). Gronn rejects being an advocate for distributed forms of leadership "in favor of a more naturalistic, organic understanding of it" (p. 18 in this volume). His aim, through description of the forms taken by distributed leadership in his research sites, was to lay out the realities of leadership practice in order to advance the claim that such practice is best understood not simply as distributed but as hybridized. At different points in an organization's life cycle, leadership may vary significantly in the degree to which it is exercised by individuals as distinct from being more widely distributed. Both individual and distributed forms will coexist but in different proportions at different times. As Gronn explains, "Leadership is more likely to be concentrated for substantial periods of time in the hands of one individual while in others it will tend to be shared" (p. 19 in this volume). Furthermore, these variations may well be adaptive responses to changes in an organization's environment and the challenges it faces at a given point in time.

From a more microanalytic perspective, Spillane, Camburn and Pareja's research supports Gronn's hybridization argument. Results of their study describe which school actors perform leadership and management work when the school principal is present but not leading the work. These results indicate that leadership and the distribution of responsibility for the work in which school principals participate varies considerably depending on the activity at hand (perhaps adaptively responding to the challenges faced by the organization, in Gronn's terms). Furthermore, their evidence makes clear that the co-performance of leading and managing activities is commonplace in elementary, middle, and high schools in the district which they studied.

With suitable nods to limitations on their external validity, these two descriptively-oriented chapters, tell us that under typical circumstances:

- leadership distribution is common in schools;
- distributed sources of leadership co-exist alongside (or in parallel with) more focused or individually enacted sources of leadership; and
- the distribution of leadership responsibility and power between individual and distributed sources typically varies in response to conditions or challenges found in the settings for leadership.

Although emerging from a descriptively-oriented line of research, these findings have significant implications for those with largely normative interests. In light of such descriptions of "typical" leadership practice, it would seem foolish to simply argue, for example, that schools just distributing leadership to more sources in schools will make things better, that individual sources of leadership are not as effective as more distributed sources, or that some patterns of leadership should be adopted because they are likely to be more powerful than others in almost all contexts. The benchmark or starting point for normative considerations about leadership distribution, in other words, may be much "higher" and more complex in schools than many distributed leadership advocates have imagined. And normal practice may already be more sophisticated and more adaptive than what some of these advocates are proposing.

This possibility should serve as a powerful stimulant for future research driven by such (descriptive/analytic) questions as: Just how complex and adaptive are typical patterns of leadership distribution? What is the normal range of complexity and adaptability in schools? Is that range sufficiently narrow or constrained to warrant intervention efforts with schools on a broad scale? If not, do we have access to interventions sufficiently robust to actually improve on normal practice – or would we be better to leave well enough alone? The instrumental value of these descriptively-oriented questions suggests that further musings about the descriptive or normative orientation of one's research is unlikely to be of much actual consequence in advancing this area of study.

Conceptualizing Alternative Patterns of Leadership Distribution

Seven of the ten central chapters in this text are framed by, develop, or otherwise depend on the concept of "patterns" of leadership distribution. And while most authors go out of their way to acknowledge how others doing research about distributed leadership conceive of such patterns, the result across the ten chapters will very likely feel, to most readers, like a "buzzing confusion" of alternative perspectives on the idea. For example, distinctions are made between additive and holistic patterns (Gronn, Chapter 2), autocratic and ad hoc patterns (Harris, Chapter 11), leader-plus and parallel performance patterns (Spillane et al. Chapter 5), planned alignment and spontaneous alignment patterns (Leithwood et al. Chapter 10), as well as pragmatic and opportunistic patterns (MacBeath, Chapter 3).

The reason for this buzzing confusion is that different chapter authors have often chosen to focus on, or highlight, different dimensions along which patterns of distribution might vary. Five such dimensions are reflected in these chapters and their authors' related works. These dimensions attempt to capture (a) differences in the range of organizational members to whom leadership is distributed, (b) the degree to which distributed forms of leadership are coordinated, (c) the extent of interdependence among those to whom leadership is distributed, (d) the extent to which power and authority accompany the distribution of leadership responsibilities, and (e) the stimulus for leadership distribution.

The Range of Organizational Members to Whom Leadership is Distributed

Spillane et al. (Chapter 5) adopt for their study what they refer to as a *leader-plus* view of leadership distribution. This concept is designed to acknowledge the leadership provided by those in both formal and informal leadership roles. In contrast, *Division of labor*, a concept of leadership distribution acknowledged by both Gronn and Spillane, for example, suggests distribution primarily to those in recognized or formally designated leadership roles. Arguments favoring the extension of leadership to those in informal roles include, for example, making fuller use of capacities often overlooked by organizations, increasing the commitment of a wider range of organizational members to the goals of the organization and increasing the opportunities members have to further build their leadership capacities.

Although these seem to be reasonable enough expectations for greater leadership distribution, we have virtually no evidence that they actually materialize in practice. Nor can we be sure that unanticipated negative consequences will not also emerge when those not in formally designated roles are awarded significant leadership responsibilities. Does the formal/informal distinction make any difference to either the enactment or outcomes of leadership distribution? Perhaps, for example, informal leaders have greater difficulty than formal leaders "signing up" willing followers. Are there unique consequences of distributing leadership functions to those in roles not formally designated as leadership roles? Perhaps informal leaders possess, for example, the credibility that comes from "being in the trenches" with their colleagues that is hard for formal leaders to replicate and this credibility adds to the influence of informal leaders. These are important issues to be addressed in future empirical research about distributed leadership.

Degree of Coordination

The four patterns of leadership distribution proposed by Leithwood et al. (Chapter 10) are intended to reflect differences in the extent to which those people engaged in leadership coordinate their efforts. These patterns, the authors claim, are likely to be more or less productive for the organization depending on the degree of coordination they represent. The *planful alignment* pattern, not unlike Spillane et al.'s (Chapter 5) *coordinated* distribution pattern, represents the most coordinated end of this dimension, followed by *spontaneous alignment, spontaneous misalignment* and finally, *anarchic misalignment*. Leithwood et al. (Chapter 10) provide some evidence in support of their claim that coordinated patterns are likely to be most productive. This claim finds some support in the results of research in non-school contexts also but the corpus of evidence about this claim is still tiny, pointing to a fruitful avenue for subsequent research. Evidence described by Anderson et al. (Chapter 6), furthermore, provides an intriguing argument for a more contingent view of the consequences of different degrees of leadership coordination; this is also the case for the taxonomy of patterns proposed by MacBeath (Chapter 3). Indeed, both of these studies give rise to a more nuanced question for future research: Under what conditions are different patterns of leadership distribution likely to be most useful?

Degree of Interdependence Among Those Exercising Leadership

The additive and holistic patterns proposed in Gronn's (2002) earlier work, patterns frequently referred to by others (e.g. Spillane et al. Chapter 5), capture variation at the extremes of the interdependence dimension. At the least interdependent extreme, additive patterns entail little or no necessary interaction among leaders, while at the holistic end, the leadership whole adds up to more than the sum of its parts. This is because high levels of interdependence have the potential to promote more collective learning, more sophisticated problem solving, and result in different and potentially more powerful courses of leadership action.

The pattern of distribution referred to in Chapter 5 by Spillane et al. as *collective distribution* also captures variation in the degrees of interdependence among those enacting leadership. This pattern, according to Spillane et al. occurs when two or more leaders co-perform the same leadership routine but work separately and independently. Spillane et al.'s *parallel performance* also signifies a place on the interdependence continuum toward the additive end.

Once again, however, we find ourselves tempted to theorize largely positive outcomes, this time in favor of more interdependent patterns of distributed leadership. More interdependence feels like it ought to be a good thing. But is it? When the leadership whole adds up to more than the sum of its parts, are things necessarily better? In "fact," we actually have no idea. There is no serious body of empirical evidence that might confirm our optimistic expectations about highly interdependent patterns of distributed leadership. If there was any doubt that such theorizing alone should not carry the day, consider other theories which suggest largely negative outcomes from high levels of interdependent work. Janis' (1971) classic work on "groupthink," a prime example, provides compelling reasons and evidence favoring negative outcomes; interdependent work, according to this line of theory can just as easily result in actions no individual in the group actually believes is the best alternative. Our future empirical efforts to explore the nature and consequences of variation in the interdependence of patterns of leadership distribution should include questions about the conditions that determine the extent to which interdependent leadership work is productive.

Degree of Power and Authority Which is Distributed

Patterns of distribution proposed by both MacBeath (Chapter 3) and Harris (Chapter 11) are primarily distinguished by variation on this dimension. Harris identifies a *formal* pattern of distribution, one in which responsibility is allocated and ownership encouraged, but within the bounds of existing roles. Harris also refers to two forms of leadership distribution that have been identified in a large UK study presently underway (e.g. Day et al. 2006) distinguished by degrees of power and authority:

- *decisional distribution,* a pattern in which full responsibility and a high degree of autonomy awarded to teachers for all decisions in a designated area of responsibility;
- *consultative distribution,* a pattern in which teachers are asked for information and advice about important school-wide decisions but the final authority for making the decision is retained by those in formal leadership roles.

Two of the patterns included in MacBeath's (Chapter 3) taxonomy are also distinguished by variation in the amount of power and authority associated with them. In the *opportunistic* pattern, as MacBeath explains, leadership distribution is unplanned (reflecting the degree of coordination dimension); "It is dispersed. It is taken rather than given. It is assumed rather than conferred. It is of the moment, opportunistic, rather than planned" (p. 50 in this volume); the outcome of such dispersal will be unpredictable amounts of power and authority. This seems likely to be the case for MacBeath's *cultural* pattern of distributed leadership, as well. The cultural pattern manifests itself in activities rather than roles: "People exercise initiative spontaneously and collaboratively and there is no clear demarcation between leaders and followers." There is a community of people working together toward a common end (p. 52 in this volume).

Does the distribution of more rather than less power and authority result in greater use of an organization's capacities? If so, what is the nature of that difference? Are serious problems of coordination likely to arise at some "tipping point" in the amount of power and authority that is distributed? Is there a minimum amount of these commodities to be distributed before much good accrues from distributed leadership? Answers to these questions have great practical value to practicing leaders shaping the distribution of leadership in their organizations. At this point, there is very little research-based evidence to help with such answers.

The Stimulus for Greater Leadership Distribution

The fifth dimension reflected in the different conceptions of distributed leadership found in the text encompasses whatever it is that either prompts or constrains fuller expressions of leadership distribution in organizations. One set of patterns reported by Harris (Chapter 11) seems to vary primarily along this dimension with organizational structures serving as the stimulus for greater distribution. Harris labels and defines these patterns as follows:

- *Ad hoc distribution:* creation of a flexible, lateral and loose organizational structure but with leadership practices distributed in an uncoordinated and random way (limited benefits).
- *Autocratic distribution:* organizational structures remain largely

unchanged but participation and involvement is encouraged (existing structures limit impact).

- *Additive distribution*: structures remain relatively unchanged but opportunities are created for limited forms of involvement in change efforts.
- *Autonomous distribution*: more flexible and loose organizational structure created with the aim of generating innovation. Leader work is coordinated and disseminated in productive ways.

Although not resulting in a unique set of distributed leadership patterns, evidence provided by Anderson and his colleagues (Chapter 6) suggest a handful of factors that influence the extent to which leadership is distributed. These factors include the extent of both leader and staff members' expertise, and the prevalence of policies and regulations that influence the direction of work in the school (what Kerr and Jermier [1978] called "substitutes for leadership"). Also influencing the extent of distribution are the leadership functions(s) to be performed and the scope of the goals to be accomplished. More significant leadership distribution seems likely, for example, when staff have significant amounts of relevant expertise, and when there are relatively few substitutes for leadership in the organization. Greater leadership distribution is stimulated when the leadership functions needing to be performed can be enacted by many different people in the organization. Greater leadership distribution is also simulated when the goals to be accomplished are complex and relatively broad (improving student performance in math across a school versus implementing a particular math program in a single classroom).

Four of MacBeath's (Chapter 3) patterns are defined largely by the stimulus for leadership distribution. His *pragmatic* pattern arises in reaction to external events that have to be dealt with but with no established lines of leadership established; this pattern has an immediate and short-term nature about it. A focus on longer-term school improvement goals prompts what MacBeath has labelled a *strategic* pattern of leadership distribution. Finally, as leaders gain confidence in being able to "let go" of their top down control and exercise their own leadership through ensuring the development of their colleagues, they are enacting a form of distribution MacBeath refers to as *incremental*.

Leadership Functions: What is Being Distributed?

Our opening remarks in this chapter portrayed the study of distributed leadership as a field of study in its adolescence. While striving for a measure of independence, we noted the field also finds itself relying on its parentage for some of its progress. A key element of that parentage is those long-studied leadership functions (or practices, tasks, behaviors, actions – we make no distinction here), along with the knowledge, skills and dispositions on which they are based. After all, these functions are arguably what it is that is being distributed. We say "arguably" because conceptions of leadership are sometimes reduced to "influence," something located it in the dynamic relationship between leader and follower (e.g. Spillane, 2006; Wood, 2005). Leadership functions, from this perspective, are not leadership per se. They are, rather, what it is that people do in order to exercise leadership.

The designs or purposes for the research reported in several chapters in this text did not require their authors to grapple directly with the question of what leadership functions were being distributed; this was the case, for example, in chapters by Gronn (2) and MacBeath (3). But most chapters did grapple with this question. In four of these chapters (4, 5, 8 and 10) a set of functions explicitly framed the collection and analysis of data from the outset. Of these chapters, two adopted approximately the same set of functions, a set based on earlier research by Firestone, including:

- developing and maintaining a vision,
- developing and managing a culture to support the vision,
- providing encouragement,
- procuring and distributing resources,
- supporting the growth and development of people in the organization,
- monitoring instruction, innovation and the overall climate.

Justification for this choice of leadership tasks or functions was provided by Firestone's earlier work. As Mayrowetz and his colleagues (Chapter 8) claimed, these functions "have been empirically tested in the implementation of a social problem-solving reform (Heller & Firestone, 1995) and the inclusion of students with special needs in general education classrooms (Mayrowetz & Weinstein, 1999)." The Firestone and Martinez study (Chapter 4) resulted in the addition of two functions to this list: *Implementing a centrally mandated curriculum* and *Responding to the issues that arise during district regime succession.*

Leithwood and his colleagues also adopted a set of functions justified with reference to a considerable body of earlier leadership research carried out in both school and non-school contexts (Leithwood et al. 2006; Leithwood & Riehl, 2005). Some 13 specific leadership practices were associated with categories of functions labeled: Setting Directions, Developing People, Redesigning the Organization and Managing the Instructional Program.

To better identify the leadership or management tasks principals carried out with others as distinct from alone, Spillane and his colleagues (Chapter 5) stipulated two categories of tasks – *administrative* (e.g. managing budgets, personnel, schedules) and *curriculum and instruction* (e.g. reviewing student work, lesson plans, classroom instruction) – to help organize the collection and analysis of their data. Evidence for this study was also collected about *Professional Growth* functions or tasks and activities associated with *Fostering Relationships*. Little explicit justification is provided in this chapter for the selection of these tasks.

Research in several additional chapters was informed by an a priori consideration of leadership functions, but also discovered others, or more specific manifestations of the original set in the course of the research. Harris' study of knowledge management practices is one of these chapters. Timperley's study (Chapter 9) aimed to discover the consequential leadership functions that were distributed without an explicit a priori expectation of what those functions would be. *Boundary Spanning, Embedding Vision in Activities*, and *Using Artefacts* such as achievement data were among the most important functions identified by this study.

The significant variation in how leadership functions are conceptualized and used begins to surface as an issue quite central to thinking about both future research and the work of current leaders. Does the choice of functions matter? Or can we learn about leadership distribution just as well with one set as another? We do not entirely rule out "no" as the answer to the first of these questions and "yes" as the answer to the second. Such research might tell us that schools are distributing to teachers, for example, the function of drawing up the extracurricular timetable. While this is a function someone in the school needs to do, it certainly would be difficult to justify it as a consequential leadership function. But knowing this says something about the current state of affairs. It reminds us that it is often not leadership that gets distributed. For those who would promote distributed leadership as part of a school improvement strategy, the value of such knowledge is to benchmark the current state of affairs.

There is, however, a range of questions beyond those serving a benchmarking function that will be quite critical to address in future research aimed at leadership improvement. These are questions about whether some leadership functions are best enacted by one group rather than another, whether co-distribution of some functions has greater influence on the organization than individual enactment, and whether the nature of the leadership context influences the most productive distribution of functions. So beyond the early but important stages of research on distributed leadership, it will be critical to select for study those leadership functions which can be justified as likely to make important contributions to the organization's directions and capacities. We think it is equally critical for leaders actually doing the distribution of leadership to their colleagues, when this is how distribution occurs, to give the question of what is being distributed careful deliberation as well. If they are not functions with the potential for significant influence on organizational directions and capacity, then most of the anticipated advantages of leadership distribution have no chance of materializing. Indeed, appreciating the importance of choosing functions for which there is adequate justification points out the limitation of conceiving of leadership simply as influence to begin with. All human relationships entail the exchange of influence – or at least the intent to influence. For the concept of leadership to have any distinct meaning, this exchange of influence must also be qualified by reference to the direction of the influence, (likely) to its relative strength, and certainly to what happens as a result.

Developing Distributed Leadership

Most chapters in the text offer insights about how the distribution of leadership is either fostered and enhanced, or discouraged and undermined. Indeed, the evidence from these chapters offers a more consistent answer to this question than to most other questions that have been raised. In a nutshell, this evidence indicates that it is often some form of external pressure that prompts efforts to distribute leadership more broadly. Gronn referred to the "need for intelligence" for example. These needs might take many forms, for example, pressure to improve disappointing school performance, or introduction of new policies and programs requiring new instructional capacities.

Typically, it seems, these needs must be recognized and acted on in some manner by those in formal district and/or school leadership roles. Paradoxically perhaps, greater distribution of leadership outside of those in formally established roles usually depends on quite intentional intervention on the part of those in formal leadership roles, although MacBeath (Chapter 3) has described conditions in which greater leadership is "taken" rather than "given," as well as cultures in which assuming leadership responsibility is a widely shared norm. We expect such conditions are still relatively rare, however. Furthermore, as Mayrowetz and his colleagues (Chapter 8) argue, stable formal leadership at both district and school levels builds the kind of trust those in non-formal leadership roles require to risk stepping outside the bounds of their "day jobs" and into the leadership world.

So district leaders, as in Firestone and Martinez' (Chapter 4) study, create new teacher leader roles or otherwise open up possibilities for more people to participate in decisions at the district and possibly the school level. School leaders can foster greater leadership distribution within their schools independent of what districts do, although school and district leaders acting in concert seems much more effective. As Firestone and Martinez' evidence indicates, school leaders can easily, if unintentionally, sidetrack district efforts to distribute leadership. Indeed, school principals figure very prominently in this leadership distribution story. Among the important conditions influencing leadership distribution that depend, in part or whole, on what principals do are: providing time to exercise leadership, acknowledging the importance of such leadership, creating opportunities to develop leadership skills, targeting or encouraging people to take on leadership tasks, and ensuring the leadership task is clear.

There are conditions in the school or district only indirectly influenced by those in formal leaders roles that also influence the extent and nature of leadership distribution. These include organizational cultures, as MacBeath indicates, in which taking on leadership responsibilities is a shared norm. Cultures of collaboration also provide opportunities for collegial exchange and mutual influence. It also helps, as Grubb and Flessa's (Chapter 7) study shows us, if those close to the school (e.g. parents) are comfortable with shared or distributed leadership, if those sharing the leadership have compatible personal relationships, and if there are adequate resources, when required, to support the activities of those taking on additional leadership functions.

As this brief synopsis indicates, there is likely a clearer picture emerging about how to foster distributed leadership than there is about any of the other issues typically associated with leadership distribution. Do we need more research on this matter? Of course we do. But a good portion of this research should adopt a decidedly ends-oriented perspective. As Timperley (Chapter 9) has argued, greater distribution of leadership is only desirable if the quality of that leadership significantly enhances teachers' capacity to provide more effective instruction to their students. Among the questions that would be most productive for future research on this matter are, for example: How can productive or effective forms of distributed leadership be developed? What sorts of interventions are most likely to encourage the emergence of coordinated rather than uncoordinated patterns of leadership distribution? Which consequential leadership functions should be the focus of professional development for those assuming distributed leadership responsibilities? Under what conditions or at what stage in a school's work is fostering leadership distribution a better option than maintaining control in the hands of those in formal leadership roles?

Final Comments

By this point in the text, most of our "hard nosed" readers will be experiencing profound disappointment at the lack of serious effort in the text to assess the contribution of greater leadership distribution to the long list of desirable outcomes typically invoked by advocates – greater student learning, more democratic practices, greater commitment by staffs to the mission of the organization, increased professional development for a wider range of organizational members, better use of the intelligence distributed throughout the organization outside those in formal leaders roles, and the like.

We have considerable sympathy for such disappointment but have come to the grudging conclusion that research focused on outcomes would have been premature, at least until quite recently. What would be selected as the "independent variable" in such research is the dilemma. Simply put, distributed leadership, we are now learning, appears in quite different patterns, includes the distribution of a potentially wide array of different leadership functions, and arises as a response to many different challenges. Without this more nuanced appreciation of the anatomy of distributed leadership it is not at all clear how one would have conceptualized and measured distributed leadership in order to assess its effects, whatever they might have been. The clarity the chapters in this text have begun to bring to these issues sets the stage for a line of research about outcomes or effects much more likely to produce useful results. To have attempted studies of distributed leadership effects in the absence of such clarity would have been a significant waste of scarce resources. We are now in a position to consider questions of impact.

Note

1 Versus the "dust bowl" empiricism label attached to much earlier teacher effectiveness literature.

References

Day, C., Stobart, G., Sammons, P., Kington, A., Gu, Q., Smees, R., & Mujtaba, T. (2006). *Variations in teachers' work, lives and effectiveness. Rb747.* London, UK: Department for Education and Skills.

Gronn, P. (2002). Distributed leadership. In K. Leithwood & P. Hallinger (eds), *Second international handbook of educational leadership and administration* (pp. 653–696). Dordrecht, The Netherlands: Kluwer Academic Publishers.

Heller, M.F. & Firestone, W. (1995). Who's in charge here? Sources of leadership for change in eight schools. *Elementary School Journal, 96*(1), 65–85.

Janis, I.L. (1971). *Victims of groupthink.* Boston, MA: Houghton Mifflin.

Kerr, S. & Jermier, J.M. (1978). Substitutes for leadership: Their meaning and measurement. *Organizational Behavior and Human Performance, 22,* 375–403.

Leithwood, K. & Riehl, C. (2005). What we know about successful school leadership. In W. Firestone & C. Riehl (eds), *A new agenda: Directions for research on educational leadership* (pp. 22–47). New York, NY: Teachers College Press.

Leithwood, K., Mascall, B., Strauss, T., Sacks, R., Memon, N., & Yashkina, A. (2007). Distributing leadership to make schools smarter: Taking the ego out of the system. *Leadership and Policy in Schools, 6*(1), 37–67.

Mayrowetz, D. & Weinstein, C.S. (1999). Sources of leadership for inclusive education: Creating schools for all children. *Educational Administration Quarterly, 35*(3), 423–449.

Spillane, J. (2006). *Distributed Leadership.* San Francisco, CA: Jossey-Bass.

Wood, M. (2005). The fallacy of misplaced leadership. *Journal of Management Studies, 42*(6), 1101–1122.

Index

283